MARK→

Thanks for the many years of mentorship and encouragement! I will always remember the day we drove to PLU and I got to take my tour with FROSTY! (in his yellow wagon) Thanks for being part of my journey and helping me start. Keep sharing your wisdom and enthusiasm!

Steve Marsh

I PLAYED FOR FROSTY

CELEBRATED STORIES OF FAITH, LIFE, AND FOOTBALL

I PLAYED FOR FROSTY

Cross Training Publishing

www.crosstrainingpublishing.com (308) 293-3891

Copyright © 2022 Cross Training Publishing

ISBN: 978-1-938254-24-6

Front cover photograph taken by Harley Soltes, used by permission/all rights reserved.

"Uniquely Memorable" written by Chuck Culpepper, used by permission/all rights reserved.

ACKNOWLEDGMENTS

Many thanks to the following people who helped make this book possible.

To the group that helped begin and continue the process: Steve Ridgway, Scott Westering, Nick Dawson, and Brad Westering.

To Jim and Holly (Westering) Johnson for your early photos and materials.

To Kirk Isakson for your help providing photos.

To the donors who provided up-front funding which allowed the book to be published:
Chad and Carolyn Barnett, Troy and Cheryl Brost, Ron and Gretchen Brown, Doug and Kristi Burton, Casey Carlson, Brad Christiansen, Nick Dawson, Jeff and Kristen Douglass, Guy and Brenda Ellison, Jeff Elston, John and Michelle Eussen, Paul and Julie Finley, Ken and Teri Flajole, Jeff Gates, David and Margaret (Nerheim) Greenwood, Tom and Sherrie Hayes, Paul and Jeanne Hoseth, Chris and Tharen Inverso, Chad and Michelle Johnson, Jeremy and Whitney Johnston, David and Anita Knight (Duske), Jon and Shelley Kral, Craig and Karin Kupp, Dave and Mari Misterek, Steve Ridgway, Curtis and Carol (Strandoo) Rodin, Jon and Jane Rubey, Gavin and Stephanie Stanley, Jim and Robin Walker, Garth and Kristy Warren, Scott and Susan Westering, and Jon and Debbie Wolfe.

To Josh Smith (PLU Archives) for your generous help with finding photos.

To Cross Training Publishing: Gordon Thiessen (Publisher), Chad Bonham (Editor), and Monte Lange (Designer).

And finally, to the writers who took time to share memories from your time with Frosty.

Editor Note:

EMAL, meaning 'Every Man a Lute,' was used to help people "buy in" to a philosophy that was very different from possibly any football program in the country. It was based upon celebrating the day, your teammates, your commitment to them and the joy of being on the 'success road,' which was distinctly different than the 'road to success.' EMAL involved every mom, dad, brother, sister and friend that was involved in the program. Being an EMAL truly made people feel part of something bigger than themselves.

FAMILY & BELONGING

INTRODUCTION

It was 1963 and I was in my sophomore year at Concordia College in Moorhead, Minnesota, where I had the privilege of playing football for a legend, Jake Christiansen. Little did I realize that years later I would be coaching with another legend. Our first football game of the 1963 season was in Fairfield, Iowa, vs. Parsons College. The head football coach at Parsons was Frosty Westering—the legend with whom I coached from 1972 to 1995.

Our journey together started in 1972. I was already in my fourth year at PLU and was on the search committee for a new head football coach. We interviewed several candidates, but none seemed to be the right fit. Finally, Frosty was invited and he brought at least two weeks of material in his briefcase for the two-day interview. Parsons College played Wartburg during the previous years and our Athletic Director, Dave Olson, was familiar with Frosty's record. He was offered the PLU position, and the Westering family moved west.

To say that Frosty made an immediate and lasting impact on many would be a huge understatement. Football was merely a means to help make a positive difference in the lives of countless individuals, many beyond the football field. He coached the Elkader High School Warriors, Fairfield High School Trojans, Parsons College Wildcats, Lea College Lancers, and the Pacific Lutheran University Lutes.

The combination of Frosty and Donna was unique. Donna was the glue that held things together and allowed him to function as only he could. Frosty received most of the credit, but Donna kept the ship afloat.

Several years ago, I was thinking about finding a way to celebrate Frosty and his legacy. In 1996, Finn Grinaker, assistant coach at Concordia, published a book titled, "I Played for Jake." Collecting players' stories seemed like a much better way to honor Frosty than through a biography. I wanted the stories to be told by those who played for him and by those who knew him well. With the help and encouragement of Steve Ridgway, Scott Westering, Nick Dawson, and Brad Westering, we pursued the project. A special thank you to the former players who donated funds to make this project possible and to those who contributed to the book.

As you read the stories, you will notice that relatively few are specifically related to football games. His wins, national championships, and honors speak for themselves. The impact Frosty had went far beyond the football field. Some stories will make you smile, laugh, or cry. The stories span a period of about 50 years and yet many threads are similar. It is clear that the legacy of Frosty Westering has lived on, continuing to impact the lives of those who knew him and those who are meeting him for the first time through this book.

Keep enjoying the trip. "Make it a Great Day!" ~ Paul Hoseth

TABLE OF CONTENTS

CHAPTER 1

THE EARLY YEARS

[1952 - 1971]

SOCK HOPS, FLAT TOPS & COCKLE BURRS

Larry Lange (Elkader High School/1952-56),
Teacher and Coach

I was born on October 19, 1938. Frosty came to Elkader, Iowa, when I was a 13-year old freshman. Here are some of my best memories:

1. The first year we went 8-0-1, if I remember correctly, and won the conference.

2. The Elkader Warriors Letterman's Club was so neat and we learned so much about sticking together and about life. We learned how to bond and play as a team. The Cleveland Indian patch on my red sweater was such a great honor. I was so proud to be a Warrior. Frosty was so ahead of his time to have a Letterman's Club.

3. I remember Frosty painting our locker room one color and our opponents another color.

4. All the signs and sayings were so neat to have in our locker room and he would change them every week. I can remember most of them by heart.

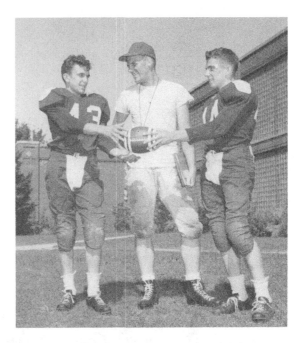

5. Our sock hops were so neat after the games. Frosty played the drums and it was so neat when he and Donna would dance. What a memory to have our coach and his wife participate with all of us.

6. I won't forget the play (24-25)—the pitch that was such a great play and how well it worked. I told Mary the night we got to see Pacific Lutheran play at our house that we ran a lot of the same plays. I could not believe we ran a lot of the same plays at Elkader, Iowa. The only difference was we ran the plays on cockle burrs and they did hurt and stick to our uniforms.

7. I remember Jack Dittmel used to come to all of our basketball games and sit in the second row on the aisle.

8. I really did enjoy playing against the team that Frosty started and played on. Those basketball games were fun.

9. Frosty's pre-game talks and halftime talks were so great and he made me say to myself, "I will run through a wall for Frosty." He was such an example looking back. In all that we went through together I never ever heard him swear or say a bad word. That is still amazing to me today the way our world is.

10. I remember Frosty telling me the story about his conversation with the basketball coach from New Hampton before the game and his final comment was, "We will take it easy on you tonight." We went out and beat them pretty good. He laughed a lot about his comments.

11. I remember that Frosty told the team if we were undefeated we could throw him in the Turkey River. The moral of the story, he always stuck to his word. That meant a lot. The water was cold.

12. He loaded most of us in cars and a couple of guys went by plane across the state. We got to see Boys Town and play his old high school in Missouri Valley. We came home with two wins. What a great trip for the boys from Elkader, Iowa. I will never forget that.

13. Frosty was always working hard so we could have the best equipment and we always had the best-looking uniforms. That was very special.

14. Those playbooks with our offense and defense that he would hand out every year were so special. I know none of our opponents had playbooks. The night we played

West Union in football, we got a few miles down the road and Frosty left his playbook in the locker room. We went back to the school. It was dark and locked. They had left a window open in the locker room and I crawled through the window and got the playbook. Frosty was so happy when he got

back on the bus. What luck.

15. I remember one night we were playing Postville in basketball and it was a close game. I had two free throws. Frosty looked me in the eye and said, "Larry, don't worry. The sun will come up in the morning." It took so much pressure off. I stepped up and made both free throws and we won the game. That was very rewarding.

16. Donna was such a great example of a coach's wife and the interest she showed in all of us. All the players loved her cookies. They were always hot off the press.

17. I will never forget the weights that Frosty made out of Folgers coffee cans and filled with cement.

18. We all liked the way he kept stats. We knew every game what we had done and he kept them for the whole year.

19. We all liked how hard Frosty worked with the Elkader Register and all the press that we received. It was also very neat the way he put in our picture or snap shot when we had a good game. I always looked forward to the day that the paper came out. That was such a great thing for the players and their families.

20. One small thing was we always had clean towels after we took a shower. I know he was involved in that process.

21. Most of the Warriors had flat top haircuts because our coach had a flat top.

22. In my junior and senior years, we won 47 basketball games and I think we lost three maybe four. I credit 90 percent of that to coaching. The fast break was so good and was well coached. I'll never forget Frosty saying, "Lange, button hook and go. Pass the

ball to the middle and get a three on two." Frosty always preached that assists were as important as making the basket and he made us believe that. That was the reason we had such good teamwork. The jump ball play was out of sight. We scored a lot of points off that play. In many games we would score on the first jump ball of the game. That was such a thrill to make that play work.

23. We had some great out of bounds plays. Frosty also taught us how to block out on missed free throws and always block out the shooter.

24. Frosty always knew when to call time outs. He would get down on one knee with the chalk in his left hand and draw out what he wanted us to do. He sometimes drew the plays on the hardwood and always wiped it up with his white towel. We also had great coaching and good drills where we would practice blocking out, rebounding, and passing the ball out to the guards to get the fast break going.

25. We had a lot of games where we scored 80 or 90 points.

26. I will never forget the night we beat Postville on the road. I had two running hook shots off the glass on the fast break. After the game Frosty said, "Lange, I think your speed has really improved. I want you to come out for track after the basketball season." After the Postville game we traveled to Dubuque. I think it was the first time a team from Elkader played in a sub-tournament game. Their coach was Johnny Orr who later went on to Wisconsin and then was head basketball coach at Iowa State. That night Dubuque had a 6-11 center by the name of Bill Engel who had his best night of his career. He hit five or six shots from the top of the key. Frosty and I said that if he hadn't been hot we would have won the game. It was still a great night to be from a small school and travel to a big city like Dubuque and give them a good game. I will never forget the thrill to be part of making history for the Elkader Warriors.

27. The one great thing Frosty did the first year was take us to St. Olaf for our football breakaway. I will never forget the practices, the homemade pull-up bars, the showers that were very cold, and all the food the mothers brought every day. We practiced hard to learn the offense and the defense. I know how happy Frosty was when they said he shouldn't do that and he was so lucky that St. Olaf was in the Elkader School District. The camp bonded us and the results the first year were terrific. Also, I always enjoyed the physical education classes

28. I went to Osage, Iowa, in 1961. The second year I became the head basketball coach after the team went 0-28 the previous year. The first year we won seven games. The third year we went to the sub-state tournament in Mason City. I could have run for mayor. Frosty would have been proud. We did everything that he taught me at Elkader. Those were the best four years of my life and I thank him from the bottom of my heart for what he taught me about sports and life.

Frosty was the finest coach and man that I have ever met or have been associated with. What great memories!

TRULY A BLESSING

Bob McNew (Fairfield H.S./1956-60; Lea College/1966-72), Teacher and Coach

I played for Coach Westering in 1956, his first year as head coach at Fairfield High School in Fairfield, Iowa.

In 1966, I was very fortunate to be asked to join Coach Westering's staff at Lea College, in Albert Lea, Minnesota. He and Coach Caris were excellent Christian mentors. They took a football team from not existing

to be winners in a short period of time. The student athletes were offered football, basketball, wrestling, and golf. Those four years prepared me well to become an Iowa high school head football coach.

Knowing and working with Coach Westering from 1956 to the end was truly a blessing.

THE BIG TIME (IS A STATE OF MIND AND HEART)

Jerry Staton (Parsons College/1959-63; Lea College/1962- 72), Assistant College Coach and High School Head Coach

In The Beginning

My first experiences with Coach Westering took place while I was a three-year starter for the Ottumwa Bulldogs. I considered him the enemy as I was for certain a Red Car player and I didn't know what I didn't know—that there even was a Blue Car! Ottumwa went 0-3 against his Fairfield Trojans and following the game my senior year as we were doing post-game handshake, which was more of a hand slap than anything else, something very strange happened to me. The head coach of the Fairfield team actually stopped the line of players as he grabbed my hand and elbow to actually shake hands and congratulate me on the great game I had played. He said that they almost had to change their game plan because of me. That felt really strange and at the same time it felt good. I did not know it but I had just had my very first ride in a Blue Car, even though I did not even know what a Blue Car was! Little did I know that I would go on to play for this coach in college and be on his football staff at Lea College.

Frosty's First College Team

His first year as head coach at Parsons actually began the summer prior to the start of practice as he took three of us seniors on a trip to Estes Park, Colorado, to an FCA Camp. I thought it was a Football Camp of America and jumped at the chance to have such an experience. The first night they had the strongest man in the world give a testimonial after lifting eight guys and some big plates off the floor at one time. I thought that was a tremendous message but wondered why they had the best speaker on the first night. The next night they had an even more inspiring speaker and I thought it could get no better than that. The lights went out on the last night and on the screen there was a movie of this athlete pole vaulting to a world record. The lights went out again and this time there was a thin man in a wheel chair standing by a huge man. The frail man said that what happened to him was the greatest thing that could happen because it brought him to Jesus and to this friend that gave up a four-year scholarship to care for him and roll him over several times a night to help him avoid getting bed sores.

Whoa! At the time I had an ingrown toenail and was complaining about not being able to do the activities as well as I wanted. I left that meeting, went out to pray, and turned my life over to God. I was never the same person from that point on and Frosty was the man who pointed me in the right direction. We returned to Parsons to a great group of players, but religion was not big on their list of priorities. Our challenge was to present our feelings in a way that would make them think about their positions and of course Frosty was doing his part as well.

We were undefeated but locked in a tremendous game with Central College, which was also coached by a college football legend, Ron Schippers. It was very late in the game and the score was 0-0. Frosty always gave players the right to express their feelings and ideas and would actually try suggestions from players. He had this metal board with small magnetic players on it. He would arrange them and explain why certain adjustments needed to be made. Central had an All-American defensive end that was really tough to trap out. I was the pulling guard assigned to block him out, but at the strategy board I asked Coach if we could hook him in and run the play outside.

"Can You Hook Him Jerry?" I replied, "Yes Coach," and he told us to run it again. We did and the play went for sixty yards and a touchdown. Frosty was always willing to listen to his players.

But that is not the most amazing part of the story. Before running the play we had discussed with Frosty in the huddle, our quarterback stepped in and said, "Fellas we have been kind of ridiculing this FCA stuff and maybe we should give it a try." Wow! Scoring a long game-winning touchdown on the next play put an end to a lot of doubters and the team was never the same again. Frosty had a way of touching the hearts and minds of many, many players. The "Frosty Way" was working again on the college level.

The Beginning Of The Breakaways

Frosty held his first Breakaway that first season and we spent a full week at Camp Arrowhead near Ottumwa, Iowa. None of us had ever experienced such a thing, but a very strong bond began forming like nothing we had experienced at Parsons. One night after dinner, a limousine pulled up to the main lodge and out stepped Pat O'Brien, the movie star. His latest film "Knute Rockne" had just come out and he spoke to our team. In the film, he had made a locker room speech that became quite famous. Hearing him give that speech had everyone ready to play right

then. Frosty never missed an opportunity to bring new experiences to us and having a Doctorate Degree in Psychology helped him. In all the time I knew him I never heard anyone call him Doctor. He was "Frosty" to everyone.

On The Road Again

Road trips are part of the football experience. Frosty always tried to make something special or educational out of our trips.

One road trip really stands out in my memory bank. I liked to sit in the front seat behind Coach Lutz and Frosty. First, Monte Versteeg who weighed over 300 pounds (no scales in Fairfield went above 300) was so big he could not fit in one seat and, me being the smallest lineman on the team, they often put me in with him. Monte did not want to sit by the coaches so I could escape his overlap and those two coaches always had a huge bag of chocolate covered peanuts. Since they could not eat all of them, they would hand them

back to me and say to take what I wanted and pass the rest back. None ever got passed on.

Being up in the front let me save Frosty from a nasty fall. He was standing by the door of the bus as it was rounding a curve and for some reason the driver made the turn sharper and the door came open and Frosty started falling out the open door. I made a grab for him, just caught the sleeve of his coat, gave a big pull, and he came back in. That was a close call and I am thankful I was in the right place at the right time.

We finished the season undefeated and could have gone to one of the 10 bowl games that were held at that time, but we believed we were the best team in the nation and wanted to take our chance at being selected as one of the top four teams to compete for the National Championship. Frosty explained to us that if we were not selected, it would be too late to go a bowl game. He supported our

decision and let us decide. We did not get invited and our season was over. We would have won it all.

After my senior season, I took the football coaching position at Pekin High School, which was about 30 minutes west of Parsons. Frosty knew we were running his offense and thought it would be good if all my players and the community could see it from the original source. He decided to have their spring training camp scrimmage at our school.

The day arrived and here came Frosty and his Wildcats in their travel bus. They pulled into the gate to the field, which is where all the school buses came each Friday night, but

the Parsons bus was much taller than regular school buses and the overhead sign with the name of our field came crashing down on top of the bus. Of course Frosty was very apologetic about their grand entrance and the next week a new and even better sign was erected.

Ish Time

As one of his players and as an assistant on his staff, I learned that there was standard time, daylight savings time, and Coach's "ish" time. The staff meetings, bus trips, practice segments and much more happened on a schedule that really operated in Frosty's head. A drill would begin at 4-ish. We would board the bus at 8-ish. It always seemed to work out well.

Assistant Coach Experiences With Frosty

Of course, as an assistant coach to Frosty, there are hundreds of memories and experiences that occurred. On one road trip we stayed at the Mark Twain Hotel in Missouri. It had been a long bus ride and after the team meal we had a team meeting. Coach

Bob McNew, Coach Bill Caris, and Frosty and I were sharing a room with two double beds. At about midnight the other two coaches turned in but Frosty and I ventured out to the team bus where all the players had left their helmets out so they could be painted. Frosty had developed the tradition of the Lancers having all silver helmets for their games. We began using spray cans to paint the helmets and placing them out to dry. There were a lot of helmets to paint and while we were doing that, hundreds of some kind of big bugs dive bombed us the whole time! Finally, at about 2 a.m., we went back to the room and climbed into bed. But, Frosty wanted to talk. He was my head coach and a father figure to me. I felt I had to stay awake to listen to him. I was really tired and actually held my eyelids open so I would not fall asleep. Frosty had a battery that most people do not have and he could go on and on and never seemed to tire. It must have been 3 a.m., or later that we went to sleep.

Breakfast the next morning was at 7 a.m., so it was a short night. McNew and Caris were well rested and were awake early. Frosty was in bed beside me facing one way

and I was on the other side of him facing away from him. I must have thought in my sleepy state that I was home. I reached back and patted my dear wife on the fanny but something was terribly wrong. "Yes, Jerry?" was Frosty's response. I might have been real sleepy but I woke up quickly and those other two guys roared with laughter and have never let me forget that experience.

Donna Memory

When you got Frosty, you also got Donna. One day after my senior season at Parsons College, Coach invited me over but was operating on "ish" time and was not there when I arrived. Donna and I had a great visit and, of course, she topped it off with milk and cookies. In our conversation I mentioned that Frosty was such a great person and that he could sure make it in the "Big Time" coaching world. Donna gave me a reply that I have often wondered if she got it from Frosty or if she gave it to him. She said, "You know Jerry, you make the 'Big Time' where you are. It is not a place but a state of mind and heart." Sound Familiar?

The Move To PLU

The road trip of all road trips came when Frosty took the head coaching position at Pacific Lutheran University. He called me to see if I could help him make that move. Of course I would help. It was mid-July and my football practice didn't start until mid August.

With my 10 years of working for Mayflower Moving Company, I packed all their dishes, lamps, and other fragile items so they would safely make it to Tacoma, Washington. We began the journey West with what looked like a wagon train. We had our car and pop-up trailer, a U-Haul moving truck, and two of Frosty's automobiles with both pulling trailers. The thing is, it took us four days to get out of Minnesota as Frosty had to make stops at various places to bid farewell to people he knew and I think he knew everybody.

After two days at Gla-

cier National Park, we continued West and the Westering boys took turns riding in the moving truck with me. They were delightful to ride with and we played many traveling truck games along the way. I started to worry that I would not have the family moved out there before my team in Oskaloosa started practice. We made it back in time, but had to hustle to get there! I was glad to have helped Coach.

Frosty's Impact

I was a senior during Frosty's first college season at Parsons. That year I was the Letter Club President and received the coaches' award for "Player To Contribute Most To Team." After my time as an assistant coach at Lea College, I returned to Iowa to coach high school football where my teams were state runner-ups in 1983 and state champions in 1996 (using Frosty's offense). I was honored to receive the National Coach of the Year award, finish ranked fifth all time in wins at retirement (I've moved down the list some since), and become inducted into the Iowa Football Coaches Hall of Fame.

After Graduation Thoughts & Influences

Graduation or leaving the program did not end Frosty caring for you. Once you were

one of his guys, you remained there forever. I had decided that it was time for me to retire from coaching and Coach McNew called Frosty to tell him that my last game was coming up. It just happened to be against Fairfield High where Frosty coached before going to Parsons. Frosty had a big game coming up on Saturday, yet, he hopped on a plane on Thursday evening and showed up to give a presentation to my high school players at our "Togetherness Night." Who does that? I was really surprised to see him. At halftime of the game, he was on the radio station from visiting Fairfield and then back on our sidelines. I think this is a tremendous example of the fact that once you were one of his guys, you were one forever.

THE STRANGE SECRET

Rick (Harvey) Boyle (Lea College/1966-69), U.S. History Teacher, and Head and Assistant Football Coach (retired)

Coach Westering once said that the strange secret is that there is no secret. It is the power of choice, which is really about our heart, not our head. When we change to a caring heart, it causes a new way of thinking, which generates faith, hope, and love. In life's journey the road is filled with lessons, hardships, heartaches, joys, celebrations, and special moments that will ultimately lead us to our purpose in life.

It has been also said, "If you don't know where you are going, any road will take you there." At Lea College, the road was not always smooth. In fact, throughout our time at Lea, we encountered many challenges. Amidst these challenges, Frosty and the coaches were our saving grace, always there to help us and bail us out of trouble locally, as well as in neighboring towns and states. They did so much for us behind the scenes—and it's probably better that those stories go untold.

The choice to attend Lea College in 1966 put

me on the road to where I am today. Initially, I intended to go to Parsons College with friends from high school, but Parsons informed me that their student enrollment was full for the coming year and I should consider Lea College. Lea was a satellite college of Parsons and they were starting a sports program. I applied to Lea and was accepted. I then called Coach Westering and told him that I was interested in playing football and he put me on the list. He mailed me all the information about when to report and a workout schedule that wore me out.

At Lea College, coming together with my teammates was the beginning, staying together was progress, and working together was our success. Each person can add their own story of how they came to Lea in the beginning. For me, being a sturdy 5-10, 160 pounds in high school and never starting (just playing on special teams), I stayed out a year and worked and built myself up to be a frisky 183-pounder my freshman year. I just wanted the opportunity to play football. For four years at Lea I was a starter—two years at tight end, two years at linebacker, and punter for all four years.

I did not know anything about Lea College was like—not the coaches (Frosty Westering, Bill Caris who coached the backs and defense, Robert McNew my position coach, and Jerry Staton with the OL and D line and one of the best wrestling coaches), not the town, or even the cheerleaders! What a leap of faith we took to invest in Lea College. That leap of faith was enormously rewarded. For me, not only did I obtain an education and an opportunity to play football, but thanks to Frosty and the coaches, through their faith

and the Fellowship of Christian Athletes, I also developed a spiritual life that is a blessing for which I am grateful every day.

It makes me so proud to read the success stories of my teammates and coaches and what we have had to endure, overcome, and continue to deal with on a daily basis. The stories of everyone's families, children, and grandchildren are a blessing to hear and behold. We still know how to keep our legacy and tradition rolling forward with loving put ups, pats on the back, and the occasional practical jokes. There are old stories that still keep us laughing when we get together even after 50 years apart!

The journey to and from Lea College has put me on the road to meet God and after playing at Lea (winning and losing), I have learned to surround myself with good people that have become great. EMAL

MERE X'S AND O'S

John Sauer (Lea College/ 1966-69), Superintendent of Iowa Schools (retired)

I met Frosty in the spring of 1966 when he persuaded me to attend Lea College. I have never regretted it. The football team helped launch a new college and the relationships with coaches and teammates have lasted a lifetime. It was a unique experience.

I believe that I learned a great deal from Frosty that had nothing to do with football. These things had a powerful impact on my life. Things like loyalty, responsibility, trust, and fellowship were more important than mere X's and O's—living life to your fullest and giving your best in whatever your challenge happens to be.

The friends I made along the way have influenced my outlook on life. Looking back, I wouldn't change a thing. I loved my football brothers and I'm in frequent contact with many of them. After over 50 years, we still get together. We used to talk about the opponents and the special plays, but now it's grandkids, vacations, and coping with retirement.

Having said that, I still know my assignments for 08, 05X, 47 Trap, and Buck 2X.

GO SEE BEV

Greg Francis (Lea College/1967-69), GRF Comm Provisions Inc. (Cable TV Construction)

I first met Frosty at Lea College in the fall of

1966 when the team was already playing. I walked on in the spring of 1967 and got a full ride. I played the best ball of my life, which I needed to, to make the team.

Frosty had a great mind for the game. I benefited from the end around pass play. It worked 95 percent of the time.

The one thing that sticks out in my mind is something that happened during summer camp in 1968. I married my wife Beverly on August 10th in New Jersey. I needed to report to camp on August 22nd. Beverly and I got settled in Albert Lea and I took off for camp.

One day at two-a-day practice, I had a bad day. Not much went right. After returning to the cabin, Coach Bob McNew took me aside and gave me his car keys and told me to go see Bev and get back before 10 p.m. That meant the most to me as a player—that the entire coaching staff had our wellbeing in mind. You cannot ask for more than that. Bev and I celebrated our 54th Anniversary on August 10, 2022.

THE BEST WORK TOGETHER

Bill Sosnowski (Lea College/1967-70), Industrial Product Sales, Developmental Football Coach, and Football Referee

Like a lot of student athletes in the late 1960s, the Vietnam conflict was raging and few if any colleges and universities wanted C+ grade average students. My guidance counselor suggested the junior college route until I got drafted. He also handed me a three-fold flyer from Lea College.

Lea was a new school and I set up an appointment with Don Hartman. He showed me clippings of athletics at Lea. He pointed out a very talented local football player and wrestler by the name of Mike Hemmerick. I had known Mike in high school before he moved to a different high school. Several times in one wrestling practice he used me for a mop. I was only too happy to find he gained success at Lea and thought if I got the chance I'd go there also.

Don and Mike helped with my decision to apply and shortly after that, the wrestling

coach called and offered me a partial scholarship. Then, Frosty called and offered a one half scholarship.

I had never been away from home. Breakaway camp was a new experience. Coaches that didn't cuss you out was another new experience. That's when the Lea College light went on for me. Those that went home missed a lifelong learning experience—a pride and drive that exists today.

Some of Frosty's expressions I'll never forget are "Ding Ho!" which means, "work together" in Chinese, and "the best" in Cantonese. Put them together and you've got "The Best Work Together."

Frosty also liked to quote American journalist Heywood Brown: "Sports do not build character. They reveal it."

He also used to say, "Fate whispers to the Warrior, 'You cannot withstand the storm.' The Warrior whispers to Fate, 'I am the Storm.'"

And finally, Frosty would tell us, "If you always do what you've always done, then you'll always get what you always got!" That one helped me defeat cancer.

A LIFE OF DISCIPLINE AND COMPETITIVE SPIRIT

Phil Klek (Lea College/1966-70), Sales Manager, Hyster Co.

I played for Frosty from 1966 to 1970. I was his left offensive tackle. My most memorable story was when Frosty was recruiting for Lea College in Chicago. He actually came to visit me while I was recovering in the hospital from a kidney infection. His presence was amazing—such a dynamic man. I was proud to join the Lancer's as a charter member. He assembled a great coaching staff of McNew, Staten, and Carris. That single experience shaped my life of discipline and competitive spirit. I will forever be grateful for the lessons Coach instilled in us as they have permeated my life through my career, raising my children and grandchildren, and beyond. Thanks for everything, Frosty.

CAPTAIN ABROAD

Leotis Swopes (Lea College/1968-72), Math Teacher, Assistant Principal, Principal, Assistant Superintendent, and Superintendent

I, Leotis Swopes, played for Frosty Westering at Lea College during the years of 1968 to 1972. I graduated from North Chicago Community High School in North Chicago, Illinois, where I was a three-sport athlete: football, basketball and baseball. I lettered in football and was the Vice President of my school's Lettermen's Club and served as a representative on the Student Council. I graduated in the top half of my graduating class.

However, a weekend mishap that did not occur on school grounds, nor was it a related school sponsored activity, caused me great consternation. The first weekend of December during my senior year in high school, I was expelled. Greater powers intervened and I was reinstated at the beginning of the second semester. Even so, the coaching staff and board of education refused to allow my Athletic Director to recommend me for an athletic scholarship to the schools that had been interested in offering me a scholarship.

It became clear that I needed to change my environment even if it meant changing my location to get away from the elements that I felt had caused my troubles.

My freshman football coach, who was also my history teacher, suggested that I contact colleges and ask to walk on. I chose Lea College on the advice of my coach and the need for a different life perspective.

Frosty's response to my query was timely. Now, I was nervous because of the unknown and the thought of being away from home for the first time and entering an arena of unfamiliarity.

Meeting "The Snowman" (out of earshot, that's how some of the players affectionately referred to him), I found him to be of the same disposition as my high school coaches (who, by all accounts, were good coaches!) and as my father projected: pleasant, purposeful and business-like. There was a discernible "just-the-facts" temperament about him. Yet, he would laugh, listen and encourage while pushing toward the goal of building team.

Playing for Frosty, I lettered my freshman year, but I wasn't a starter. My sophomore year, I wasn't starting but still getting playing time. I became flustered and challenged him. That's when I discovered his affection for the "Upper Classmen/Seniority System." Another troublesome weekend had Frosty visiting the confines of the local Police Department to retrieve a few Lancers from the throes of their club activity. Thereafter, the "Upper Classmen" rule met a timely demise—at least as it related to the position I held on the Lancer's team. I respected him even more for that.

The end of my junior year football season, I had been convinced by a rival head coach to join their team. Out of respect for Frosty I went to him to inform him I was leaving at the end of the first semester. He told me that my teammates had honored me by selecting me as one of the Tri-Captains—the first time ever that the Lea Lancers had tri-captains.

Needless to say, I remained at Lea College.

Our opening game that following season was a home game. While chilling before the game, Frosty came to me and asked if I minded if I not go out for the coin toss and let the other Tri-Captain go out because he had family in the stands. I did go out for the coin toss at the away games. My travel roommates christened me the "Captain Abroad!" Frosty caught wind of our teasing on a trip and questioned us. We never relinquished our humorous retort. He responded, "Well, let's go, men!"

Christmas my senior year, I went to Frosty with a fictitious story about not being able to get home. He had me meet him at the business office in downtown Albert Lea. He blessed me in a positive way. I felt truly guilty for

taking advantage of his empathy toward me.

I played for Frosty, the coach, leader of men, and motivator. I was Player of the Week 15 times, Honorable Mention NAIA All American, and Defensive Player of the Year at Lea College.

I received a Doctorate Degree in Education Administration from the University of Nebraska-Lincoln in 1986. A few accolades that came along the way: Superintendent of the year, National Alliance of Black Educators; "Break the Mold Award" (technology for creative uses for minority children) given by the Illinois State Board of Education; and Youth Empire Community Educator Award (local award for innovative discipline programming). I retired after 40 years as an educator.

Years	School	Record
1952-56	Elkader High School (Iowa)	26-8-1
1956-60	Fairfield High School (Iowa)	21-13-2
1960-61	Athletic Director, Parsons College*	n/a
1962-63	Athletic Director/Coach, Parsons College*	15-4-0
1964-66	Graduate School, Northern Colorado**	n/a
1966-72	Lea College***	29-22-2

*Fairfield, Iowa
**Greeley, Colorado
***Albert Lea, Minnesota

CHAPTER 2

THE 1970's

[1972 - 1979]

A LEGEND IS BORN

Doug Ruecker (Pacific Lutheran/1970-73), Thrivent Financial (36 years) Senior Partner in the Pacific Northwest Region

December 1971 (The Beginning of the Legend): Coming off a 5-4 season, the Pacific Lutheran University football team was informed that our current head coach would not be returning the next season and the athletic department would be forming a search committee to find a new head football coach. Soon thereafter, team captain Ira Hammond asked me to serve with him as player representatives on the search committee. Little did we know at the time, but this was the starting point of something with enormous significance for the Pacific Lutheran community. It would begin the making of a legend.

I am not sure if it is common knowledge, but Frosty Westering was not the first choice for the new PLU head football coaching position to begin the 1972 season. In the early stages of our search, the committee had the chance to interview an experienced coach with a National Championship and National Coach of the Year award on his resume. The committee (consisting of Athletic Director David Olson, assistant football coach Paul Hoseth, a faculty advisor, Ira and me) decided this was a too good of an opportunity to pass on. We offered him the position. Only problem: he chose not to accept the job. A setback in our search? Perhaps. But in hindsight, I believe the hand of God was in motion, guiding us to consider someone different, someone special for Pacific Lutheran University.

There were dozens of resumes from prospective coaches to consider. However, I distinctly remember one specific profile that stood out from the others. This particular applicant not only talked about his experience and success in coaching (like all the other applicants), but he also elaborated on his Christian faith, including his involvement with the Fellowship of Christian Athletes. There was something intriguing about this man from Minnesota. His personality and his genuineness seemed to jump off the pages of his resume. We had to learn more.

Frosty was the third candidate the committee invited on campus for interviews. We learned quickly that Frosty Westering was the real deal. He was authentic. His optimism was contagious. He was a brilliant football mind, a man of principles, a man of faith—a man soon to be named the Head Football Coach at Pacific Lutheran University.

September 1972 (The Birth of a Legend aka The Towel Play): Frosty entered his inaugural season at PLU with a team made up mostly of us "inherited" players. However, his first

home game foretold of the legend he would become. Preseason saw Frosty immersing himself in the community—speaking at every function and organization that would invite him. He was the new face in town, with an infectious enthusiasm that engaged people with PLU football. He specifically invited folks to the season home opener against defending National Champion California Lutheran by sharing the details of a play he would call during the game. He diagrammed the end around pass play to his audience, explaining he would telegraph the timing of the play to them by throwing a towel high on the sidelines just prior to the call.

Midway through the second quarter with the Lutes at mid-field, the towel was tossed. The crowd grew excited. Seemed everyone but Cal Lutheran knew what was coming. Quarterback Rick Finseth took the snap and handed the ball to the pulling end Ira Hammond, who then dropped back and threw a perfect pass to wide receiver Dave Greenwood for a touchdown. The crowd went crazy; a love affair began, and a legend was born!

I was on Frosty's team for only two years, but I am proud to say—I Played for Frosty! EMAL

THE TOWEL TOSS

Dave Greenwood (Pacific Lutheran/1972), Biotech CFO and CEO, 14 Boards of Directors

In his first year as PLU Coach, Frosty introduced a sideline event: Tossing a towel in the air. People would wonder, what's he doing and why? The purpose was to gain attention to a special play. Turned out to be a success, a touchdown, on an end-around by Ira Hammond, with the pass to me, good for 50 or 60 yards. Victory over Cal Lutheran! Frosty got everyone's attention with his towel toss.

Many years later, Margaret and I were on Maui, climbing up Haleakala. We stopped at a cafe and heard a loud voice. Margaret and I looked at each other with surprise because we heard Frosty talking to Donna. We had a wonderful visit with Frosty who was, as usual, excited about everything.

THE LONG WALK

Steve Adelson (Pacific Lutheran/1972-73), Retired teacher, counselor, and football coach in Montana; Park Ranger at Little Big Horn Battlefield National Monument

My very first practice at Pacific Lutheran University under new coach Frosty Westering took place in August of 1972. I will never forget that day as long as I live.

Toward the end of practice we had a little 11-on-11 activity. I was a linebacker. The quarterback rolled out to the right and I chased him and caught him from behind, dragging him down. When I got up, after the play was dead, an offensive lineman hit me in the back. I angrily turned around and shoved him, screaming, "What the (expletive) are you doing you (expletive)? Frosty blew the whistle and walked over to me saying, "Steve, we're not about that here. Hit the shower."

65 guys witnessed the event and you could've heard a pin drop. I headed for the showers and man it was a long walk across that field.

I had transferred to Pacific Lutheran University from Wenatchee Junior College where we had won the state championship with a 9-1 record. Cussing and fighting were part of that program. Dog eat dog, chew them up, and spit them out. That's what I knew. Now I was walking off the field, thinking to myself, "What kind of a fruitcake program is this?" I thought I was done.

I had showered and was getting dressed when one of the players came to me and said, "Coach Westering wants to see you in his office." I thought, "Now I'm really going to get it!" And then I thought, "I don't fit in here anyway."

I walked into Frosty's office and he said, "Steve sit down, let's visit." Then he picked up a big jar he had on his desk that was full of cookies and said, "Here Steve, want a cookie?" I took the lid off and put my hand in the jar with the intent of grabbing a handful of cookies when Frosty said, "Now Steve, don't try and take all the cookies or your hand will get stuck in the jar. You know there are enough cookies for everyone if you understand that it's not all about you. It's about us."

He then proceeded to tell me that he had heard so many good things about me and how excited he was to have me part of the team. We stood up and he put his hand on my shoulder and said, "Steve, we are all about building guys up and not putting guys down. See you tomorrow at breakfast."

I walked out of that office and could hardly believe what I just experienced. Nowhere in my football past had I ever had a coach who talked to me like Frosty did. It was just the beginning.

I coached football for 33 seasons. There was never a day when I didn't feel Frosty's hand on my shoulder as I shared with young men what Frosty Westering shared with me nearly 50 years ago.

BURN OUT

Rick Finseth (Pacific Lutheran/1972-74), K-12 Teacher (1975-2018), Coached high school and middle school football and baseball

A Memorable Moment: Senior Year 1974

As co-captains, Dud Lutton, Dave Anderson, and I noticed that Frosty seemed more stressed than usual, and we wanted to talk with him about it. We were concerned about his health because we knew he wasn't eating well or getting enough sleep. We were able to catch him alone for a few minutes. We let him know we thought he was pushing himself too hard and we were worried about him.

After listening to what we had to say, he paused for a few seconds, and in true Frosty fashion, he said, "Well, guys, ya know, I sure would rather burn out than rust out!" Certainly, a Frosty quote that sums up one of his philosophies in a nutshell.

Cherished Memories from Frosty's Later Years

I didn't go to a lot of PLU football games after I graduated, but I tried to go to at least one game most years. After Frosty retired, whenever I went to a game, I knew where I could find him at the top of the stadium. He always had plenty of visitors who wanted to talk to him, but he would make time for everybody. I cherish those years when I approached him. He always greeted me with a big hug and we would catch up on the latest family news as well as some serious football talk. Although our conversations weren't very long (it was halftime after all), we would

often get into X's and O's just like we had when I was his first quarterback at PLU in 1972. Those were wonderful moments that I got to spend with the man who I loved like my father.

MORE THAN X'S AND O'S

Jim Crary (Pacific Lutheran/1973-74), Attorney for the Municipality of Anchorage (14 years), BP Contracts Department (17 years)

When football practice started in August 1973, I was actually still in the Army, so I was a bit skeptical about Frosty's PMA approach to football. When, instead of two-a-days and pads, the entire team went down to Seaside, Oregon, for Breakaway, I did not know what to think. But it turned out to be a wonderful way to meet my teammates and start forming team bonds.

I was not a starter my first year, so I mostly played Bomber football. Upon reflection, one of the most amazing things about the

Bomber games was who coached us. Frosty very easily could have sent us out with an assistant coach but, no, he coached us himself! As the head coach I am sure he was not looking for additional things to do, but he was there when we went to Central Washington, McNeil Island, UPS, and other games.

All my life I have pretty much taken what people say with a huge grain of salt because words can be cheap. Instead, I put much more weight on where people spend their time, as a person's time is valuable and limited. You can tell a great deal about what is important to a person by how they spend it and Frosty's presence at the Bomber games spoke volumes about his commitment to us as football players.

I also thought, when things did not go our way, Frosty's PMA would melt away faster than a snowman in the August sun. But I was wrong. Frosty remained positive even when things got tough or went awry.

I played two years for Frosty and he proved to me, with his actions, that he was a whole

lot more than X's and O's on a white board and that when he spoke you could believe his words because he backed them up with his actions.

Breakaway, Bomber football, Crazy Hat days, away games and "Frostyisms" helped us form bonds that continue almost 50 years later.

I was a starter in 1974. In 1975 I still had two years of eligibility remaining, but I wanted to take a semester abroad, so I went to Norway instead. One day in Oslo I went to get my mail and there was a tube from PLU. I could not for the life of me think what it could be. When I opened it up there was about an 8"x12" length of paper rolled up inside the tube. On the paper were greetings and signatures from everyone on the team! I could not believe that Frosty would, again, use his limited time to organize such a mailing for someone who wasn't even on the team.

Frosty was not only a great antidote for my Army induced cynicism, but he was Ted Lasso long before Jason Sudeikis was.

Thank you Frosty.

FOOTBALL PLAYERS SECOND

Dave Cornell (Pacific Lutheran/1973-75), Teacher and Track and Volleyball Coach (42 years), The Dalles, Oregon

My first year at PLU started a tad different than I expected. While finishing my second year at Columbia Basin Community College, I was recruited by Joe Broeker to play

for Coach Carlson. I was excited to have the opportunity to continue my football career at PLU.

I vividly remember our first team meeting. All of the players were assembled in a room awaiting the coach. In walks, not Coach Carlson, but a new head coach: Frosty. I thought, "What kind of a name is Frosty?"

He walks in, puts his briefcase down, and stares at all of us for what seemed like ages. Then, the first words from our new coach were: "It doesn't matter if you are agile, mobile or hostile, because if you are not eligible you aren't playing."

We spent the better part of that meeting setting up study groups. Frosty expected us to be serious students and good human beings first—football players second.

Frosty was a great coach, but more importantly he was a great person and used coaching to equip his players with life skills. He walked his talk and is someone we counted on for honesty, integrity and direction. He never let us down.

As a dad of three athletic boys and over 42 years of coaching volleyball and track, I have carried Frosty and his teachings with me. He has never let me down.

FLYING CHALK AND Y BLOCKS

Craig Fouhy (Pacific Lutheran/1972-75),
Sports Director and Sports Anchor, ABC15
KNXV-TV, Phoenix, Arizona

I was fortunate to be recruited by Joe Broker as Frosty was going through the hiring process, and needless to say, upon meeting Frosty, I was blown away. I had never met anyone as positive and as deliberate in his message as he was. From the git-go, the focus was on developing a PMA. It changed my life forever. I was also fortunate enough to co-direct the Frosty Westering Team Camp for a number of years with Scott and Sue Westering. An entire extra set of special memories live on from that experience.

On to some favorite memories:

Oil change and car service please: Steve Adelson and I had sports cars (along with a couple of other guys on the team) and we were constantly working on them in our spare time. Oil changes in the parking lot, battery replacements, carburetor tune-ups, tire changes... you name it, we did it. Word got around and we were soon helping teammates with their cars and trucks. It wasn't long before Frosty heard through the grapevine and Steve and I were enlisted to work on Frosty's Wagon— even if it meant missing practice time because we were in the middle of an oil change or a tune-up. Hey, the car needed some extra attention!

Take a bag lunch and spend the night or eat out and travel game day: This happened occasionally on road trips that could have been turned into an overnight affair, but the budget was tight, so we had a few opportunities to make a choice. We could take a bag lunch and stay overnight (four players per room), or we could eat a breakfast on the road and travel on game day. We experienced both!

Push the bus and hope the lights stay on: Spokane was one of my favorite trips and, of course, staying at the Ridpath Hotel. The only problem, on Saturday morning (game day), the bus wouldn't start. So, after making sure everyone was on the bus, Frosty said, "Everyone off the bus, we're going to push start it." So, we all got off the bus and pushed it down the street in downtown Spokane so we could go play the Whitworth Pirates. Turned out to be a great pre-game warm-up.

And the lights: Traveling from College of

Idaho in Caldwell, Idaho, isn't always done on main freeways or thoroughfares, so for much of the trip across Eastern Washington, you're on some pretty dark roads. On one trip, the lights would flicker on and off regularly for much of the trip. Thankfully, we had a cloud-free night and our bus driver was able to keep the bus on the road and keep us safe! Phew!

Bus driver and hot creamery butter: Traveling through Eastern Washington, Oregon and Idaho can be, well, boring, without some sort of distraction. While some players liked to play cards (despite Frosty's displeasure with card games and gambling) or listen to music, a handful of us discovered a microphone the driver had to share important travel information to passengers. Once we found it, life after a game, on the long trip home, changed permanently. Repeated chants like "Bus

Driver!" and "Hot Creamery Butter!" by myself, Ken Flajole, and Roger Pasquier became so distasteful that players actually threatened our lives if we didn't shut up. Where all of that started, I have no recollection, but it was clearly annoying and was certainly meant to be. And it worked! Nobody, and I mean nobody, wanted us to ever find the microphone on a bus after a road game.

The Hoogalites: Never one to play it safe at Breakaway. Most of us in the early years pushed the limits, working to find Frosty's limits—sometimes to our own detriment but never maliciously. At one Breakaway at Fort Worden (near Port Townsend), a few of our Dogpatch team members were walking along the beach and discovered a couple of concrete tablets that resembled the 10 Commandments. How and why they were there on the rocks and sand, we'll likely never know, but they were there, and the Hoogalites were born later that night. The 10 Commandments tablets became the centerpiece of our skit. We attacked every other Dogpatch team throughout our skit with the 10 Commandments directing our script, playing off each team, one at a time, as though they were evil in the eyes of the Hoogalites' 10 Command-

ments. It worked well and accomplished lifelong memories.

Mimicking Frosty: This was likely the most favorite pastime of all players as we waited for Frosty to start a meeting. He always reminded us of Lombardi, so most of us would arrive early to meetings and practices if possible. The one thing Frosty was known for in those days was being late to a meeting. So, what does a roomful of college aged football players do? Someone steps to the chalkboard (often times me) and pretends to be Frosty. By the time Frosty showed up, there were a hundred lines across the board and chalk was flying everywhere. Like Frosty, almost as much chalk ended up on our clothes as on the chalkboard. Chalkboards were fantastic for Frosty. White boards destroyed the element of a great meeting. No chalk flying and chalk dust on your clothes!

And speaking of Spokane and Whitworth College: Frosty had clearly devised one of the best cross-blocking systems in all of football. It was innovative and clever and gave us the best opportunity to open a hole for our

running backs. But there was one Saturday at Whitworth College that didn't go as planned. Jon Horner was our fullback that day and the cross-blocking system wasn't working so well. Frosty must have taken a liking to Jon because he got so frustrated with those of us on the offensive line that after he had chewed us out for not doing our job and opening holes for Jon, he told us we were going to "Y" block for the rest of the game. We'd call a signal opposite of the hole, but it was simply a decoy. The plan worked and I think Jon finished that game with 200 yards rushing, or so it seemed.

Fouhy's two pass receptions in the Fall of 1975: I had finally made it to my senior season and Frosty and the staff decided to incorporate a tackle eligible pass play for me. Unfortunately for Craig Dahl (our quarterback), the first time Frosty called the play, Craig missed on the pass. Frosty met him at the hash marks and gave him the what for. The next two times (that was it for the season), Craig completed both. I finished with two catches for somewhere around 47 yards. Not bad for an offensive tackle!

1,000 WAYS CHANGED

Larry Green (Pacific Lutheran/1974-75), PLU Assistant Coach (1978-80), Teacher and Coach, Lutheran Brotherhood (eight years), Thrivent Financial (28 years)

Frosty and Paul helped all of us Lutes live the Big Time!

Once upon a time in Luteland, there lived a miracle worker named Frosty. He came to Luteland from far away and he brought special gifts—gifts of fun (Crazy Hat Day), PMA, love, and adventure. This Frosty was amazing and he would change Luteland forever. This is my story and how Frosty made me better from the first day we met. He took a young former Marine and former UPS football player and turned him into the best version of himself.

I landed at PLU because I walked away from the University of Puget Sound (UPS) and hitchhiked across the United States. Upon returning, I found that, while NCAA rules left me with only one year of football eligibility at UPS, NAIA rules allowed two. I asked the UPS coach for the location of the closest NAIA school, and his response was, "Pacific Lutheran University." Looking at the coach, I said, "Thank you" and drove directly to PLU. I knew nothing about Frosty or his program, but Jesus knew about Frosty and how he would impact my life forever. I needed Christ and then I needed men like Frosty, Paul Hoseth, Steve Ridgeway, and Dud Lutton to mentor and help me to follow Jesus. Thank you Jesus!

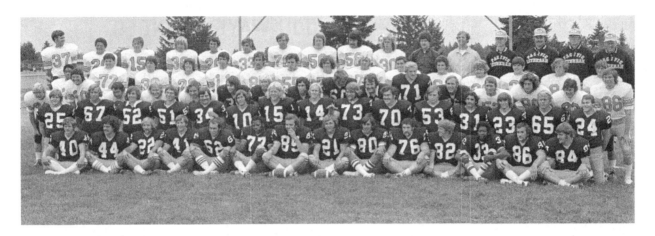

I played organized football from the age of eight to my last year at PLU when I turned 27, but I never played my best football until I played for Frosty, Paul, and Jesus. EMAL football.

How did I change? The Bible tells us to forgive others 7x70, or 490 times. I changed 10x100 or 1,000 ways! Love, serving, giving (time and money), being your best self, make "the Big Time" where you are, the pick up game, self talk, visualization, loving Jesus, helping others improve, "the man in the arena," red car/blue car, "I am only one but I am one," "see the Jesus in everyone," mirror house/window house, there is no "I" in the word team…. Well, do you get the idea?

You probably noticed I've said nothing about football. Football was a by-product of everything Frosty and Paul taught us. We all knew how to play football, but the real change and coaching took place at Breakaway, team meetings, and the post game Afterglow (known as Locker Room in the '70s). If you change how you look at things and grow your faith in God and your teammates, playing football only gets better. "Don't change for the sake of change but change if change is needed." Or as Proverbs 23:7 says, "As a man thinketh shall he become."

Thank you Frosty. You are missed. Paul, I want to thank both you and Frosty for all that you taught me, but not just for all you taught, but also for showing me how to take what you taught and "make it a lifestyle." I have learned to live my life, "for a loving and not for a living."

COMMANDING THE ROOM

Walt Zeiger (Pacific Lutheran/1974-75), Teacher and Coach (four years), Real Estate/ Mortgages (25 years), Commercial Building Maintenance and Operation (14 year), Boiler Technician with the Puyallup School District

I remember a gathering at Frosty's house where he had games for us to participate in. There was black magic, white magic, and numerous others. They weren't really magic, but you had to think outside the box to figure out the keys to solve the puzzle. I have been able to use them myself at gatherings over the years. Speaking of useful skills learned, hanging a spoon from my nose has come in handy many times.

Frosty always taught us to honor and respect everyone no matter their status or position. That is good advice for everyone, and you never know when you might need their help. He would lead a team yell for almost everyone we came in contact with: Hey (name), go (name), attaway! He left people feeling noticed, appreciated, and important.

Frosty was in his own time zone. The team operated on what became known as "Frosty time."

He had many sayings. "Sometime is no time" and "do it now" come to mind.

Frosty was a take charge kind of guy and always seemed to know the right thing to say or do. He had a lot of great stories such as the time he got caught in a pickle between

home and first in a baseball game. He commanded the room in every situation. He loved to have fun and was able to get even adults to do silly things.

Frosty would hold a special game film review session for wives, girlfriends, mothers, sisters, etc. He would also design a special play for the upcoming week that only they knew about. When it would come time to run the play during the game on Saturday, he would throw a towel in the air so all the ladies knew the play was coming. I assume the ladies took that opportunity to explain to the men around them what the upcoming play would be, making them look like football geniuses, especially if the play worked.

ICE CREAM ON THE DOCK

Doug Girod (Pacific Lutheran/ 1972-76), Math Teacher, Coach and Athletic Director (40 years including 37 years in the Hillsboro School District)

My first year at PLU was Frosty's first year, 1972. I have this memory that I think of

often, but you know how it is with memories, sometimes they may not be all that accurate. So, I called Rick Finseth, told him how I remembered it and he said, "Yep, that was how it was."

Frosty was a bit unorthodox. Often on the day before a game, he would take the quarterbacks (Rick Finseth, Craig Dahl and me) in his car to get a double scoop ice cream cone at Baskin-Robbins. From there, we would go to Spanaway Lake, sit on the dock and talk game situations until we were all thinking the same way. I really enjoyed the laid-back vibe, the camaraderie, and the clarity it provided us on how we would attack different situations. I came away feeling valued because at that time, I was the third string QB. This was just one of many systems Frosty had in place to let us know we mattered.

In our football program there were so many things that needed to get done and Frosty did them in a unique way, where people came away better because of the experience.

THE STEVE WILLIAMS WORKOUT

Ken Flajole (Pacific Lutheran/1973-76), College Coach (21 years), NFL Coach (24+ years, including Kansas City Chiefs and Super Bowl Champion Philadelphia Eagles)

I would like to start off with a story about Breakaway at Cannon Beach, Oregon, my senior year at PLU. As all previous football players knew, Breakaway was a tradition at PLU when Frosty was our head coach. It had multiple functions: it was our conditioning test on the sands of Cannon Beach (1.5 miles in 12 minutes) as well as team building/ca-maraderie events (softball games in the surf, dog patch Olympics, etc.), and it was a great time and certainly was a unique approach to setting the stage for the upcoming season.

My story starts with doing dishes on Friday night after the team meal with two of my teammates (Mark Brandt and Brad Wes-tering). We were talking about how Steve Williams (Olympic sprinter) had been in-terviewed for an article in Sports Illustrated about his training regimen. He had stated in the article that his best training sessions occurred when he trained on the beaches of Southern California at midnight with no clothes on (completely naked). You can probably guess the rest. We decided that we would sneak out later that night and replicate Steve Williams' workout at Cannon Beach.

We took ourselves down to the beach and found a log that we thought would be easy to find when we came back from our run. We stripped down to our birthday suits, stashed our clothes behind the log, and commenced on our "Steve Williams" workout. Problems occurred when we came back to that log and our clothes were gone. Thinking we were at the wrong log we continued to go up and down the beach searching for that log where our clothes were stashed. After about a half hour we gave up and decided that we needed to find our way back to the FCA lodge where we were staying.

Making our way on the streets of Cannon beach back to the lodge (completely naked) was an effort in itself. Car headlights coming down the street would require us to dash into somebody's yard or behind a bush. We actually came around a corner and bumped into some guy with his girlfriend walking their dog. Thinking we had avoided the worst and now coming upon the backyard

of the lodge we thought we were home free, and no one would be the wiser.

Unfortunately, when we got to the backyard, Frosty and Paul Hoseth were on the back porch having a conversation. They saw us. Frosty was disappointed and Paul was shocked to say the least. The only thing that saved Mark Brandt and me was that we were with the head coach's son, Brad. He caught the majority of Frosty's wrath.

When we had our skits the following night at Breakaway, one of the other teams had overheard our plan to go to the beach and recreate the Steve Williams workout. They followed us down to the beach and stole our clothes and that was their skit for the night. We all had a good laugh and have enjoyed telling that story for many years.

THE TIME OF MY LIFE

Dan Pritchard (Pacific Lutheran/1973-76), Math and Social Studies Teacher, Football, Wrestling and Track Coach, President of Cy-Tec, Inc., (print roll manufacturer) from 1984 to present (soon to be retired), DeKalb, Illinois

First Practice

In the fall of '72, I was a running back on the freshman team at the U.S. Air Force Academy. My best friend and future roommate, Gary Crockett was a guard on the Bomber team. We played Colorado, Wyoming, Mississippi State, Colorado State, etc. The Bombers played; well, they played a Bomber schedule. At USAFA, football was a job, a way to avoid being a fourth-class cadet. I was miserable. Gary was in Frosty's program. He was having the time of his life.

A freshman cadet at USAFA was used to being yelled at, sworn at, demeaned, and conditioning at 6,700 feet was tough enough without getting your butt chewed regardless of effort. I visited PLU during spring break and knew I needed to be there.

The first practice on campus after Breakaway the next year was very different than any I experienced at USAFA. But the most incredible thing was when conditioning started. Frosty explained we were to run gassers (sideline to sideline) in, I believe, 45 seconds. Rest for one minute and then do it

again. Five times. There was a big clock at one end of the field. We were to time ourselves. And then, Frosty, Paul, Joe, and Duane walked off the field. Are you kidding me? Never had I been in conditioning without yelling and screaming. Frosty wanted self-starters. I had just completed the first day of having the time of my life.

Road Trips

Yeah, yeah, yeah. We've heard all about the international trips to Europe and Asia, the cross-country plane trips to Wisconsin, Texas, California, and most notably the five straight road games culminating in Salem, Virginia, to win the 1999 National Championship. Of course, everyone knows it's a "quick trip from the penthouse to the outhouse." But before there were plane trips and passports and Frosty having to use a Sports Illustrated for ID to get on a plane, there was the 10-hour bus ride to College of Idaho in Caldwell on October 28, 1976.

Frosty gave us two options at our Monday team meeting. We could leave early Friday and stop for a crazy-hat-day practice in

Ellensburg before continuing to Caldwell, or we could each kick in $10, get a brown bag dinner from the UC, leave right after practice on Thursday for a quick three-and-a-half-hour ride, and spend the night at the luxurious Red Lion in Pasco (four to a room).

A leisurely ride into Caldwell on Friday sold us all on the deal. Now, it was not the ten bucks or the sack lunch that any of us were concerned about. It was how do four football players squeeze into two queen size beds, especially if Brad Hauge, the married guy, was one of your roommates. The easy solution was to throw the mattresses on the floor and draw straws to see who got the mattress and who got the box spring. It wasn't just the players that were a little phobic about sleeping with the married guy because the coaches, all married, did the same thing.

And that is when the Penthouse was found. Frosty was mortified. But every time he threw it away, it miraculously reappeared (did he ever lock his briefcase?). That magazine just never died. As I recall, it made an appearance at the PLUTO (PLU Traumatic Occurrences) Awards the following spring. And thus, was born the classic Frosty misquote: "A quick trip to the outhouse with the Penthouse."

Post-Game Locker Rooms

In the beginning, PGLRs were just coaches and players. Soon, dads were invited. It wasn't too long before moms and then girlfriends were attending. Eventually, PGLRs were held in the bleachers or field houses instead of locker rooms and everyone was invited.

I played football because my dad played football. I wore #42 because my dad wore #42. I am a lot like my dad, maybe too much like my dad, kind of like that song, "Cat's in the Cradle." But I don't drink because my dad drank. Because he drank, my mom, sister and I moved away in the spring of my sophomore year in high school. He saw me play only one high school football game.

My parents divorced and I did not talk to my dad basically from March of 1970 until Nov 6, 1976, in Walla

Walla. But, on that day in that tiny, smelly, poorly lit, Whitman College visitor's locker room, after the only college game my dad saw me play; because of all the love that I had experienced in four years of PGLRs, I was able to stand up, in front of my team and their families and friends and cry, hug my dad, and say that I still loved him. I can't tell you one thing about that game. I will never forget the hug. And 46 years later, the letters I am typing are suddenly blurry. Thank you Frosty, I love you too.

Frosty's Influence

I became a running back in eighth grade. I was recruited to play at the U.S. Air Force Academy. When I transferred to PLU in '73, I had to sit out the first semester. I could practice but not dress on game day. So I was a practice team RB during the week and a cheerleader on game day. By the end of the season, our two fullbacks, Dud Lutton and Gary Tortorello, were out with foot and shoulder injuries. All 150 pounds of Doug Wilson became our fullback and there I was, riding the pine because of transfer rules. Don't get me wrong, Doug was a great player

and fun to watch, I was just disappointed that my 200 pounds wasn't going to get a shot and I loved being a running back. The fall of '74, Doug returns to halfback, Gary is the starting fullback, Dud is voted captain, and JUCO All-American Jon Horner transfers in. Suddenly, the backfield is a little crowded.

I accepted Jesus as my Lord and Savior as a junior in high school. Unfortunately, it did not really change my life until I met Frosty and found a man that modeled a Christian life daily in real time. I had never done daily devotions until then. During the second week of preseason practice, the lesson in "The Daily Bread" was to work without seeking recognition, be humble, and recognize and appreciate those who toil without acclaim. My first and only thought was to thank the offensive linemen for doing their job instead of being critical if they missed a block. As I walked into Olson Auditorium for the morning practice, Frosty was at his desk and called me in.

"Dan," he said, "we've got a lot of running backs this year and not a lot of offensive linemen. Would you be willing to move to guard?" My second and final thought was,

"Hey God, thanks for the heads up." I would do anything for Frosty. I was not a very good offensive lineman, but three years of OL experience helped secure two of my three coaching jobs.

What I wouldn't give to do it all over again.

Criminal Activity

At the PLUTO awards in the spring of '77, I thought for sure I was winner for what happened at Pacific University where I was in the wrong place at the wrong time. At halftime, I couldn't find a bathroom in their field house. I came back out to the field and saw Scotty on the far sideline, ran over and asked where the restrooms were. He told me, "Right around the corner." I finished what I had to do in the nick of time. I knew that Forest Grove stadium was old, but I was surprised it did not have urinals in the restroom. Evidently, I wasn't as surprised as the lady walking in as I was hustling out. I guess I got second place at the PLUTO awards because during a car wash fundraiser that Frosty organized, Jon Horner washed the PLU police cruiser down by the maintenance buildings and, while vacuuming the backseat, pulled the door shut behind him. He spent over two hours trapped in the back seat of the really, really clean Lute cruiser.

One last thing: Did anyone ever find out who taped the nut to the lid of the jar?

PRINCIPLES AND PRIORITIES

Ron Brown (Pacific Lutheran/1972-76), Recently retired CEO and General Manager for Earl Brown & Sons (the largest grower, packer, and shipper of apples in Oregon)

Frosty Westering was an incredible man, coach, mentor, teacher, and friend. He had a huge impact on my life, my career, and my family.

The principles and priorities Frosty lived by and taught not only applied to EMAL (Every Man A Lute), and not just football, but to life in general. These are just a few of the principles I recall:

• Respect for your opponent: If you put a good hit on your opponent, extend a hand and tell him good job.

• Punctuality: If you were not 15 minutes early to practice, you were considered late, and not prepared.

• Strong work ethic: In almost every game we knew more about the opponent's playbook than the opposing players did. We were prepared.

• Leadership: Leading by example. This was Frosty's "walking the talk."

• Spiritual relationship with God: This was Frosty's first priority for all of our lives.

• Family, friends, and teammates: This was Frosty's second priority for all of us—to love one another.

• Excellence in your performance: This was Frosty's third priority—whether playing football or working in your career.

In summary, I have included three scriptures (paraphrased) that sum up Frosty's impact on my four years at Pacific Lutheran University:

1) Genesis 12:2 – I will bless you, and you will be a blessing.

2) Isaiah 40:31 – But those who hope in the Lord will renew their strength, they will soar on wings like eagles, they will run and not grow weary, they will walk and not be faint.

3) 1 Corinthians 13:6-7 – Love does not delight in evil but rejoices with the truth. It always protects, it always trusts, always hopes, and always perseveres.

I look forward to playing again for Frosty on his heavenly team. Save my number (#24).

BEING BENCHED

Steve Ridgway (Pacific Lutheran/1973-76), Executive Director, The Northwest Network Foundation (faith-based non-profit in Puyallup, Washington)

I was a transfer player from the University of Colorado. I was a highly decorated high school player. At Colorado I was injured within the first month and my personal values did not align with the overall philosophy of the football program. Transferring to PLU was not on my list at all. However, another

local college coach encouraged me to go and meet this new coach named Frosty. So, I did.

Over the next four years (during the season and many times in the off-season), Frosty and I would run errands on Thursdays. We would jump into his avocado-colored station wagon with the faux wood paneling on the sides and run to McDonald's for lunch and pick up the free lunch coupons that would be given out each week to the Players of the Week.

We would gas-up at one of the gas stations and he would yell out to the attendant to "put it on his bill." I am not sure he had an account.

Then we would stop by Baskin-Robbins to say hi and to let them know that we had every intention of being there on Monday after the Saturday game. Because they served 31 flavors, Frosty worked out some deal that if we scored more than 31 points in a game, we could get free ice cream for the whole team.

With the deals he had going on with McDonald's and Baskin-Robbins, etc., I think Frosty tapped into this NIL (Name, Image, and Likeness) thing long before the NCAA even thought of it.

Finally, we would drive down to the football stadium, and we would walk the field and we would talk about his football players. We never spoke about football. Then we would sit on the bench, and we would pray for each of those players by name. At times he would cry.

In those moments my character began to take definition. My faith was solidified and my vision for what should motivate me became clear. I knew in those moments that, no matter what I would do in my life, love and compassion needed to be the cornerstones. For four years I looked forward to being

"benched" on Thursday afternoons with Frosty. It was the best day of my week. It is where I was shaped and molded.

FATHER AND SON DAY

Prentis Johnson (Pacific Lutheran/1973-77), Director, The Boeing Company (retired after 37 and a half years), Senior Pastor, Greater Christ Temple Church in Tacoma, Washington

How Frosty Influenced My Life, Part 1

Frosty was a man of high standards and quality. He understood the value of life and the beauty of God's creation. He always seized the opportunity to recognize the simple things of life that we so often time overlook or just take it for granted.

I remember we had a road game to the College of Idaho. We had two busloads of football players. We were in the mountains of Idaho where there were deep cliffs on the left side of the road as we begin to ascend up the mountain. All of a sudden Frosty yelled out frantically to the bus driver, "Stop the bus; pull over to the side of the road, now!"

Both buses finally pulled over to the side of the road. Frosty, with his military Marine voice commanded us to get out of the bus quickly and line up on the opposite side of the road. We thought maybe there was a mechanical problem with the bus, or someone was seriously ill. Cars were passing by wondering what was going on.

Frosty commanded us to quickly turn around and we saw the deep cliff below us. What was going on?

Frosty, in a calm and pleasant voice, stated, "Look at that sunset. You will never see such a

beautiful sight. The handiwork of God."

We stood there for several minutes watching the golden sun slowly descending over the rigid mountaintop. It was a beautiful pictorial view of a simple activity that we take for granted every day. Frosty taught us that any time is the right time to take the time to appreciate the beauty of God's creation. I will never forget that moment. It changed my life. That day, that moment, instilled in me the attitude of appreciating the simple things in life we take for granted every day. I am continually grateful, thanks to Frosty.

How Frosty Influenced My Life, Part 2

My father died when I was seven years old and he left my mother with nine children, all about one year apart. I was the fifth child with two older sisters and brothers and two younger sisters and brothers. Growing up was not easy and we had to work hard to survive. My mother only had an eighth-grade education but made sure we all had the opportunity to go to college.

In my freshman year at PLU playing football, we had one home game as Father and Son Day. All of the football

player's fathers would come early on game day and spend time with their sons. Not having a father, I felt isolated, and I would withdraw myself from the team feeling left out and alone. Frosty saw my disposition and called me over to him. With a big smile on his face, he spoke and said, "Prentis, I have good news for you today. I know you have a heavenly Father and, along with Him, I will be your father this day forward."

As tears ran down my eyes, I hugged Frosty, and he made an open statement to the team that he was now my father, and I was his son.

LOVE, FIREWORKS, AND NOT CRASHING THE BOMB

Randy Rochester (Pacific Lutheran/1974-77), Corporate Trainer, The Boeing Company

How Frosty Influenced My Future Family When I Was a Teenager

The day we hit the road for SoCal influenced not only me, but also those around me for years to come because of what Frosty said to me before we drove away. He leaned into the car and grabbed my hand. He looked at me with a big warm smile and the first thing he said was, "Randy, I love you. Now, you better take good care of this new car." That was the first time a grown man had said that to me in that way. I was flabbergasted. I didn't hear the word "love" as a teenager. So, in my startled state, I just uttered, "Thanks, Frosty."

Sitting behind the wheel of Donna and Frosty's brand new Chevrolet Malibu, I was feeling really special. Frosty had arranged for Brad, Scott, Steve Ridgway, and I to serve as high school counselors at the National FCA Conference. And now we were going to drive there in style! And I was the first driver.

Raised in the '60s, my environment included a lot of beer drinking and macho talk by my dad, uncles, and cousins. It was such a personal turnoff that I just decided that I am not going to indulge. So, it was refreshing to get into the PLU environment.

But that powerful phrase haunted me and challenged me and inspired me as I grew into adulthood. It was some years later that I actually said, "I love you" to my own dad. Talk about shock! Once the dam was broken, God's plan was realized. I couldn't wait to share that feeling with my own son a few years later. And I made sure I expressed those words to him way before he became a teenager.

The Day I Wish I Drove The Bomb

Whenever Steve Ridgway and I are in the same room, he doesn't hesitate to ask everyone with a grin on his face, "Did you ever hear how Randy crashed Frosty's brand new car on the freeway in California?"

Then I explain. It all started that day in the summer of 1975. Steve Ridgway, Brad and Scott Westering and I were scheduled to be high school counselors at the National

FCA Conference in SoCal. The Westerings were kind enough to offer their family car for us to drive. Well, I assumed we were loading up The Bomb for a never-to-be-forgotten party bus road trip. But to my surprise, the boys were loading up the brand new (fresh off the showroom floor) white Chevrolet Malibu that Frosty had just bought for Donna. Wow!

Well into the trip, we were approaching SoCal. I had never driven anywhere that had such traffic. A little distracted by the great fellowship we had going on in the car, my instinct was telling me that it's getting slower, but traffic never actually comes to a complete stop. Does it? But it did that day.

Someone yelled my name to watch out and as I slammed on the brakes, we skidded up to the stopped car in front of us and barely tapped his bumper. It was so minor I didn't even get out of the car. But Steve, Brad, and Scott shot out of their seats to greet the guy in front. After a quick analysis by the four of them, everybody got back in their car razzing me for some time about "crashing" the new car. It's a razzing that I accepted as true love for a brother in Christ. But for a few brief seconds on that SoCal freeway, I was wishing I had "crashed" The Bomb instead.

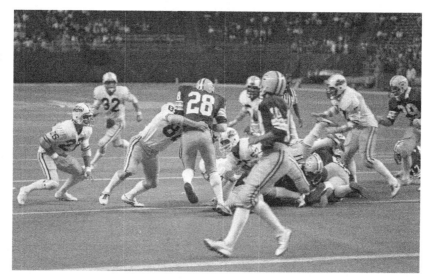

Thanks To Frosty, Thousands Are Still Enthralled

Mark Accimus and I were walking by Frosty's office one day and he yelled out to us, "Hey, do you guys want a summer job?" We looked at each other and said, "You bet, Frosty." He handed us the phone number of a guy

that had just called Frosty looking for some big football player types to build the wooden stands that they sell fireworks out of on the Fourth of July. We called, interviewed, and got the job driving all over the state setting up these stands. That job led me to pursue the same Red Devil fireworks company for a job the next summer. They hired me to be the Central Washington warehouse manager that season.

That being my senior year at PLU, I was about to graduate with a degree in Education. Red Devil offered to match any teaching job salary to come to work for them year-round as the Corporate Distribution Manager. Offer accepted.

I was able to hire scores of part time summer workers to help us through the fireworks season over the years. I went straight to my source of PLU football players and among many, hired Scott Westering. Scott got the bug to shoot the professional fireworks displays. He got licensed to become a head pyrotechnician and continued to shoot shows ever since.

I got out of the business for a while but wanted to show my kids what real fireworks were. I called Scott one day and asked if he still shot shows. He said yes and would love to have me join the team at Liberty Bay and Ft. Lewis. So to this day, thousands of people are entertained by a Westering, thanks to that wonderful phone call that Frosty shared with Mark and me back in 1976.

JUST AS IMPORTANT

Tom Alexander (Pacific Lutheran/1975-78), Retired Teacher, Coach and Athletic Director (38 years), Manson High School; Owner and Operator of a 20-acre apple orchard (35 years)

Tough Love

During practice on a Hat on Dummy pass blocking drill, I got beat by "Big Wally," John Wallace, three times in a row. On the third block, he pushed me back into the bag that Frosty was holding and it knocked him to the ground. When I helped Frosty up he really lit into me. This was something I had not seen him do before as I was expecting him to "flush it" or coach me up as he always did after a mistake.

After practice on my way back to my dorm, I passed by his office, and he called me inside. With tears running down his cheek, Frosty gave me a big hug and for 15 minutes explained to me that he was trying to make me better and that he overreacted to being knocked down. It was a great lesson for me in my future coaching on how to treat athletes when they make mistakes.

My Story

The summer I graduated in 1979, I was working construction and interviewing for teaching jobs throughout the area. I got a phone call from someone in the PLU placement office telling me that Frosty wanted me to apply for a teaching and head football coaching position at a small school on Lake Chelan. He said I needed to call them that day. I was somewhat reluctant because I wasn't really thinking of being a head coach, but I called and had the interview two days later.

Fifteen minutes into my interview, the district secretary came into the office and told the superintendent that he had an important call. I left the office and after 15 minutes he called me back in and told me that I had the job if I wanted it. He handed me the phone and Frosty was on the line. Through his recommendation and great words, I signed the contract that afternoon.

Frosty and I stayed in contact throughout the years. He would check in with me to see how I was doing, and I would also call to ask for his advice. Like PLU was Frosty's Big Time, Manson was my Big Time. Many years it was just me along with a great assistant and sometimes 62 players.

A great honor Frosty gave me was asking me to talk to the 1988 PLU team prior to the only Alumni game I played (we actually tied) about how lessons learned from him, and the program helped me in my coaching and how it affected hundreds of my athletes and

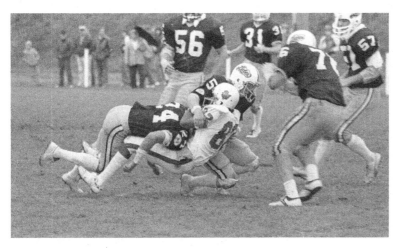

thousands of my students. Four of my players had the honor of playing for Frosty (Paul Finley and Wai Tim Petersen being two of them). Frosty also allowed me to bring my team to practice in the field house so they could experience turf before our 1986 state semi-final game in the Tacoma Dome.

After 18 seasons and 14 state playoff years (119-47), I had to retire from coaching football due to open-heart surgery and later two artificial hips. When I awoke after my heart surgery, I received from a PLU player a great Attaway sign with messages from the 1992 PLU team. Next to my father, Frosty had the greatest influence on my life. I still have my PLU Oil Can Award sitting on my desk and all the plays and advice in his handwriting that he gave me in preparing for my first season at Manson.

Every year at Manson, I wrote a summer letter to our incoming team. It was my way to share Frosty with my athletes. The letter included dates and times for meetings and our practice schedule, plus three to four motivational articles from notebooks Frosty would send me.

When I was interviewing at Manson, there were six other candidates for the coaching position. One was Al Bessette who interviewed the day before me. I tried to convince the superintendent that he was a better candidate. He was an All-American and set so many receiving records at PLU and I was just a four-year backup lineman. My future superintendent told me he was looking for a great teacher and coach, not a great athlete. Frosty must have seen something in me.

I was always trying to be an important part of the program. I would stay after practice and catch punts, field onside kicks, and challenge Brad Westering in passing distances. We would start at opposing 30-yard lines and see who could force the other to get into end zone first. Occasionally I would win. Great times.

I learned from Frosty that I was just as important to the team as a player like John Zamberlin as long as I gave my maximum effort. That's the greatest lesson I learned. Because of that, I always tried to make my four-year JV players feel as

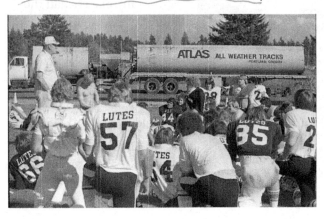

important to the team as my all-state player. I knew it would make the team better and help that student athlete in his future.

By the way, I sent John Zamberlin one of my best players after he pressured me as one of his former PLU teammates and weightlifting partner. That player ended up being an All-American at Central.

Thanks again Frosty for being a part of PLU football and my life.

FROSTY PRAYERS IN THE DESERT

Ray Pulsifer (Pacific Lutheran/1975-78), Air Force Officer, Head Baseball Coach, Lathrop High School, Head Coach and Program Manager, Alaska Wild Baseball Club

After graduation from PLU, I became an Air Force officer and earned my wings as an Electronic Warfare Office in the F-4G Advanced Wild Weasel Aircraft. With Prentis Johnson and Greg Price, I used my leave from USAF to join them at the Alumni Games for many years. It was a blessing to rejoin Frosty and see old friends at these games.

I was deployed to Desert Shield with the Wild Weasels and used my phone privileges to call Frosty and inform him that for "reasons I can't go into," I would be unable to join him and the Lutes for that particular Alumni Game. Frosty asked if I could tell him where I was and I was not allowed to say. He immediately asked if he could pray for me on the spot and of course I welcomed his prayers. He said he would watch the news even more intently now that he knew I was "involved."

His love and support were wonderful, and I thought of him and my loved ones praying and supporting me as I flew combat missions during Desert Storm. I flew 45 combat sorties. I received the Air Medal, Aerial Achievement Medal, Presidential Unit Citation, and a "V" for Valor device due to the hazardous nature of those missions.

I have tried to emulate Frosty's philosophies as the Head Coach of Lathrop Baseball and Head Coach and Program Manager of Alaska Wild Baseball Club (American Legion). Frosty's valuable insights help me every day as I try to influence and develop my young men.

TOE TO TOE WITH FROSTY

Brad Westering (Pacific Lutheran/1975-79),
President and Creative Director, Incite the
Mind, Inspire the Heart

All I have ever known is that Dad and football went hand in hand. My earliest memories are when he would take Scott and me under his arms, throw us in the car, truck, bus, or whatever mode of transportation with "low on gas" status, he included us. I believe that he wanted us close to him. I believe that he wanted us to share in the experiences of what he knew (or didn't know) each day would hold. It was the unexpected thrills, fun, relationships, and experiences of being wherever he was—because wherever he was, there was the Big Time.

I saw him serve so many people over so many years. He received immense joy out of making every experience unique, yet his ways were quite simple. I "suited up" in a Lea College football uniform when I was ten to be on the sidelines watching the intra-squad football game. He put me in on the last play to run the 09 pitch-out where I ran for a touchdown amidst blocking and diving college players and made the local paper the next day. I finally figured out they were organized in their efforts to make sure I scored.

He perched himself high on top of the press box with the 16mm team camera when I was in junior high taking movies of me playing. He came and apologized to my high

school football team after he had come to the sidelines to give me a coaching point during one of my games and the head coach thought he had crossed the line as a parent/coach.

He gave me great freedom to become a decent college quarterback amidst our battles as father/son, coach/player. It was a difficult distinction to make clear during our years, yet we worked through it together with insights and love from my mom and Coach Hoseth. Mom would often tell me that when Dad and I went "toe to toe' it was as though a mirror was between us reflecting an exact image of the other.

Hanging around my dad, all I knew was the Big Time—because it was wherever he was.

FROSTY'S NOT SO HAPPY VOICE

Brian Troost (Pacific Lutheran/1976-79), Superintendent, Soilfreeze Inc., Woodinville, Washington

Frosty Westering made an impact on my life the day I met him. That particular moment was just the first of many that I remember, and that made an indelible imprint on my life. Many of those memories are moments of laughter. Some were tearful. Some were intense learning moments, and others were simply moments of peace, and appreciation of what God has given us. It would be hard to pick one moment that stands out above all others, as I am sure most EMALs would agree that Frosty has said or done many things that have made an impact on their lives.

One moment in particular, as I recall it, stands out in my mind. It was on a Saturday evening in Ashland, Oregon, after a victory over Southern Oregon University. Our team spent the night in a hotel before the next day's trek back to PLU. Keep in mind that this hotel visit was after a game, a win nonetheless, and many players did not feel the need to get a good night's sleep. Needless to say, the evening was jovial and celebratory, and the jocularity lasted well into the evening—and apparently into the morning for that matter.

One player in particular, seemed to have the unfortunate ability to be involved in notable and controversial moments that occurred during team activities. Most of my teammates would agree that he was legendary in his ability to be front and center during most notable events.

I was awakened in the wee morning hours to Frosty's voice (his not so happy voice) echoing throughout the hotel parking lot. My roommate and I rushed outside to see what the matter was, as did the rest of the team that had decided to turn in earlier, along with most of the other hotel guests, staff, and

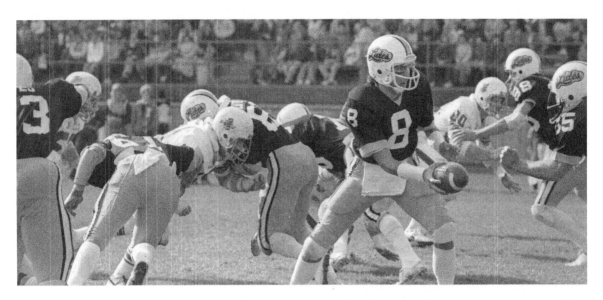

everybody in the all-night diner next door.

There we saw Frosty, bestowed in minimal nightwear, standing dead center in the hotel parking lot, calling out the names of the late night/early morning revelers that were being such a nuisance. He used both their first and last names, (I'll just call them "Jeff and Scott" for referential purposes), along with a couple of standard Frostyisms: "C'mon guys!" and "Let's go!"

I was able to hear him so well because all

of the traffic on the adjacent interstate had stopped during the commotion, as did the Amtrak line and the commercial airliner flying above. Even the local crickets dared not interrupt Frosty's short-lived articulation. Rumor has it that "Jeff and Scott" froze in the positions they were in (I believe it was a half nelson) and remained as such until their morning alarm went off. It goes without saying that the rest of the evening went without any additional frolicking or carousing.

The situation was just an example of how much respect Frosty garnered when he engaged us as players. He didn't need to say a lot, but what he did say carried a lot of weight. Perhaps even more impressive was his ability to let things go, or "flush it." As the new day arrived, nothing was said about the previous night's proceedings.

Years	Record	Postseason
1972	6-3	
1973	6-3	
1974	8-1	
1975	7-2	
1976	6-4	
1977	8-2	
1979	9-2	NAIA Division 2 Second Round (1-1)

CHAPTER 3

THE 1980's
PART I

[1980 - 1984]

TEAM RECOGNITION DAY

John Bley (Pacific Lutheran/1977-80), President and CEO, Compliance Services Group, LLC; Director of the Washington State Department of Financial Institutions

It was late afternoon on a clear but cold December 18, 1999, day as Frosty, his assistant coaches and the 1999 PLU football team made their way across the football field after the Amos Alonzo Stagg Bowl in Salem, Virginia, to shake hands with the coaches and players of New Jersey's Rowan University.

PLU football was 1999 NCAA Division III Football National Champions; a feat made even greater not only by being the first team in NCAA history to win all five playoff games on the road (logging 15,200 flight miles in the process), but more importantly that the game turned out to be a national

showcase for Frosty's brand of stewardship, devotion, fellowship, and hard work known as "Double Win" football.

PLU's story reached the offices and halls of the state Capitol and at the end of January 2000, the Governor's office and the state legislature extended invitations to Frosty and the football team to be honored on PLU Football Team Recognition Day, March 3, 2000. That day would be like no other day in Washington legislative history.

The mid-morning was spent with Governor Locke who was regaled with stories of the 15,000-mile journey to Salem, Virginia, from the players and coaches. At the end of the festivities, the Governor signed a proclamation declaring March 3, 2000, *PLU FOOT-BALL TEAM RECOGNITION DAY!*

The next stop was the chamber of the House of Representatives where Frosty and the

team were presented with legislative resolutions honoring the team and its accomplishments. There is always a certain decorum that is strictly followed in the legislative chambers and in that context Frosty was asked to say "a few" words.

A few words turned into Frosty leading attaway cheers and running from one aisle of the chamber to the other. The co-speakers of the House, the Honorable Frank Chopp and the Honorable Clyde Ballard also got attaways. Then the toy PLU footballs began to fly and we learned that receiving was not a strong talent among the legislators. A few words ended up being a wonderful 30 minutes of Frosty's win-win stories and a few more ad-lib antics that echoed throughout the halls of the legislature.

It was another feel-good moment, by a feel-good team with a feel-good coach. ATT-AWAY! (WINS)

JUST DON'T GET WET

Scott Davis (Pacific Lutheran/1977-80), Sales Manager, Climatec, LLC + AZ

Eric Carlson (Pacific Lutheran/1978-80), Teacher and Coach (Retired)

GEORGE ATHONS / KON HOVING

In the end, this story is about Frosty Westering. Along the way, and in telling it as an observer and unfortunate participant, there is a supporting character who is central to it's telling.

James Jefferson (Jeff) Walton III (aka Walt, James, and James the third) showed up on PLU's campus during the interim of 1978, having transferred from the University of Oregon. I first met Jeff in what used to pass as a college weight room. For

those old enough to remember, he looked like a 19-year-old Mark from the TV show "Gentle Ben."

For the era, Jeff was big at 6-0 and 240 pounds. His suit jacket was a 50 and he could barely keep his socks up for having such small calves. Frankly, he looked like a bird with a house on its back! Since it was just the two of us in the weight room, I went over and introduced myself, starting a friendship now stretching 44 years. Little did I know the trouble that my new friendship would cause, or better said, the trouble that Jeff would suck me into.

This anecdote begins James the third's first week of his first season as an EMAL in the 1978 season. What could possibly go wrong? A better question might be how did a second-team Bomber get on Frosty's radar?

Hmmm, was it because Jeff lost his jersey on picture day or was it when Frosty called him out for having lost said jersey?

Could it have been at Breakaway where the Dogpatch team's all had to come up with a skit and Jeff elected to portray a Samurai

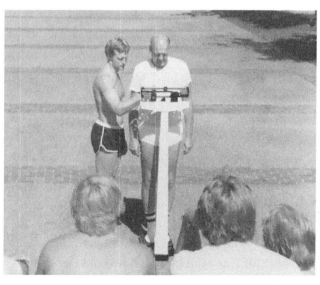

gynecologist in a parody of John Belushi's various samurai skits on Saturday Night Live?

Jeff did his best to put his hair in a ponytail, donned gym towels as a loincloth, and ad-libbed the rest, keeping all of us in stitches. The coaching staff found no humor in this however, particularly Frosty. Due to Walt "not knowing he didn't know," Frosty felt obligated to admonish the team that there was a line of good manners where one does not cross, and that line is clearly crossed when it degrades the female body.

There was never a room that Frosty entered that he did not own. If you knew him, enough said. This included classroom 101 in Olsen Auditorium where we had our team meetings. There was another side of Frosty that seemed to be reserved for his players. It was a side that the public never saw. This was when he was "not maaaaad. Just disappointed."

Let's now continue with Jeff's first week as an EMAL.

The setting is classroom 101. Frosty is pretty darn close to being mad, but clearly disappointed. He had a Cardinal rule: you brought your football notebook to every meeting. In addition to the X's and O's of the game, he seldom was without an article to help us with the "winning edge" that he would hand out, already three-hole punched, for our "Hot Button" section of the notebook.

On this fateful day, Frosty held up a football notebook that was clearly someone's from the defensive team based on its disheveled look. "Whose is this notebook?" Frosty bellowed out, as Jeff frantically tried sneaking in late to the back of the room. "This was found in a trash can. Whose is it?" We all wanted to turn invisible for fear even though it was not our

notebook. From the back of the room a familiar voice said, "It's mine Frosty." I blacked out and have no memory. So what happened next is a mystery. But it could not have been good.

The story does not end there—although it would be reasonable to expect that by then Frosty would have said goodbye to Jeff and whatever career as an EMAL that he might hope to have.

On the way up to Bellingham to play Western Washington University (WWU) for the first game of the season, we stopped at a Girl Scout camp on Lake Samish. There we had baloney sandwiches that Donna Westering made for us with an apple and a bag of chips. This should tell you something about the budget that Frosty had while at the helm.

Frosty showed a 35mm film by Reverend Bob Richards, a former two-time Olympic gold medalist, to inspire us before the game. After the film, there was still time left before we had to set off for WWU. As clear as day I can hear Frosty saying, "Guys you can go down to the water, but just don't get wet." The words were barely out of Frosty's mouth when a 6-0, 240-pound blur went past my eyes.

Assuming that was my cue, I turned and jogged down to the lake. By the time I got there, Jeff was in the lake-end of a canoe, perpendicular to shore, in a half-squat, not yet seated. in the shore-end of the canoe, Steve Kirk, one of our defensive tackles was putting one foot into the canoe to enter, with the other still on solid ground. The canoe started to quiver, then it started to shake, then it proceeded to tip over and Jeff (who was sitting now) wisely put his hand out over the side of the canoe to keep it from tipping over… and completely disappeared. Gone.

"Just don't get wet."

Jeff pops up spitting water and the thick wool sweater he was wearing had to be holding 20 gallons of water. Mike Catron was standing next to me and almost wet himself from laughing.

"Just don't get wet."

We got Jeff up to the bus to find some dry clothes and to keep him out of Frosty's sight because we all knew that if he was caught, Walt was done with PLU football! Someone lent him some shorts, one guy gave him a shoe, and another a shirt. Frosty was none the wiser.

But the story does not end there.

When we pulled up to the stadium, the bus driver parked near the end-zone on a severe blacktop slope pointed at the goal posts near the locker rooms at the field. As was his protocol, Frosty would dismiss the first team guys first, then the second team guys, then the Bombers. Jeff stayed behind to stay out of sight and was one of the last two people to exit the bus. Mike Westmiller was the other, who was on crutches from an injury suffered the first week of practice.

As Jeff walked to the exit with Mike right behind him, somehow, as only Walt can do, he released the parking brake, and the bus started rolling down the steep incline toward the end-zone. Springing to action in a panic, Jeff jumped into the driver's seat, searching for a solution and finally slams the brake on, saving the day just as the bus came to a rest in the third lane of the track on it's way to the end zone.

Mike said afterword that he thought he was going to shoot headlong through the front

windshield. Had Jeff not stopped the bus, it certainly would have sunk to its axles under the goalpost in the waterlogged sod from all the rain. The game for certain would have been canceled!

This was only the first week of PLU football for Jeff Walton. He went on to play three more seasons, several as a starter, with no fewer escapades to follow. Jeff has a bad case of attention deficit syndrome (ADD) and is in constant need of stimulation. He claims to be a victim but certainly he was the instigator of so many things that the not-yet-fully-developed male brain could conjure up. I shake my head to think that he graduated.

So how did Jeff's first week at PLU end? After the game, in which we were victorious, we were in the locker room, having the traditional Locker Room. We were all crammed into an extremely small space, with parents, family, and girlfriends included. This was a time where Frosty and Paul Hoseth gave the players a chance to talk about the game, the week leading up to it or really any topic, as nothing seemed to be off limits.

Many players took their turns sharing and then came a point where several players started calling on Walt to share. Jeff sheepishly stood up and recounted his first week in the first-person, beginning with his lost jersey, then the lost notebook, Frosty finding it, playing the Samurai gynecologist, falling into the lake, to almost canceling the game due to a bus being stuck in the end zone. While telling the story, I peeked over at Frosty and he had his hands on his hips, eyes closed, head tilted back, with a belly laugh bellowing out of his mouth.

Frosty was one of the most accepting, color-blind, fair men that I have ever met. If you knew him, you know he had his faults. You know that he was not a candidate for sainthood. Jeff went from the outhouse to the penthouse that day because that was the kind of man Frosty was. In the years and decades after our class left, Frosty would still call on Jeff Walton to speak if he saw him in the group after a game or special event. For me, Jeff helped to prove what a wonderful man, coach, and mentor Frosty was.

BEARING FRUIT

Eric Dooley (Pacific Lutheran/1979-80), Missionary, Southeast Asia (28 years); Pastor; Licensed Psychologist, New Life Counseling Center

The First Time I Met Frosty

On a sunny Friday morning towards the end of my senior year of high school, I squeezed my 5-foot 9-inch, 160-pound frame into my car to go visit PLU for the first time. It was the spring of 1979, and only a couple months after Mt. Hood Community College had let me know that they had dropped their football program, and

that they were sorry if I felt I had been strung along. My dad had told me that PLU had a football program. So, I drove to PLU to talk to the admissions counselor and meet the PLU football coach—whoever that was.

I don't remember how we ended up on the PLU football field watching a high school track meet, but Frosty had graciously taken time to talk to me as I approached him uninvited that Friday afternoon. I remember sitting on the grass as I told Frosty that I wanted to play college football. Frosty listened patiently then he gently said, "Well, Eric, we have already done all of our scouting in the area, and we already have our team for the fall." As I persisted in pleading my case, Frosty finally said I could walk-on in the fall. In hindsight, it was classic Frosty that he gave me those 15 or 20 minutes of his time.

That fall, Frosty was speaking at the opening night of freshman orientation. I approached him afterwards and he told me to come down to the football field the next afternoon. And so, I got a chance. Frosty truly cared about people—even an uninvited boy who just wanted one more chance to play football.

1980 National Championship: Recollections From the Bench

In hindsight, one of the most striking things about the 1980 National Championship season was how calm, steady, and humble Frosty was, and how the team instinctively resonated with that demeanor and attitude.

Football was fun! Frosty projected his usual optimism week by week. He would say, "There are 13 goal sheets in your playbooks this year, and that isn't an accident." Frosty frequently repeated the mantra, "The only pressure you have is the pressure you put on yourself." There was no noticeable difference in how each week's practice progressed as the season moved on and the playoffs began. One of the most memorable moments that year was playing Linfield in McMinnville on November 1st. It was a highly anticipated rematch after beating the Wildcats by one point the previous year. Down 19-20 at the end of the game, Frosty decided to go for two points to win the game. Although the conversion failed (resulting in the only loss that season), the play demonstrated Frosty's attitude and belief in his team's ability to win.

Two weeks later as talk turned to the playoffs, someone mentioned that we might play Linfield again during the first playoff round. I saw Frosty's attitude reflected in his son Scott who responded with iron determination: "I'd love it!" Three weeks later, we played Linfield again in Tacoma and won 35-20.

The following week's game was also at home. Trophies arrived at Olson Auditorium in preparation for the game, one set for the winners, and one set for the losers. Someone in the athletic department, apparently trying to mirror Frosty's positive attitude, picked up the box of trophies for the winner's and boasted, "Here are our trophies!" But that wasn't the kind of attitude Frosty had. He humbly said, "There's no place for that kind of talk guys." And even the following week after winning the national championship, nothing changed. We were all just enjoying the trip.

How Frosty Influenced My Family and Career

Although Frosty is often known for his love of one-liners, it was the stories he told that have stayed with me the longest. Stories with catch phrases such as "you're gonna be glad and you're gonna be sad" or "whether the bird is dead or alive, the answer is in your hands," have been repeated by myself (in various languages) across Southeast Asia during a 28-year missionary career, and for the past decade in my office as a counseling psychologist. I have told church members and patients alike about Frosty and the fact that he told these stories over 40 years ago. However, Frosty's influence and legacy aren't merely contained in the things that he said, but in his impact upon the lives of others.

When I returned to the Pacific Northwest

after being overseas from 1986 to 2014, I was surprised to find how many of the college kids I had known at PLU had grown up and become leaders in education, coaching, insurance, and ministry. Moreover, even those who hadn't played on the football team but had been influenced by Frosty and The Lutes continued to carry a unique and recognizable positive attitude, servanthood, sportsmanship, and faith across decades and into an amazing number of spheres.

This truly is an example of the words of Jesus in John 15:16 (NKJV): "You did not choose Me, but I chose you, and appointed you that you should go and bear fruit, and that your fruit should remain."

A DIVINE GIFT

Scotty Kessler (Pacific Lutheran/1979-80), PLU Coach (parts of 1981-82, all of 1984 and 1992-96); Missionary; Adjunct Professor, Faith International University and Seminary, Tacoma, Washington

My Testimony

I am a Northern Californian who met the Westering Family at summer camps run by The Fellowship of Christian Athletes. I had previously not heard of Pacific Lutheran University until I met the Westerings and other alumni of the PLU football program at these camps. I attended two other colleges prior to transferring to PLU with three semesters of schooling left to graduate in order to play football in the EMAL community.

The bottom line is that my life was completely transformed, spiritually and otherwise, while playing two seasons under the leadership of Frosty Westering and Paul Hoseth. The impact of the PLU football program upon my life and family line was more than I could have ever imagined and to this day is by far the single greatest influence upon my life in all regards.

Bottom Lines

1) I am who I am due to my relationship, past and present, with the PLU football community that has been overseen and stewarded by Frosty Westering over many decades. Frosty has been the primary impactor of my adult life and is the most influential person in my life story.

2) The PLU football and the EMAL philosophy is the single most powerfully and eternally impactful philosophy of competition, and more importantly philosophy of life, that I have ever read about, heard of, seen or experienced in all my work and travels. Nothing is even close to its direct impact upon the lives of men and women, boys and girls, and the subsequent ripple effect upon parents, families, and others in the outer circles within the program's reach.

3) Frosty Westering was a divine gift to the PLU community specifically, and to the world of sport in general, and I mean divine in every sense of the word.

Breakaway

Breakaway was a genius approach to team building—bonding with new players, laughs, making memories, singing and skits, and creative competition. It was so much fun to look forward to the start of football. Breakaway was completely opposite of the world's normal way—blood and guts, sweat and work and pain, and no fun at all. Still to this day, I've never heard of anyone who approaches pre-season this radically.

It was the complete elimination of all things football related (no football schematic talks, football related training or conditioning, etc.). I call it "anti-football" because it was everything other than football. However, it in fact affected the football team so directly in every way. Breakaway was the foundational keys to the team's season.

Pre-season Practices

Two-a-days were as low key and non-physical as anything I've ever heard of or seen in 50 years around football. There were limited or no pads, limited or no team conditioning, limited or no contact. Full speed 11-on-11 contact full scrimmage the first Thursday and Saturday of two-a-days and then never again for the season.

For a player, this was as player friendly as could be imagined. Healthy players played better and the limited hitting was a great player benefit to the early season.

Football people would say these kinds of behaviors would never prepare a team to compete at the highest level, however, in every way, Frosty's philosophy did just that, with less wear and tear on coaches and players than I have ever heard of or seen—ever. Genius!

Post Game Locker Rooms (Afterglow)

More Genius. The PGLRs (or Afterglows) were a post-game time of sharing and caring and debriefing the game day with coaches and players (in the early years) and then family and friends in addition (in the later years). Frosty would take a long, long time to milk the moment. These processes would take hours. Sometimes the players did not shower until many hours after the game.

These were very intimate, vulnerable, and supernaturally powerful and palpable sharing times player to player, coach to player, player to coach, player to family and friends, etc. You never knew what might happen. You simply knew it would be long, emotionally powerful, full of laughter and singing, and just about anything that could happen when people come together to share and care.

Player Notebooks

Once again, counter-culture, the player notebooks were mostly filled with handouts regarding heart and attitude, not with football schematics (though there was a comparatively small section in the back of the playbook that was specifically related to football).

It was very clear both by verbal acknowledgment from the coaches and their practice that attitude and effort, relationships, and servant leadership were more important than the football related information (though that was important also).

Team Meetings

Team meetings were part inspiration, part attitude development, part logistical, and part football related (but mostly not the football part).

Post-season Competition and National Championships

In all the playoff seasons and all the games in the postseason, I never once heard Frosty say or hint anything like, "We need to win." I never heard winning mentioned in a way that was like the world. It was always mentioned as a sidebar—for sure at most a by-product of the process.

He would often say things like, "Enjoy the trip," "Let's play as long as we can so we can be

together as long as possible," and "They come to *beat* us. We come to *be* us!"

He made away games an asset instead of a liability. He created a culture where players loved away games (more time together!). Frosty made it an advantage to be away and together. He disabled all the traditional thinking that when you are at someone else's, "house," that you were at a disadvantage.

SHARED PASSIONS

Tom Wahl (Pacific Lutheran/1977-81), Teacher and Coach, Port Angeles High School (41-plus years)

I believe the first time I met Frosty was in his office at the front entrance to the gym. Besides him being very friendly and upbeat, I immediately noticed on the wall behind him a picture of him playing the drums. I grew up playing music and especially the drums so I knew we shared two passions, a love of football and a love of playing music. I have coached football and several other sports for 41 years now and still play the drums in a

worship group at a church where I live and occasionally for the student body at the school I work at.

I also followed in Frosty's footsteps and completed a Ph.D., degree in the field of education 20 years ago. Frosty was an excellent role model, which I still strive to be also as a teacher, coach, grandparent, community member and still competing athlete.

I was a four-year starter and honored to help Frosty win his first National Championship my senior year.

TOUGH LOVE TIMES TWO

Garth Warren (Pacific Lutheran/1977-81), Chief Development Officer, EFCA

Tough Love

One day in the locker room, I was running a little late for practice when Frosty scampers through in a hurry and says "Come on Garth! Let's go, let's go, let's go!" Foolishly I said, "I thought we were on Frosty Time." I felt an immediate moment of silence as he screeched to a halt, did a 180-degree pivot and like a heat-seeking missile stormed back to my locker bay saying, well, it really doesn't matter what he said. You can imagine my comment was not taken well and I learned firsthand about tough love.

The Human Side of Frosty

During the recruiting season after my senior year, Frosty asked me to serve as the recruiting coordinator, a role Scotty Kessler had filled the year before. I was happy to do it and think I did a good job that pleased

him. We had agreed to a salary for my work, something like $100 per month for four months.

When the time came to get paid, Frosty told me to wait for him for 15 minutes inside his office. I didn't realize he needed to go to the bank to get $400 from his own account. I took the money, thinking I needed it, but honestly was embarrassed realizing he likely never had my position approved from Dr. Olson and so he needed to absorb the cost himself. I suspect part of what I took away from being a Lute was that even when painful, Frosty taught me that we do whatever we can to honor our word. In his case, I am convinced his integrity came at great personal sacrifice to he and Donna over the decades.

Paul and Jeanne

I have served in a number of roles in my career where I was in the second chair. I marvel at how well Paul and Jeanne served in that role with Frosty and Donna. From my perspective, Frosty did a good job of giving Paul a voice and an influence upon all things PLU Football, but it was still Frosty's program.

Having said that, the program came to life for me, had tangible and sustainable impact on me, and shaped the course of my professional career, marriage, and role as a father as I witnessed Paul's relationship with Jeanne, Karl and Mari. There will never be another Frosty. He was bigger than life and I consider it one of the greatest gifts of my life to be a part of his legacy. Yet, in the best of win-win scenarios, I feel like being exposed to the EMAL football program that Frosty envisioned and brought to life was extraordinarily complimented by Paul and Jeanne's practical, humble, and quiet influence. Frosty and Donna in their own ways, and Paul and Jeanne in their unique ways, had an immeasurable impact on my life and the life of my entire family.

Tough Love: Lister

One day during the week immediately following Breakaway, we took two PLU vans full of players to talk about leadership with the students at Lister Elementary School. Still fresh from the egg-throwing antics of the Breakaway trip from Tacoma to Gearhart and back, the seven or eight guys in the van I was driving thought it would be hilarious to egg the other van right after we finished at Lister. I have no idea what we were thinking, but the eight of us strategically boxed our fellow Lute van into the after-school bus line so they could not get out. We then methodically unloaded all of the eggs and laughed the entire way home.

It was only when we pulled into the PLU campus that we began to think Frosty was about to be called by Lister. Realizing this, Greg Rohr (one of our team captains) and I went into Frosty's office two minutes before practice started. We asked if he had a minute to which he said, "I've got a minute, but that's all." We told him what we'd done and it was as if time had stopped. Getting to the practice field was no longer his priority.

He said in an escalated voice, "You did what?" We truly thought he might blow a gasket right then and there. He was hot! He said, "That is like sticking your head down the toilet bowl and flushing it! What were you thinking?" And then, almost immediately, miraculously, he went into the film room right next to his office and sat down.

We started thinking about how we could solve this problem. Greg and I proposed to Frosty that we would talk to the entire team on the bleachers before practice and acknowledge the foolishness of our acts. Frosty felt like that was a good plan and he would handle the administration both at PLU and Lister.

Once that was settled, he sat back in the chair in the film room and he said, "Tell me again what happened?" We told him, fearing his reprisal. Instead, a big smile took over his face as he envisioned all that happened in front of those impressionable Lister kids (as they were

all sitting on their buses). Frosty's smile grew into a big grin as he envisioned what those kids were thinking as we were declaring egg wars on our fellow Lutes.

Reflectively, he said, "It is not so much the event as the way everyone holds us (EMALS) to a higher standard." In retrospect, I can only recall two other times in my life where I felt so much grace in light of the huge cost my foolishness had on Frosty and the goodwill he had worked so hard to build. One last note: Frosty dearly loved Greg Rohr and the entire Rohr family. I am so glad Greg was with me that day.

LEADER OF THE BAND

Scott McKay (Pacific Lutheran/ 1978-81); PLU Coach (1982-83); Teacher and Coach in Washington (40 years, retired in '22)

I first met Frosty in late March 1978, on a visit to PLU to find out about the football program and the university. My high school football coach told me that he had heard about Frosty from a former Everett player (Randy Ayers) and that he really enjoyed his PLU experience and that Frosty was a coach like no other.

We started in Frosty's office in Olson Auditorium and he began to share what the college experience and being a part of EMAL football would be like. He took out a plain pink sheet of copy paper and began writing as he talked. It was incredible! I watched and listened as he talked and wrote and talked and wrote and soon the paper seemed completely covered with words, lines, and squiggles. His enthusiasm, warmth, and positivity were amazing and genuine.

I come across my pink sheet every few years it

seems, usually when cleaning and organizing, and it takes me back to that day and my first time meeting Frosty, my first time on campus, and his way of making you feel like this is exactly where you belong. Frosty really was a coach like no other.

In November 1981, we flew back to Kansas City, Missouri, for a National Quarterfinal playoff game against the William Jewell Cardinals. Part of the trip was a visit to FCA National Headquarters the day before the game. I remember very little about the building and what we saw but toward the end of the visit Frosty introduced us to then FCA President, John Erickson.

He talked to us for a few minutes and bantered back and forth with Frosty.

As it became time to leave, Erickson took out his guitar and began playing. He sang Dan Fogelberg's song "Leader of the Band" as a dedication to Frosty—a song Fogelberg wrote about his father as the leader of their family. John Erickson was commending Frosty, the leader of the EMAL family.

I hear the song from time to time and to this day it triggers memories of Frosty, that trip and others, and the amazing love and support he gave so freely to all of us.

COMING HOME

David Knight (Pacific Lutheran/1979-81), Owner and Team Leader, Landman Inc.

Meeting Frosty

I met Frosty for the first time at his office at PLU and what struck me about him was how warm, open and authentic he was. I felt like he truly listened to my story and understood me and cared about my situation. I learned from him that, "People don't care how much you know until they know how much you care."

I had heard about Frosty from one of the players at the college I was playing football for at the time. I was very successful on the field but not happy there. I was exploring what to do with my football career and looking for another school to play for. I felt I could trust him and follow his recommendations and guidance.

As we shared and talked, I found that Frosty was putting into words what I felt about football, life, and the world we live in, but I did not have vocabulary or the ability to express it. I guess you could say I found a kindred spirit. Meeting Frosty felt like coming home. I knew right away I wanted to be a part of what Frosty was all about even though I knew or understood little of what was going on. It felt right. It felt like Frosty, PLU football, and many of the coaches and players were about something much bigger than football and I wanted to be a part of that. My time at PLU proved this to be the case.

My Faith Journey

I did not grow up in a family of faith. We did not go to church and I was not exposed to faith options, yet I had a hunger and longing in my heart to know the God who created me. Frosty (along with many coaches and players) was a man of faith in God who was open, honest, real, and transparent about that journey—the good, the bad, the ugly, the struggles, and the victories.

It did not feel fake or religious in a bad way. I did not feel pressure to believe nor was I pressured to reject the faith. It was presented and lived in a down-to-earth authentic relational way that resonated with me and drew me in to embrace faith. I made a specific declaration of my faith at my first Breakaway, took communion at the beach from Frosty with some of the other players, and it is a special day I will always remember.

Since that time I have continued on my faith journey. I strive to be authentic and not religious. I have been intentional to provide an atmosphere in my family, business, churches, and ministries for a similar experience to happen for others like I learned from Frosty at PLU.

About Paul Hoseth

Paul Hoseth also had a profound effect on my family and me. I took Paul's Family Centered Childbirth class one interim and it really impacted me. It exposed me to the concept that there are so many options in life, so many choices, and if I explored the world more I could find what fit me.

I was not married at the time yet had a heart to be married and have a large family one day—to create my own sports team. A couple of years later after getting married, I called up Paul to see if my wife (a PLU grad) could take the class. My wife was a biology major and was of the mindset that we should not have very many children because it would contribute to overpopulation. After taking

the class, my wife had a change of heart and we ended up having six boys in 10 years. Five were successful home births! Thank you Paul, and the rest is history! Paul's example and heart for faith, marriage, family, and others played a huge role in who I have become and the impact my family is today.

Frosty's Impact

It is said you become the average of the five people you spend the most time with. Frosty was one of my five at a critical time of my life. From a young age I had a vision for my life. At 13, I made a list of things I wanted to accomplish, places I wanted to go, and the life I wanted to live. I had no idea how to achieve these things but at that young age I saw that football and education were the paths in my life journey.

My success in football got me to Frosty and PLU. Frosty introduced me to countless others (who became my fives) that greatly shaped my life and kept me on my journey. People like coaches, politicians, business leaders, pastors, teachers, and other great people who did great things and became great people. These were my people group. They were my mentors, teachers, business coaches, and friends.

It became a daily habit to spend each day with these people via cassette tape (podcasts today), in person, seminars, sermons, personal development classes, etc, I found a greater community that was able to express what I was thinking and feeling and help me to adopt, achieve and continue becoming.

I had a heart for God and He gave me a heart for people. My primary calling was to family and marketplace ministry through business. These became the vehicles through which I served God, loved and served his people. I worked in the medical and pharmaceutical field for 13 years while flipping properties on the side and got my real estate license eventually and have operated my own real estate company up until now. Landman Inc., became an expression of what I have previously shared. My company has funded ministries, missions, helping others, and traveling to many parts of the world.

I am so grateful for who I am and who I am becoming because of who Frosty became for me and for others. I am paying forward what was paid into me.

THE CANNON BEACH CREW

Dave Reep (Pacific Lutheran/1979-81), Licensed Financial Advisor, Mt. Vernon and Anacortes areas (32 years, now retired)

As activities at the Breakaway lodge in Gearhart, Oregon, came to a close, a few of us Lutes jumped into our vehicles and headed south to Cannon Beach, only 10 miles away, to see the world famous Haystack rock. This idea, of course came from someone who grew up near the Oregon coast in Salem. I cannot say his name but his initials are—Jeff Walton.

Upon arriving at our destination, we were able to drive right down onto the beach and take part in all of the beach activities first hand. We were tossing the Frisbee, throwing a football, watching Jay Halle play hustle golf, all by himself. It was inevitable that someone suggested going swimming. So since we were at the beach, we did. By now, we needed to hurry back to Tacoma since our side trip took additional time.

Finally driving on to lower campus we saw the entire team standing outside Olson Auditorium with all the coaches and staff and cheerleaders. There was an impromptu dinner arranged upon our arrival but somehow our Cannon Beach crew ended up being over an hour late. And everyone was waiting for us before dinner would begin. Before we could sneak and mix in with the rest of the team, we were intercepted and confronted by none other than, Frosty.

"Well?" Frosty demanded. "Where have you guys been?"

Everyone was looking down at their shoes or trying to hide under a rock. Not sure why he was compelled to answer. Maybe it was the 10 people hiding behind him. But Scott Davis quipped to Frosty something right out of the Wally Cleaver handbook. "Well gee Frosty, I guess we went south instead of going north."

Needless to say, Frosty got excited and in a hurry. We experienced a true tough love session in front of the entire team. I now can say I have never heard a person raise his voice and shout as much as he did without uttering a single swear word. Truly amazing.

HITTING THE JACKPOT

Chris Utt (Pacific Lutheran/1979-81), Teacher, Glacier Peak High School in Snohomish, Washington

Anyone who knows me knew that Frosty and I did not always see eye to eye. Whether it was a team meeting or a game, we would have our moments. I did not totally buy into the PLU system. I just wanted to play on a successful football team, and did I hit the jackpot.

The year I joined, there were six or seven

transfers who would make an immediate impact. I was fortunate enough to be part of a National Championship in 1980 and two other playoff teams in 1979 and 1981. I played with some pretty good football players and great people. There are 12 of us who meet every summer for a three-day golf fest and Lute session. It is one of the highlights of the year for me. These guys are my brothers. We go away and come back the next year and it is just like it was during our time at PLU.

I am finding myself using a lot of the Frostyisms in my classes and the teams I coach. I, along with many others, had the privilege of playing for Coach Frosty Westering. One more thing: he did a great job preparing us for life, but he was also one of the best coaches I ever played for. He was an offensive genius, and truly a great man.

ONE EVENT: A LIFETIME OF IMPACT

Guy Ellison (Pacific Lutheran/1977-82),
High School Coach and Teacher (eight years);
Thrivent Financial (34 years)

A jar of beans with a walnut was an interesting prop for a keynote speaker—a large bear of a man holding forth with captivating tales at my Auburn High School Fall Sports Banquet. Intriguing. What was this Frosty going to share with a room full of student athletes, teachers, and parents? In a word, "Inspiration!" A positive mental attitude, goal setting, and comparing yourself to your own best self and no one else, were just a few of the motivational themes woven into his stories. I went on to play for, coach with, and later in some capacity even advise this force of nature that was Frosty Westering.

On Frosty's football field of life, I married my high school sweetheart at the old age of 20 years. Frosty and Donna shook our hands, hugged us both, and at some point delivered a working refrigerator to our first home in married student housing.

Our daughter (born on the sidelines of Frosty's field) played in the sun with Frosty and Donna's third grandchild. The girls were separated by time and space until Clare was accepted to PLU 18 years later. Upon hearing the news, Frosty all but shouted, "Does she have a roommate yet?" Heather and Clare

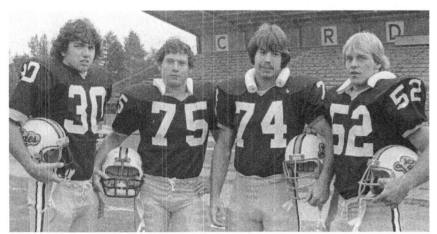

*Be kind to your web footed friends
For a duck may be somebody's mother
Be kind to your friends in the swamp
Whether the weather is cold and damp*

I can't remember the ending but it was repeated many times and led by Frosty. As a greenhorn freshman and having put on my game face even before I got on the bus, I was in shock! I wondered what I was getting myself in to.

shared their first dorm room, enveloped in Westering Family love. And more happy stories ensued. My career with Thrivent would eventually find a few of us around the kitchen table with Frosty and Donna, helping them plan and enjoy some dreams of their own.

An Auburn High School Sports Banquet keynote speaker caught my attention one evening in 1976 and that has made all the difference for this "Man In the Arena." It's been an honor and a privilege learning from and playing football with Frosty Westering.

It wasn't long before I realized I had gotten myself into this amazing experience called PLU football—led by this amazing man, Frosty. A magical tour!

SEEING THE BIG PICTURE

Jay Halle (Pacific Lutheran/1978-82), Corporate Chaplain (retired)

I met Frosty during the summer of 1972. I was 12 years old and attending a summer FCA camp with my family in Ashland, Oregon. My dad was involved with FCA and was helping run the camp. I remember Frosty's energy and positive approach to life even at that young age. Thanks to Frosty's influence, as well as other athletes I admired at the camp, I decided to follow Jesus.

A MAGICAL TOUR

Eric Anderson (Pacific Lutheran/1978-82), Counselor and Disability Services Coordinator, Skagit Valley College (retired)

As a freshman, I made the traveling squad. On my first bus trip with the team to an away game, we had just started off. I was nervous and was expecting it to be a quiet, intense and focused ride. But instead, soon after our departure, Frosty stood up in the front of the bus and said some positive Frosty words and then, out of nowhere, he led us in a song and it went like this:

After high school, when it was time to decide what college I would attend, I prayed and asked the Lord to guide me. It came down to two: Huskies or Lutes. One offered me a football scholarship. The other did not. I chose the one that did not offer me a

scholarship because Frosty was the coach. I figured that, if I was to go on and play college football, I wanted it to be fun.

Frosty made it the most enjoyable experience I could have ever imagined. It wasn't just about football for Frosty. He taught us how to be men of God and see the big picture. I am extremely thankful for God's leading and helping me make the decision to play at PLU. Through the way Frosty ran the football program and his life, I grew in my relationship with God, which influenced how I would continue to run my life.

I have used many of Frosty's one-liners through the years and one of my all-time favorites is, "Winners do things that losers don't want to do." What a blessing and an honor it was to have played for Frosty and Paul Hoseth. Paul was also very influential in my life. My hope and prayer is that I would continue to use some of the many tools they shared with me as I continue to run this race called life. God's best to the whole Westering and Hoseth families and thank you!

A GUY IN BAND

Curt Rodin (Pacific Lutheran/1979-83), Orthopedic Surgeon

We all have many great and memorable stories about our time at PLU and our experience of Frosty as our coach, leader, and mentor. These were priceless times and our memories and stories include tales about meeting Frosty, playing for him, seeing him expose himself (literally, well, down to his underwear when getting weighed at the start of the season), great and unorthodox coaching and strategies, team meetings ("Frosty Time" and Donna's doughnuts for those of us on the offense), crazy antics during road trips, having him yell at us outside the hotel in the middle of the night (ask Jeff Walton about this one!), sideline chaos, and of course great football with lots of winning, and yes, for many of us, a national championship.

I have lifetime friendships with many of my teammates, and whenever we get together, we share our stories from this time like it was yesterday. I'd like to share a couple of stories that may be a little different and may reflect a slightly different side of the great man and coach.

At one point in my time at PLU, I really missed playing music. I don't remember the exact sequence of events, but I got an audition with the University Jazz Ensemble. I was elated when the director asked me if I'd like to play the baritone sax with the group. The problem I hadn't considered, though, was that the rehearsals overlapped with the beginning of football practice.

I set up a meeting with Frosty to see if we could work out a solution but figured I would get the typical coach talk about dedication and responsibility, and that if I wanted to succeed in football, I would have to prioritize my commitment to the team.

I couldn't have been more wrong, and I learned a lot about what a great coach and leader Frosty was that day. He urged each of us to be our own best self, and he walked the walk and supported me in pursuing that. As we sat in his office together, he thought out loud and said, "Well, you know, that first little bit of practice is just individual skills, so as long as you get that done another time, it should be okay for you to be a few minutes late." No problem.

Then, as he stood up to see me out of his office, he clapped his hand on my back, and with the classic Frosty grin and endless enthusiasm said, "This is so great, Curt. We've never had a guy in band before!"

There is no "I" in team. Playing football for Frosty, it was all about team, and our team succeeded because we supported each other and stood together as brothers. We had a lot of very talented players, and yes, there were many individual achievements and accolades. But the focus was on how we were all better together.

Decades after my playing days at PLU, I got a package in the mail. It had very familiar telltale block print handwriting and arrows, so even after the passage of time I knew it was

from Frosty. I had no idea what it might be. Maybe a book? Something inspirational? What could have made him think of me now?

As I unwrapped the brown shipping paper, I saw that it was a plaque—an award for First Team Academic All-America, College Division. There was a classic note from Frosty telling some crazy detailed and long-winded story about how this plaque had been on an epic journey, got lost, and then eventually found (when in reality it had just been in a box in his garage or office all those years). The note ended: "Just wanted you to know how proud I am of you and of your success and achievement in life."

I sat quietly and looked down at the plaque. I thought about Frosty and about life's journey. In that moment, much more profoundly than it would have been when I was a young college football player, it meant the world to me.

MENTOR FOR A LIFETIME

Kirk Talley (Pacific Lutheran/1981-83), College Head Football Coach (39 years); Athletic Team Consultant

Introduction to Frosty

I was in Frosty's program for one year, however, Frosty impacted me for a lifetime.

My cousin Dave Olson played for Frosty in the mid 1970's. While my parents were visiting extended family, they chose to visit PLU where Dave was attending and playing ball. My parents ran into Frosty that day in

1975 (I was in ninth grade and back home in Minnesota). He gave them a tour of the campus. When they got back to Minnesota, they told me of this gregarious head football coach named Frosty. They were so excited about Frosty that I set my sights on attending PLU and playing in his program.

Fast-forward six years: I was a PLU student-athlete. I had transferred as a junior and was excited (and nervous) to finally be under Frosty's tutelage. I learned so much from him. He had me mesmerized. I was learning how to coach while in his program and while attending his football class.

Though I did not play my senior season due

an ACL tear, God saw that one year in the program was enough for me to grab a hold of Big Time football and begin my coaching career. Because of Frosty, I had 39 years of opportunity to impact and influence young men and those around them! Thank you Frosty!

Though this is a condensed version of my Frosty story, I want people to know that other than my Lord Jesus Christ, my wife, and parents, Frosty has had the biggest influence on my life. Because of Frosty, I chose to attend PLU, met other coaches, professors, and friends that influenced my life, coached college football, and had a unique coaching philosophy. I will always be grateful for Frosty Westering being my mentor for a lifetime.

Frosty's Impact

I could sit and listen to Frosty for hours. He was such a great storyteller, and his stories were not only funny at times, but they also had a message about being the best that one can be in life and in sports. And though so many stories were hilarious (like the one about him and Brad throwing interceptions), the way he displayed his love of life in front of us was even more captivating. Like when he would tell the team to stop singing "Frosty the Snowman" at a restaurant, as if he were embarrassed, and then he would begin playing an air trombone. He was bigger in life that way.

With the hilarity of his stories and his bigger than life personality, Frosty also had a serious side that would let one know that he was serious. As an example, one better had not been late for a meeting, or you would feel Frosty's heat. And so with his alluring personality and his unique approach to life,

athletics, and football, I learned to be myself in life and in coaching.

Though I learned quite a bit from Frosty by how he ran meetings, led practices and games, and directed our road trips, I also gained invaluable knowledge in his classroom, specifically the football class. Frosty had a huge impact on my coaching philosophy, which I gained by observing him and learning from him as a student. I still hold the same philosophy to this day. He also guided me through the fundamentals of how to put together a program. More than anything, Frosty taught me how to be a man of God and live for Jesus Christ, and how to be the best that I can be in that process.

A NEW WAY TO COACH

Kirk Westre (Pacific Lutheran/1980-84), Department Chair, Kinesiology, Whitworth University; High School and College Football Coach (31 years)

Frosty's Influence on My Career

When I arrived to the PLU program in 1980, I was introduced to a new style of coaching and an entirely different culture surrounding competitive athletics. At the time, the predominate, almost exclusive style of

coaching was autocratic and militaristic. The sports culture was very Darwinian.

The contrast to my previous athletic experiences was startling (in a good way), overwhelming, and even difficult to absorb at first. Frosty implemented a democratic style of coaching that relied on persuasion rather than coercion, put ups rather than put downs, mutual support and respect, and an experience that focused on the journey rather than the destination. His program exposed thousands of athletes (PLU players and opponents) to a different sporting experience through the most effective form of socialization—modeling.

Frosty and Paul demonstrated what a player-centered approach to coaching was all about. As a result, the others and myself had the philosophy and practice to coach in a new way. I implemented his style in the 31 years I coached and continue to teach his style in my collegiate coaching classes (38 years and counting). I wrote about it in my doctoral dissertation and have published many articles (and given presentations) about his methodology. I know many others who have also replicated this way of coaching and leading.

As a result, his coaching and culture-creating techniques have spread exponentially and by now have positively impacted tens of thousands (and counting). That is Frosty's professional legacy. Pretty amazing for a guy who just followed his heart, convictions, and faith.

About Paul Hoseth

Although I played on offense exclusively during my five years at PLU, I had (and still have) a special relationship with long time Defensive Coordinator Paul Hoseth. I interacted with Paul and the defense at practice regularly as I spent a significant

amount of time serving on the scout or Bomber offense. But the bulk of Paul's influence on my life came from off the field interactions and experiences.

As a physical education major, Paul was a professor of mine in a number of my classes and he also served as my student teaching supervisor. Paul also hooked me up with a baseball coaching opportunity while I was still an undergrad to help with my professional development. I even attended the same church as Paul and his family while attending PLU. Occasionally, Paul and his family would be in charge of the entire service that Sunday. I watched how he conducted himself as a husband, father, and spiritual leader. Those initial college interactions laid the foundation for an ongoing personal and professional relationship that continues to this day.

After graduation, I was fortunate enough to get a high school football job as the head coach. Paul spent hours with me on his backyard patio teaching me about defense and how to implement a defensive system into my program. Throughout my entire professional career, I would contact Paul regularly for advice, wisdom, insights, problem solving, and fellowship. He always had time, space, and energy for me. For the bulk of my coaching career, however, I served in the role of an assistant. Paul modeled for me how to effectively, professionally, and with integrity function in that position. Although Frosty's program initially changed my life, it was Paul Hoseth's example that solidified and entrenched that change.

BEYOND THE SCOREBOARD

Dave Templin (Pacific Lutheran/1981-84), PLU Assistant Coach (1999-2003, 2014-17); High School Teacher and Coach; Army Contractor, Cognitive Performance Specialist with the H2F Program

In 5th grade, my brother and I rode our bikes to PLU and ended up watching football practice. It was 1973, one of Frosty's first years of coaching at PLU. Some of the players, including Steve Ridgway, took the time to say hello. I kept going back to practices. The kindness of the players, who would take the time to play catch and ask how I was doing, along with Frosty's great stories would always keep me coming back for more.

After a while, I became a ball boy for the Lutes. My dad was kind enough to take me to the PLU games home and away. There was something intriguing about the games, the attitude, but what sticks most in my mind was the Locker Room as it was called back then. I remembered sitting in the actual locker rooms and listening to players and coaches talk about what just happened in the game. Sometimes there was laughter, sometimes there were tears, but there was always a level of authenticity about what they'd just been through that really struck home.

I remember sitting in a locker room at Franklin Pierce after a loss to UPS. We could hear them hooting and hollering and celebrating their victory. Frosty shared how

much he cared about the guys in the room and how he wouldn't want to be in that other locker room.

He also shared about Christ. Growing up in a Christian family it was wonderful to see coaches and players who shared about their faith through the game of football. And while the world around me was saying that you only had value if you won, Frosty redefined what winning and success should really be about. Every Locker Room ended, as it should, with everyone holding hands and praying.

Fast forward to high school and 1980 where Don Coltom (another long time Lute) and I drove down to watch PLU vs. Linfield. We got there really early so we could stand along the field. Both teams were undefeated and ranked #1 and #2. Before the game started, I was asked if I could help with the game balls. I thought, "Are you kidding me? I get to watch the best game of the year from the best seat in the house. This is going to be awesome!" Then someone told me I'd have to be on the Linfield sideline during the game. "Ugh!" I thought, but reluctantly said yes.

Linfield jumped out to a 20-0 half time lead and they were living it up. The Lutes continued to play hard regardless of the score

and the Wildcats couldn't figure out why the Lutes didn't give up when the score was so lopsided. Well in historic Frosty fashion, the Lutes "found a way" to battle back to score their third touchdown that made the score 19-20. Frosty hated ties, so of course the Lutes went for two. Linfield stopped them and won the game on the scoreboard.

But at the end of the game I saw something that changed the way I looked at sports forever. Frosty rallied the team in a huddle as the clock wound down. I could not hear what he said, but when the game was over the Lutes congratulated Linfield on an excellent game. Instead of hanging their heads after the loss, or disrespecting a worthy opponent, the Lutes met their adversary with heads held high and honored the incredible game that was just played out. If you looked at the players on the field, and not at the scoreboard, after the game you wouldn't have been able to tell who won and who lost. Since that day, I have often used this story when teaching athletes and coaches about what winning and success are all about.

From ball boy and fan (1973-1981) to player (1981-1984) and coach (1999-2003 and 2014-2017), I was blessed to play a variety of roles

in the completely unique football program that Frosty built and passed on to his son Scott. Frosty found good people who believed in what God was doing at PLU. Paul Hoseth, Craig McCord, and Scott Westering were just a few of the many who served during my tenure. Frosty was incredibly creative and was constantly seeking new ideas and ways to share.

We always made fun of Frostyisms and Breakaway skits were full of attempts, many very successful, to make fun of the corny sayings and practices that made PLU football what it was. But he would not waiver. He continued to recite the same lines, tell the same stories, and make us laugh 'til our sides hurt or scratch our heads to think, "What in the world?"

His relentlessness and choosing what was really valuable in life made the ideas stick for many, many years for some of us. But most of all I truly believe that he tried his best to honor Christ in his coaching and to coach as he would have liked to have been coached. I can only hope that at some level I can do the same.

Year	Record	Postseason
1980	11-1	NAIA Division 2 Champions (3-0)
1981	9-1	NAIA Division 2 First Round (0-1)
1982	7-2	
1983	9-3	NAIA Division 2 Semifinals (2-1)
1984	6-3	

CHAPTER 4

THE 1980's PART II

[1985 - 1989]

56-COUNTER-CRISS-CROSS

*Jud Keim (Pacific Lutheran/1981-85),
Assistant Coach, Pacific Lutheran*

My last visit with Frosty was literally at his bedside in the hospice facility where he was placed towards the end of his time with us. I knew this was the end of the "game" for him and the last time I would be in his presence. EMAL

His daughter Sue was there and Frosty had several of his visual aids all around the room: both a Blue and Red Car, the beans and the nut in the jar, and of course, the little plastic toy toilet he used for the "flush it" equation. Made me smile.

As we all know, Frosty had such a joy and energy that filled the room with light. It was palpable and just oozed from him. Given the context here, I didn't expect that, but man it was off-the-charts and charged up as I walked in the room and caught his eyes. Big thumbs up and we both almost simultaneously belted an "Attaway!" (Sue told me

later he really, "made the big time" for me and fired up, like when any former player visited.)

We had a cherished but short conversation (totally sensed his energy was only so much), but what put it over the top was he had a gift for me. He looked at Sue and asked her to get the card. It was a folded over blue piece of card stock paper. On the front it read, "Would you believe you're getting an..."

Frosty put on some glasses (I had never seen him in glasses). They looked like they were from the 1960's (they weren't super cool). He started to write something down in the body of the card. After a minute or so, he hands me the card and whatever he had done inside it. I opened it and it says: "Attaway! We are so proud of you!"

I got an Attaway card, but what he had drawn below the words was an actual football play from the old PLU Offensive Playbook. He literally drew out, in detail, 56-Counter-Criss-Cross (all you halfbacks back in the day know this one). It's a double hand-off-QB-to-Halfback-to-Halfback counter/reverse play that usually popped for

big yardage. He had the #26 tagged on the Wing, who gets the ball last). That was my playing number and where I aligned for that play 35 years ago!

Holy smokes! Frosty is a few days from taking his last breath and he draws a play to gift me. Man, I teared up big time. I hugged him and thanked him for all the selfless love he invested in me and in my family.

The card is right here on my desk in my office. It always will be.

Frosty, as we all know, had very little concept of money and time. My sophomore year, I was in need of a ride to Lincoln Bowl for a practice we were holding there. Somehow, I got in the Frosty Bomb with Kevin Skogen who was the quarterback at the time. Of course, there was no gas in the car.

Kevin had a little note of paper. We stopped at the gas station at Pac Ave and 112th. Skogen handed the gas guy the note. It said "Frosty $5" in Frosty's handwriting. We filled up and were off. I guess Frosty had a tab there or I thought. I didn't know you could do something like that. Everyone knew Frosty and where to find him and I'm guessing he had to be reminded to pay for it.

Frosty had a very small staff—really no position coaches. He'd send us halfbacks and receivers (we were one and the same) over to the old soccer field during practice. He'd be with the o-line crew. "Guys, do the hit and spin on the Crowther sled and the hand-down drill!"

Multiple times in my career he'd forget about us over there (there were probably 15 of us). It was 45 plus minutes of hand-down/hit and spin. We certainly weren't going to remind him ("Are we good?"). We just kept going

and kept trying to live out Frosty's "self-starter" principle. We were certainly great at it though, but I never ever did those two drills again!

IT'S UP TO ME

Tim Larson (Pacific Lutheran/1981-85), Teacher and Coach, Sedro-Wooley School District

In the summer of 1980, I attended an FCA camp that was held at PLU. I was headed into my senior year and had started to think about what my goals were beyond high school. I knew I wanted to continue playing football if I was given the opportunity and had previously been talking to the recruiting coordinator at the University of Washington.

I decided to attend the camp after hearing about the PLU's national championship the previous season. I had also heard that football was played "a little differently at PLU." This sparked my curiosity and led me to the FCA camp.

As the camp got under way, I spotted someone who was distinctly different from the others around him—a balding man dressed in all yellow with a big grin on his face. I watched him as he maneuvered through the crowd and seemed to have something important to say to everyone he encountered. People stopped and took notice. "Who was this?" I had to find out.

Without having to wait much longer the man walked to the top of the stairway, then turned and hollered out in a loud but comforting voice, "Welcome to PLU, home of the EMAL's. My name is Frosty Westering, and I am very excited to have you all here."

Frosty went on to talk about some camp specifics and what our next step would be, I later was given the opportunity to talk to Frosty one-on-one in the next couple of days and he sold me on PLU football, even though I would most likely have to be a walk on to be part of the team. He left me with a single thought that drove me through the year to the next spring, he said, "Tim, remember, if it's gonna be, it's up to me."

FAMILY CONNECTION

Jeff Elston (Pacific Lutheran/1982-85), Senior Vice President of Global Accounts, Corporate Visions

Scott Elston (Pacific Lutheran/1985-88), Vice President of Business Development, FCTG

My brother Scott and I had the honor and pleasure of playing for Frosty Westering from 1982-1988 with 1985 being the year that Scott and I were able to play on the same team. We were not unique. There were many brothers that followed their older sibling and chose to play PLU Football for Frosty including: Brad and Scott Westering, the Grambos, the Coltoms and many others before and after.

One of my favorite memories occurred in my senior year during a game against our nemesis, Linfield. In the heat of competition, I looked across the defensive huddle to see my brother Scott, a freshman, run in to join our battle. A huge wave of pride came over me at that moment. I still get that feeling now.

The brother connection was just one aspect of how Frosty and the program touched the Elston family. Frosty had a very special way of making everyone he encountered feel like they were part of the team. He was the epitome of inclusiveness. No one was ever left out.

In our case, that included my older brother Mark and my younger sister Maria, but especially my parents. For eight years during PLU Football seasons, my parents, Ed and Judy Elston, attended every game. No matter where the game was, they would be there. No exceptions. They absolutely loved Frosty and the entire program including all the "Attaways," quirky one-liners, and after game Locker Rooms. They especially loved how Frosty always led our team with a faith-first approach and let everyone know how much they were loved.

My parents were thankful that I stumbled onto PLU Football quite by chance. I was not recruited by PLU. I actually didn't even play football my freshman year. After seeing my roommate John Duppenthaler from high school have such a great time playing for Frosty, I decided to turn out the following fall. And I'm so glad I did. Frosty, Paul Hoseth, Greg Rohr, and so many others made a lasting impression and helped shape the man I am today.

Here's the rest of the story from Scott: The impact on our family was so positive and not only on our direct family, but a few close family friends that joined our EMAL family over those years.

One epic memory and journey was the chartered flight to Helena, Montana, for a playoff game against Carroll College. They had crazy crowds, and the Lutes won a back and forth game. The flight back was a blast, including the pilots literally "buzzing the town!" When our time on the field ended, I think our parents needed counseling to deal with withdrawals from being part of the program.

Additional brothers that made the program special were the Sweets, the Gradwohls, the Krebs, and others. And then children of players have returned to play, and the story and tradition gets to continue (Keims, Welchs, others).

The impact that EMAL football had—starting with an idea, a belief, passion, and commitment—and the team that Frosty created (his family, outstanding coaches, volunteers, etc) was so awesome and it touched everyone associated. We all remember lessons learned and have a desire to pay it forward. My brother and I have a bond and memories from our time together at PLU that we will always appreciate.

A ROAD TRAVELED SLOWLY

Drex Zimmerman (Pacific Lutheran/ 1982-86), Residential and Commercial Real Estate Broker

This is a story of Frosty's tough love and grace:

Pre-season 1985

As we caravaned south to our annual team weekend meet and greet at Gearhart, Oregon, the captains had been assigned driver duties of PLU vans. Just north of Kelso, by way of eye contact and audible, we skillfully aligned the vans across all I-5 lanes and proceeded to slow down to approximately 25 miles per hour. After two minutes of driving in Blue Angelesque formation, the multitude of obnoxious, blaring car and truck horns blocked out our ability to verbally communicate, so we changed to a silent count and broke formation.

Little had we considered that "PLU," "Pacific Lutheran University," "Lutes," and the campus phone number were strategically plastered all over the vans.

Soon after arriving at Breakaway Lodge, Frosty called a captains' meeting in the front bunk room. I'm protecting the identity of the other captains, but you know who I'm referencing!

"Guys, we had a situation come up that we need to hit head on. It's not a *big* deal but…"

Frosty went on to share that one of the irate (obnoxious) drivers that had interrupted our bumper fest had called the university to lodge a complaint. Within minutes, the complaint had found its way to the offices of President Rieke and Dr. David Olson, PLU's Athletic Director. Somehow soon thereafter, Frosty had been alerted.

Back in the bunk room, Frosty shared his disappointment in our decision-making and the negative impact it might have on our

teammates and the athletic program. He told us that when we returned to PLU we were to write an apology letter to the disgruntled (obnoxious) driver and schedule visits with both President Rieke and Dr. Olson. We of course apologized profusely to Frosty.

Little did we know that this was the dawning of "The Great Apology Tour." Frosty's bunk room closing remarks were, "Guys, I love you. Now *admit* it and *flush* it!" That was grace.

When we returned to PLU, we mailed the disgruntled driver an apology letter. The following day, we paid a visit to President Rieke's office. He was extremely cordial, giving us all the time we needed to grovel over our stupidity. He accepted our apologies, kindly questioned our judgment, but never our character. That was grace.

Our drive out to Dr. Olson's Lake Lawrence property was a quiet one. When we arrived, Dr. Olson was lakeside with his fire pit ablaze. He invited us around the fire pit and gave us all the time we needed to grovel over our stupidity. He followed up with a few of his own thoughts then wrapped up "The Great Apology Tour" with two haunting questions that I will never forget. 1) "How well cooked do you like your hamburgers?" and 2) "Would you like a Lake Lawrence boat tour?" That was grace.

To my knowledge, Frosty never discussed our I-5 folly and its consequences in front of the team. He could have resurrected the incident at any time to be used as a teachable moment but never did. Frosty never shamed you to motivate. He loved you to motivate. Now that was grace.

THE FROSTY PLAYBOOK

Mike Vindivich (Pacific Lutheran/1985-86), Tacoma Screw Products, Inc.

I transferred from the University of Washington after two major knee reconstructions. I think we often do not recognize the most significant moments of our lives when we are young. Frosty's philosophy on football was not confined to the playing field. His teachings were life skills and I still use many of his quotes and positive attitudes. My son is a basketball player and I've had the honor of giving him and his teammates the inner game skills right from the Frosty playbook.

NUGGETS OF GOLD

Terry Marks (Pacific Lutheran/ 1983-87), Principal, TMarks Design

In the days before laptops in the classroom, people used to write down their notes on paper. I've captured information both ways and maybe it's because I hail from that time before, but I get so much more out of writing things down by hand. I think it's because whatever you're writing down has to go through your mind and to your hand before

landing on the paper. You remember it better. You comprehend it.

That's the way it was when I was a Lute. Frosty dropped nuggets of gold all the time and we were in the classroom not just to study plays and the week's opponent. We had our playbook and then we had our inner game notebook. You can guess which one was thicker when you played for Frosty.

I've always been able to draw. When you're scratching down all the notes while Frosty was on a tear, imparting enthusiasm, and truth, it helped. Not only was I able to capture all the information, but I was also able to make it legible. I suppose that this was why Frosty asked me to recreate most of it when he wrote his books.

If it's not apparent, it was a privilege to work with him on it, on them. They weren't on the New York Times best-seller list—although I've worked on books that were—but these mean something more.

They weren't the pinnacle

of design. They didn't go into my portfolio. But for all the work that I've done and long forgotten, I hold those dear—more so now than at the time.

The few years you spent playing football for Frosty looms large on your mental landscape. By the time I was done playing, I had 16 years of football under my belt. I don't remember much of most other than snippets. But I remember my time playing for Frosty. It wasn't perfect. But it was special. I can't help but think it helped us be better men.

It's a common thing for people to have stress dreams. Many people have that dream where they are naked in public. Others walk into class on test day without having known that they were even in school, much less prepared for a test.

I've had that one. But my most common one is that I find myself on the sidelines of a game in a perfectly white away uniform. Sometimes it's in a stadium, once in a while at my lousy junior high field. The long and short of it is that I am a middle-aged man and I'm being told that I'm going in the game. I'm freaking out because I don't even know if I can get into my stance, much less blow someone off the line.

So, I start running onto the field and I realize that I don't have my helmet. I look around at the bench and I can't find it. Then Frosty's there.

"Terry! What are you doing? Get in the game!"

"I can't find my helmet, Coach."

"What? You can't find your helmet? Oh, for cryin' out loud!"

I'm sweating and freaked out. Then Scott shows up.

"Dad! What's going on! We're on the clock. What's the problem?"

"Scott! He can't find his helmet!"

"WHAT?"

It's about then that I wake up.

ONE MORE SATURDAY WITH FROSTY

Steve Valach (Pacific Lutheran/1983-87), English Teacher and Head Football Coach, Liberty High School

Over the course of my five years at PLU, I'm not sure how many Saturdays I spent with Frosty. What I am certain of is that my last Saturday with him is the one I'll remember most.

In late January of 2013, I received the news that Frosty was at home, but in fragile condition. The end was near. I shared this with my wife, Natasha, and she replied, "You should take the boys and go see him." So, around noon on Saturday, I piled our boys, Isaiah, 10, and Elijah, 6, in the car and we headed to Parkland to see Frosty.

The last time I had been at Frosty's house was a pre-season barbecue sometime back in the mid-80s, so I needed to call his son-in-law Jim Johnson for directions. Donna answered the door and led us to the front room where he was lying on the couch. He was quiet and a bit foggy, but in classic Frosty fashion, the longer we stayed, the better he got!

Donna was busy preparing a care package of her goodies to send to their granddaughter, Taber, who was playing basketball at Tennessee. She offered the boys and me some samples of her chocolate covered peanut butter squares, and memories of Donna's goodies and Tuesday night offensive film sessions in Olson Auditorium came rushing back.

In preparation for the trip, I had each boy draw a picture for Frosty and prepare a question to ask. Isaiah presented his picture, a drawing of Frosty and him, with "God made me, and he doesn't make junk" printed across the top of the page. Then, Elijah sidled up next to the couch and handed Frosty his drawing, which showed Frosty and him in a rocket, headed for the moon where they would "play

football together." Needless to say, the boys and Frosty began to really hit it off.

As Frosty and I caught up, the boys wandered down to the basement, which, if you haven't been down there, is like a PLU Football Museum. Before too long, they began hauling up different items. Elijah bounded in the living room holding a toy blue car: "Hey, Frosty, why do you have this?" Of course, that led to me explaining the best I could about the blue car vs. the red car mentality. The whole car comparison didn't become a Frosty staple until after I graduated. As far as I can tell, red car means you're a negative kind of guy, and blue car means you're a PLU kind of guy.

The boys listened respectfully and then disappeared for another foray into the basement.

Pretty soon the boys scrambled upstairs holding a starfish: "Frosty, why do you have this?" It had been a while, but who can forget the story of the starfish? I summoned up my story telling skills and told the boys the classic, just as I imagined Frosty telling it. Story over. They bolted out of the living room to do more digging.

Moments later, Isaiah appeared with a mini toilet that actually makes a flushing noise. "What's this for, Frosty?" Well, I explained that the toilet really symbolized the EMAL attitude of being fearless, and that fearlessness and freedom to give it our best shot enabled us to make many miraculous comebacks. "Isaiah," I said, "when you make a mistake, you flush it, and you move on." Frosty had been pretty quiet, but he piped in, pointing a finger at me for emphasis, "But first you have to learn from it, Steve. Then you flush it and move on." Of course, I'd missed that important step. Dang.

And so it went for the next hour or so, the boys hauling up treasures from the basement, me explaining the significance of different items or deferring to Frosty. Isaiah holding a leather helmet with autographs and messages to Frosty from Eddie Robinson, Tom Osborne, Ara Parsegian, Joe Paterno, Bobby Bowden, Lou Holtz, and other all-time greats; Elijah wearing an original 1972 PLU helmet; both boys holding a handmade PLU train.

I told the boys to take a break from their searching around and ask their questions.

Elijah went first, asking Frosty to share his favorite coaching memory. "Oh, boy, that's a hard one. There's so many, Elijah. I can't really pick a favorite."

Isaiah asked next: "Frosty, when did you and Donna meet?" What a great question, and it captured Donna's attention right away, as she took a break from her kitchen duties and leaned in to listen. Frosty and Donna met in kindergarten. They began dating in high school, and Frosty took Donna to the prom. Here's the kicker, Frosty had wrecked his dad's car so he wasn't allowed to drive (for those of you who experienced driving with Frosty, are you surprised to hear he wrecked his father's car?). Well, Donna, told him, "You're taking me to the prom, even if you have to take me in a wheelbarrow." And what did Frosty do? He picked her up and drove her to the prom…in a wheelbarrow.

The boys begged for one last trip to the basement, so they vanished and Frosty and I continued to talk. Moments later the boys appeared with another prize from the basement—a pair of drumsticks. Elijah loves the drums. "Frosty, why do you have these?"

Seeing the drums reminded me of our team's trip to the French Riviera in 1985, and I shared the story with the boys. We'd just finished a team dinner at some restaurant, a band was setting up to play, and everyone's making their way out to the parking lot, excited to explore the city. All of a sudden Frosty crawls up behind the drum set and begins pounding out an impressive drum solo. Who knew?

"Elijah, let me see those," Frosty extended his hand to my son. "Steve, clear off this table." Then, while lying on his side, Frosty proceeded to pound out, skillfully, two different drum rhythms as my boys sat mesmerized.

Not soon after, it was clear that he was tiring, and it was time for us to leave. In classic Frosty form, he chose to rally and engage with us. I hugged him. The boys hugged him. I hugged him again and kissed him on the head. "Love you, Frosty. Thanks for investing in my life," I whispered.

Since we were in the area, we drove to PLU and looked at the new practice fields and walked through Olson Auditorium. Nothing had changed in Olson since I first arrived in the fall of '83— same lockers, bathrooms, and showers. A recruit from Colombia River High School was waiting outside "Frosty's office" for his visit and campus tour with Scott. I let the boys run around in the darkened gymnasium for a while as they shot imaginary baskets. Then it was time to go.

On our way out of Parkland, I surprised the boys by stopping at Baskin and Robbins. Isaiah ordered a single scoop of birthday cake ice cream, and Elijah had bubblegum ice cream on a sugar cone. As they quietly licked their way through their cones, I asked, "Did you guys have fun meeting Frosty and Donna?" They nodded. A pause.

Then Isaiah looked at me, an ice cream "soul patch" forming under his lip, and said, "Dad, can we come and visit Frosty next Saturday?" As I sit here this morning, I'm consumed with an overwhelming sense of gratitude. It happens to me pretty regularly these days. I feel it when I can't sleep and tiptoe into my boys' rooms to watch them sleep. I feel it when I

look at my wife and think about the miracle that she said, "yes" fifteen years ago. I feel it when I think about myself as a 17-year-old PLU freshman walk on, learning I didn't know that I didn't know. And, I feel it right now, as I think about a divinely appointed Saturday afternoon, as I got to sit beside my coach and share him with my boys.

LIKE NOTHING ELSE

Jeff Yarnell (Pacific Lutheran/1983-87), Software Engineering Manager

I first met Frosty in the summer of 1981 at a week long Fellowship of Christian Athletes camp hosted by PLU. The following fall, PLU played a game at Southern Oregon University in my hometown of Medford. I felt like something of a VIP when I was invited to watch the game from the defending national champion Lutes' sideline.

After scoring early in the game, the Lutes kickoff team took the field. A Southern Oregon player received the kick and began running up field. At some point, he veered toward the PLU sideline. The PLU defender responsible for "contain" had drifted to the center of the field. He sprinted toward the sideline and made a diving attempt at a tackle, but he was unable to stop the return man.

As this scene was developing, Frosty came running down the sideline toward the action. But rather than continue to watch the Southern Oregon player run the ball up the sideline, Frosty dropped to his hands and knees next to the Lute who had failed to prevent a sideline return. I knew of Frosty's Christian faith, but still expected he'd let the player know what he thought about his performance—just without cursing. Instead, Frosty

shouted, "You're better than that!" and helped him up. I'd never seen anything like that from a coach in the heat of competition.

After the game, I experienced Locker Room. For well over an hour, the players (still half-dressed in their muddy uniforms), coaches, and friends and family who made the 400-mile trip from Parkland tossed verbal "bouquets." Some recognized the successes of their teammates. Others humbly admitted their mistakes and were encouraged to "flush it" by their peers. If I was a PLU fan after FCA camp, the game left me an aspiring EMAL.

I communicated with Frosty during my senior year of high school and planned to join the PLU football program in the fall of 1983. That summer, Frosty offered to give me a head start on the season. We met at a hotel conference room in Eugene, Oregon. He gave me a playbook and talked me through the "O" series and more. We moved tables and chairs out of the way so I could practice the all-important quick pitch. "The key is to deliver the ball softly and lead the running back," he explained.

In late August, I arrived at PLU and was soon on my way to the Oregon coast for Breakaway as a member of Frosty's PLU football team. Like so many others who played for Frosty, the following four-and-a-half years were like nothing else I've ever experienced. Frosty's teaching and coaching continues to influence my life—as a husband, father, professional, and follower of Jesus.

HUMILITY AND STRENGTH

John Wolfe (Pacific Lutheran/1983-87), CEO, NW Seaport Alliance

Coach/Teacher: I first met Frosty during my recruiting trip to explore PLU Football. I was familiar with the program's winning record, and I had heard about the coach named Frosty Westering. Recruited by other programs, yet not hearing from PLU, I assumed PLU was not interested in me as a player.

What I came to understand is that the program under Frosty's leadership philosophy promoted itself. There was no need to recruit, as players were drawn to this special program without fully understanding why. Once I met

Frosty and had the opportunity to sit with him, hear about his philosophy on football, life, and the PLU program, I was sold on PLU.

I didn't know what I didn't know: That Spring, I set a goal to play as an incoming freshman. What I did not know is that it was not all about whether I stepped on the field or not. I learned to accept the role as a "Bomber" and serving a bigger purpose. Being introduced to Frosty's "Inter-game" and learning what it meant to be a servant leader would transform my life during the five seasons of PLU Football. Great leaders are great teachers, and Frosty was an elite leader, teacher, and coach

Humility: I played linebacker and had great passion playing the position. My junior year, the coaches asked me to switch to defensive end. I was resistant to the change and shared with the coaches that I wanted to remain playing linebacker. Frosty pulled me aside and provided me with some well-deserved tough love. After reflection, I realized my selfish attitude and sought out Frosty to let him know that I was open to change positions. I will never forget the lesson I learned from this great teacher and coach about servant leadership. Humility—that low sweet root from which all heavenly virtues shoot. Frosty modeled humility.

Strength: Frosty was a strong man, a marine, a competitor who knew how to bring the best out of the team. He taught us to step into the arena and give it our best shot. The by-products of that strength of character were wins, awards, accolades, and championships. None of that was as important to him as the development of young men.

I reached out to Frosty after his retirement. He was late in his life and I had not talked to him in a few years. I invited him to lunch. He said, "John, come over to our home. Donna will make us lunch and we can visit downstairs." We sat in his basement for hours, surrounded by the history and memories of PLU Football. Looking around at the pictures, awards, recognitions, I realized that what mattered most was the trip. We shared story after story of the years I played at PLU. I was amazed at his recollection in detail of games we played, specific players, trips to France and Australia. We laughed together over the many precious moments of the journey. It was one of my most special memories of PLU Football.

Frosty taught us to compete in life with humility, to care for others, and to enjoy the journey every day, forever.

FROSTY KNOWS BEST

Dave Parkhill (Pacific Lutheran/1985-87), Senior Safety and Health Coordinator, Chelan County Public Utility District (Wenatchee, Washington)

I was a walk on from Wenatchee and Frosty welcomed me with open arms. I red shirted in 1985 and he always encouraged me to give it my best shot.

After moving to defensive line later in the season, I was able to play in varsity games in 1986 and 1987. These were some of the best years of my life. The camaraderie of our team was the best. Frosty told us that college football was only a few years of our life. However, he gave us life skills to be better men, husbands, fathers, businessmen, etc. I have used these skills he ingrained in me even 35 years after playing for Frosty. Thank You Frosty! EMAL

Breakaway Memories: In the spring of 1985, I found out that I would be able to attend Breakaway in the fall. I was so excited to be part of the team that got to go. I had heard so many fun stories from past Breakaways.

After our team completed all of the physical testing when we arrived in camp, we took the team buses to Gearhart, Oregon. One specific memory that I remember on the trip down was bringing a bunch of water balloons and throwing them out the windows at the other team buses—probably not the smartest idea when traveling 60 miles per hour on the freeway.

Breakaway was the best experience. Great food, great bonding and not talking about football during those few days. During skit

night, our cabin recreated "Frosty Knows Best" based on the "Father Knows Best" television show. Terry Marks played Frosty and nailed the part to a tee. I never laughed so hard in my life.

When we got back to Tacoma, our team was mentally ready for the 1986 season, and we all grew closer together.

CHOP IT UP

Keith Krassin (Pacific Lutheran/1984-88),
Account Executive, Microsoft (retired 2022)

I have so many fond memories of my time at PLU—almost all of them around my football experience with Frosty and Paul. However, my memory is horrible (hence now retired), so I'll do the best I can.

Breakaway: After arriving at the Oregon coast for Breakaway my first or second year in the program, Frosty had some insider knowledge of the plumbing at the lodge that he wanted to share with the team. He asked us to judge our activity on the toilet and if required go find a stick outside and come back and "chop it up" before flushing.

I gained so much respect and admiration for Frosty on our first trip to the beach competing in the beach games. After we competed in Izzy Dizzy, we all chanted for Frosty to take his turn and of course he did. We all had a good laugh with him stumbling around like the rest of us. Frosty seemed to have an inner child in him that would come out when he was around us and he could always laugh at himself.

Trip to France: After participating in a local parade, I believe in Nice, someone may have accidentally fallen or cooled themselves off in a large fountain, so Frosty seeing this decided we needed to get some go-drills in. He instructed us all to hop in the fountain and we proceeded to do our go-drills, splashing as much as we possibly could and entertaining the locals in our USA football jerseys.

Coach Hoseth: Playing defense my whole career, I ended up spending so much more time with Paul and Jeanne. I played a lot of sports growing up and Coach Hoseth was the best of them all. In his mostly mellow approach at coaching, I learned how much knowledge can help you be a good football player. Always making it fun and respecting your teammates was in the DNA of both Frosty and Paul. I always looked forward to the weekly defensive meetings at the Hoseth's home.

France/Australia: Our team was fortunate enough to travel to the French Riviera and Australia and New Zealand during PLU's interim two years to play football against clubs in those countries. Looking back on all the highlights of these trips, I would say now that I am most thankful for Frosty and the coaching staff for allowing parents to tag along. My parents were never big travelers, so for them to be included was amazing and created lifelong memories. Even though the football wasn't the highest caliber in France or New Zealand, we grew together as a team and a family.

SERVANT LEADERSHIP

Mark Miller (Pacific Lutheran/1984-88), Technology Leader and IT Director, Port of Tacoma

I was truly blessed to play for Frosty. He inspired and challenged me like no other coach or teacher in my life. Like all players, I learned so many valuable life lessons playing for Frosty such as "Mark, you are better than that."

Like many in my era, I red-shirted and had the opportunity to serve as a Team Captain in my fifth year. It was serving as a captain that perhaps provided me the most significant Frosty lesson. Frosty often had talked about servant leadership. The opportunity to work closely with him in the captain role helped me start to understand the servant leadership concept.

As I grew in my technology business career, I started to work as a manager of people and teams. I wrestled with being an effective leader. This led me to read and learn about lead-ership, where I found the book "The Servant" by James C Hunter. This book seemed to align and reinforce Frosty's servant leadership philosophy. Finally, I started to understand the wisdom and impact of Frosty on my life. I give thanks for the opportunity to play for Frosty and share his philosophies with family and colleagues.

THE LITTLE THINGS OF LIFE

Guy Kovacs (Pacific Lutheran/1986-89), School Administrator

A Lesson Learned: I clearly see in my mind the first time I met with Frosty. It was in his small office in the gym's foyer. I was returning home from school and football in Colorado Springs and looking for something different. I had spoken with Frosty on the phone and we set up this meeting to talk about the possibility of me joining the team. The meeting went as planned. I spent my next four years there in an incredible environment.

The unique piece I recall from that first meet-

ing was a moment when Frosty said something that had nothing to do with football or PLU. Frosty was a talker. I was not. However, the meeting was going long, and I had to pause our conversation to call my chiropractor and let him know I would be running a bit late for an appointment. All of a sudden, Frosty and I were now talking about "the little things" of life. He shared how important that phone call was to show respect to my doctor and to be someone who holds himself accountable. We went on to talk about the way we treat our significant other, how we handle ourselves under pressure, the way in which we carry ourselves in public, etc. I was sold. This guy was different.

That meeting went from me asking Frosty, "how might I fit into the current team?" to Frosty sharing, "that was an important and proper phone call to make," and, "at PLU, we are about much more than winning football games." Looking back, I believe God sat me in that chair in Frosty's office that day. That was the beginning of a new life for me, and I am forever grateful to have played for Frosty.

Coach Paul: Playing on the defensive side of the ball, my time was spent heavily with Coach Paul. Paul Hoseth became a father figure to me, and he completely changed my life. Football at PLU was partially all-team time with Frosty leading the philosophical teaching, but we would soon break into offensive and defensive groups. Some of my fondest memories and growth opportunities came from these times with the defense.

Coach Paul was brilliant at defensive schemes, and he was an incredible teacher of technique. I grew immensely as a player under Coach Paul's mentorship, but more importantly I grew as a man. Paul was an impressive balance of fierceness and calmness. Nobody got more fired up than Coach Paul, yet nobody loved as much as Coach Paul. I listened, watched, absorbed, and did everything possible to soak up what I could from him. He strived for perfection.

An example of Coach Paul's get-better-every-day mantra comes from a Sunday film session. It was my freshman year. I had a pretty good game the day before. I was especially

looking forward to watching a big hit I had on the quarterback. Unbeknownst to me at this time, I had a lot to learn. So, the big play comes, my huge blindside hit takes place, and Coach Paul lays into me. What? We watched that play over and over as Coach Paul used it as an example for how players need to strip the football and create a turnover when in that situation. Needless to say, I changed how I made tackles, and I changed how I watched film. For Coach Paul, it was about growth and becoming better—better at playing football, better in our relationships, and better at making the world a positive place, one good decision at a time. Corny, but true.

International Travel: I list my favorite parts of playing at PLU as the relationships I built with teammates, as well as the impact the program's philosophy had on my life. However, one can't deny the effect of international travel. I was fortunate to be at PLU at the time when our team went to Australia, New Zealand, and Hawaii. Oh, the memories! I think of Bondi Beach, teaching football to the locals, koalas, and kangaroos, having local hosts teach us about the culture, the Austra-

lian Open, PT with soldiers in Hawaii, and so much more. This was a trip of a lifetime. A week each in Sydney, Melbourne, Auckland, and then down time in Hawaii instilled in me a lifelong passion for international travel.

One of my favorite memories of this trip was when a few of us went out for dinner one night. To our surprise, a few coaches and their families were being seated just a few tables away. Knowing Frosty's image and his commitment to clean living, we chuckled at how funny it would be if we sent him over a drink. We laughed at what that would look like and how daring and bold we would be if we gave it a go. The courage was flowing. I ordered a glass of wine to be delivered to Frosty. The waiter handed it to him, looked at us and nodded as if to say, "Compliments of the Lutes at that table," and we all waited with great anticipation. To our surprise, Frosty picked up the glass of wine, tilted it our way in a toasting manner, nodded, and smiled his big ol' smile. I never waited to see if he put the glass to his lips, but our crew left on cloud nine as if we had accomplished some wonderful mission.

TAKING THE HIT

Craig Kupp (Pacific Lutheran/1986-89),
Regional Sales Manager, Kwik Lok

It was 1987 and we were on a six-game winning streak after dropping the home opener against UPS. We were on a roll and a struggling Lewis and Clark team was in town to play. With the score 49-22 late in the game, things were looking good for the Lutes. Frosty decided it was time to let some of the young bucks play.

As our backup quarterback, Frosty gave the great news. I was going in. "Craig, we've got a big lead so we're just going to keep the ball on

the ground to run the clock out."

We slowly moved the ball down the field to about the 10-yard line aided by a sideline infraction called on LC's coach. He was extremely frustrated with the officiating and life in general at this point. As the clock ticked down, Frosty and the rest of the team began to make their way onto the field for post-game handshakes and the fans began gathering their game day blankets to head home.

Meanwhile, us wet-behind-the-ears backups were huddling up. I looked for the play call from the sidelines but there was nothing coming in. As I looked around the huddle, I saw Bill Pubols and Andy Wedding—huge smiles on their faces with a look of, "What's the play call? Hurry up!" I looked up at the clock as the seconds ticked down. 10-9-8. All reason and logic went out the window.

"Everyone get on the line! We're running 11! Flanker Right 11! Hurry up get to the line!" I yelled out half out of my mind. LC's linebackers are looking at me like, "Are you seriously doing this?" I took the snap with one second left on the clock. As I dropped back to pass (yes pass), all I saw was complete chaos. With no clear vision I took off running, broke a tackle at the two and dove across the goal line for our final touchdown of the day.

I was so excited. All of us young ones hugged in the end zone. As I looked towards the sideline it hit me. That score just made the final 55-22. Frosty was on his way over to shake the hand of a very frustrated coach to try to explain why his team rushed to the line to try to throw a pass in the last seconds of a game already leading by 27 points. I met Frosty as he was walking to the opposite sideline and all he said to me was, "Craig, you probably shouldn't have done that."

After the game Frosty absorbed criticism from LC's coaches, fans, and media. He took the hit for me that day. He took the hit for my lack of judgment, lack of awareness, and ultimately lack of class in that moment. My actions made the program and him look bad, but he chose to show me grace. I'll never forget what he did for me.

CONTAGIOUS

John Gradwohl (Pacific Lutheran/1987-89), PE Teacher and Football Coach (31 years)

My first one-on-one meeting with Frosty was in his office in Olson Auditorium. This was the first time I had been in his office. The plaques, pictures, trophies, and signs were everywhere. It was cluttered but somehow very cool. It was hard at first to stay focused because my eyes were scanning every corner of his office and all the football paraphernalia.

Frosty showed up to our meeting a little late (ish). He was high energy and excited to talk with me. We sat down at his desk, and he brought out a piece of poster paper. He began talking to me about what I wanted to do in school and then would talk about what position I should play. He went back and forth between those subjects all the while drawing on the poster paper.

He explained a number of acronyms and other areas of his philosophy. I was locked in. His energy, friendliness, and command of thoughts had me fired up.

I should go back a little. I showed up at PLU as a 21-year-old transfer. I chose PLU because my younger brother was there and talked so highly of the program and the people. I had been to a few games and was excited to get involved. I was a "Red Car guy." I had no idea what I wanted to study. It had been a few years since I had played so I wasn't sure about what position I might play. I had spent the past couple of years working construction and had put on a few pounds.

I met with Frosty for about one hour. When the meeting ended, the poster paper was completely full of his writings and plaques and pictures and I was so excited to get started in school and football. Frosty helped me decide on my major (Physical Education and Health) and we had decided that playing tight end would be the best place for me. I walked into his office with no clue about either and I walked out with so much confidence in my future.

Like most people who played for Frosty, I have so many stories. This one stood out to me because Frosty brought out the best in all of us. His positive attitude, energy and confidence were contagious. Frosty changed the course of my life. I am thankful for him every day.

GETTING OUT OF SCHOOL

John Heller (Pacific Lutheran/1986-90), Vice President of Asset Management, LCRA

I first met Frosty Westering in early January 1986. There were a couple of players on my high school football team who set up a recruiting visit with him and they asked me if I wanted to come along. I initially said no. I had never heard of Frosty or Pacific Lutheran University. Then what my teammate said next enticed me to participate, "John, you can get out of day of school."

So away I went, along with two other teammates on a recruiting visit about 45 minutes away from my hometown of Olympia to get out of school because in my mind I had already decided to go to another school across the state (Washington State University).

However, that day changed the course of my life. Frosty was like nobody I had ever met before. He captured my attention with his beaming voice, his abundant energy, and his positive attitude. I thought to myself, "Is this guy for real?" I had never seen somebody talk

with such enthusiasm and, at the same time, work a chalkboard like no other. He was drawing arrows everywhere—from one point to another!

After the trip, I still had not changed my mind. He requested that I send a couple of game films, and I think I had to be reminded once or twice, but I eventually did. Soon after, I started receiving calls from Frosty on a regular basis, but not until about May did I commit.

I will always remember that phone call from Frosty like it was yesterday. Frosty told me that he was finalizing the upcoming recruiting class and asked me if I decided yet. I really hadn't, but for some reason I asked my parents to get on the other phone lines (before cell phones) and I committed to go to Pacific Lutheran to play for Frosty. Wow, I shocked myself.

Little did I know that decision would drastically change the trajectory of my life. Although not right away, through his influence I recommitted my life to Christ. He not only affected me, and my wife and children, but many in my circle of influence.

Until Frosty, servant leadership was something I had never heard of before. Frosty not only talked about it, but he lived it. He showed us. I am forever grateful for getting out of school that day because it led to one of the best decisions I've ever made.

Miss and love you Frosty! EMAL

ENJOY THE JOURNEY

Arne Valdez (Pacific Lutheran/1986-90), Alaska Account Manager, Burkhart Dental Supply

As a defensive and special teams' player, I didn't get quite as much on the field time with Frosty as the players on the offense. Looking back, I see that he spent a great deal of his own time sharing his insights about football and life with every player, knowing it would continue to serve us long after graduation.

I have a photo of Frosty holding the national championship trophy at my office desk. Seeing him when I start my day brings me great happiness. I still hear him saying, "Make it a great day!"

My favorite Frostyism is, "They don't care how much you know until they know how much you care." Frosty would remind us of this when asking us to volunteer to help students move into the dorms or visit the classrooms at Lister and McIlvaigh. Frosty lived the principles that he taught showing a genuine interest in everyone he met, always looking for ways to help others.

Frosty's understanding of teamwork and the

value of serving others was the foundation of his program's success, enabling him to keep excellent assistant coaches, develop great players, and build support from the community. It's likely why so many members of his program have been so successful in their chosen careers and personal lives.

Although my role and contribution to the team was very limited, Frosty and everyone else in the program always made me feel like a very important player. Even when I stopped by Frosty's office unannounced multiple times years later, he always recognized me and greeted me by name—unbelievable.

The level of professionalism and respect that Frosty established still brings everyone fortunate enough to be involved with his program pride and happiness. In the 80's, a time where respect for competitors was hard to come by, Frosty taught us to respect our competitors and understand that without their hard work we wouldn't have the opportunity to enjoy the challenge of facing them.

The true magic Frosty provided the world is how much he cared for everyone he worked with in his huge circle. As players, he taught us to serve others, have faith in God, treat everyone with respect, have a sense of humor even during difficult times, work hard, know that your struggles make you stronger, set measurable daily goals to reach your desired accomplishments, and to "enjoy the journey" and the people in your life. Even Frosty's moments of well-earned tough love had a bit of humor added to the delivery, letting you know that you would be forgiven for poor effort or an error in judgment.

Frosty lived his life with a positive energy and sacrifice for others that made him an amazing leader.

THE HARDEST HIT

Peter Gradwohl (Pacific Lutheran/1986-90), Senior Client Strategist, Lumen Technologies

My teammates and other coaches on staff would agree that Frosty and I had a unique relationship. My respect and admiration for

Frosty and Paul was undeniable. However, everyone would also agree with the fact that I drove Frosty crazy—Paul too. Any chance for coaches to knock me down a few pegs was not just welcome but expected.

One such gift was delivered to Frosty in 1989 when the entire team was waiting to start a team meeting my junior year. As often occurred, we were running on Frosty Time, so five, 10, 15 minutes passed. We all were becoming a bit restless; well perhaps just the DB's became restless. The offense was accustomed to Frosty Time, so they were diligently filling out Goal Set sheets, discussing game film, tying washers on a string to doorknobs.

I am sure what occurred next was most likely instigated by Chris Gant ('90) or Greg Goodman ('91). Brian Larson ('90) and I started a game while waiting for Frosty. The game in simple terms was take turns punching each other in the arm. Not sure if we had discussed any rules, yet we began taking turns, hitting each other in the arm, increasing our approach and impact with each turn. To the enjoyment of everyone, especially the offense, the excitement of two DB's consciously and by choice hitting each other created quite a stir.

It goes without saying Brian Larson can hit. On and off the field he was one of the best DB's to play at PLU, so when it was my turn to respond to his debilitating, arm numbing delivery to my left shoulder, I was ecstatic.

After 30 to 40 seconds of Red Car prepunch theatrics and taunting, I punched Larson in the left shoulder. I punched him good and without remorse. I raised my hands in glory! I got Larson good, really good. To my dismay the cheering and excitement stopped suddenly, and an immediate silence took over the room. Unfortunately, or fortunately, my back was to the door of the classroom. Frosty had walked in and was witness to the whole episode.

"Gradwohl!" he yelled. (3-5 second pause for effect) "That's the hardest you hit all year!" The laughter was immediate and deafening.

DEATH OF THE RED TEAM & NELLIE THE EMAL

Paul Finley (Pacific Lutheran/1986-90), Vice President of Enterprise Sales, FlexPay

Death of the Red Team (October 1987): EMAL QBs had the privilege of riding in the back of Frosty's White Ford Galaxy (the original Bomb) to and from many off-campus practices. Jeff Yarnell, Craig Kupp and I (fortuitously wearing our girdles and practice pants) were packed tight in the back for the trek back from Sparks Stadium. As usual, Scott was sharing post-practice feedback and upcoming game notes from the passenger seat. Being a hand talker, Scott set his red clipboard (affectionately called "The Red Team") on the Bomb's generous dashboard for the 15-minute ride.

We all know Frosty was a man of action (and had an unnaturally heavy right foot), so we moved quickly through the streets of Puyallup, including a light-beating, rushed right turn onto South Meridian, which Frosty actually accelerated through. As we clung to any available grab-able feature of the Galaxy, the one untethered object in the cabin, The Red Team, rocketed left along the dash, aggressively wedging itself between the A post and Frosty's fully-right-cranked steering wheel. And it wasn't budging.

Unable to correct, the Bomb continued past 90 degrees and jumped the curb onto the (fortunately) over-wide and empty sidewalk. The front right wheel's hard contact with the clipboard shattered The Red Team, sending fiberglass shards into Frosty's lap. He slammed on the brake, avoiding a storefront collision and stopped with the Bomb facing the opposite direction from the highway. Wide-eyed, mouths agape, we stared at each other. Frosty broke our stunned silence with, "Well, okay. Let's just go then." As if nothing had happened, Frosty looked both ways and drove off of the sidewalk.

The capper was the incredulous, eyebrows-raised look Scott snuck us as we pulled back into traffic. "Well, that's the death of The Red Team!"

Nellie the EMAL: It was Homecoming Week 1988 at Cascade Hall. I was asked to help judge the decorations of each wing of the dorm. As I walked through 1st West, I spied, sitting at his desk, the young man I'd seen tooling around campus in his automated wheelchair. I decided to introduce myself and learn his story.

He shared about his past in Singapore, the couple that brought him to California where he received a critical surgery, finding foster parents in Tacoma, and the neglect he experienced throughout his school years, but of the hope he had with the opportunity to attend PLU.

John was curious about PLU Football, so I invited him to check our game that week—CWU at Sparks Stadium)—and our post-game Afterglow. He showed up to both!

But most surprising was that at Afterglow, John spoke up in a really vulnerable way. He was depressed, not feeling he fit in at PLU. It blew him away that despite our loss that day to the Wildcats, we were happy to be together, enjoying each other's company and exhibiting a sense of well-being and peace he was looking for.

Frosty had us give John an Attaway cheer (of course), and he met a number of EMALs that night. In the days that followed, we met for lunch, talked more in his room, and he got to know a group of Tinglestad players including my brother Andy, Craig and Kyle Kupp, Mark Hodson, and Pete and Matt Gradwohl. It wasn't long before John began coming to practice. Soon John became Freddy (his middle name was Frederick), then finally Nellie, as his love for the EMAL inner circle grew. Lunches with the guys became off-campus dinners and movies, and trips home with EMALS for Christmas and Spring Breaks.

When the Class of '90 cycled out and left Parkland, Nellie went through a bit of a crisis, but in true EMAL fashion, the next guys up embraced Nellie. During his more than 20 years in the program (supported and encouraged by Frosty and the other coaches) Nellie grew emotionally, intellectually and spiritually, as his focus evolved ever outward, continually less about himself and his struggles, and more about PLU football, the new Bombers each year, and sharing his faith in Jesus—from justifiably self-conscious to the giving, thoughtful, and caring servant warrior we loved and admired. Talk about a great Second Act. Nellie's impact was immeasurable.

Year	Record	Postseason
1985	10-1-1	NAIA Division II Semifinals (2-1)
1986	8-2	NAIA Division II First Round (0-1)
1987	11-1-1	NAIA Division II National Champions (4-0)
1988	7-3	NAIA Division II First Round (0-1)
1989	6-2-1	

CHAPTER 5

THE 1990's
PART I

[1990 - 1994]

GREEN AND GROWING

Gregory D. Hall (Pacific Lutheran/1989-90), Adjunct Bible Professor; Author; Host of the "Rethinking Scripture" Podcast

I attended PLU to play basketball and baseball. I knew I wanted to end up coaching someday, and I figured the more experience I had the better. So, my sophomore year when I found out the football coach taught a two-credit coaching class, I was intrigued and I signed up. I had no idea what was about to happen.

At first, Frosty's teaching method seemed a bit random. He used a bunch of handouts with hand drawn graphs, pithy sayings, and overplayed clichés. Oh, and he told story… after story… after story. Needless to say, I was quickly hooked. He had me at "Attaway!"

That class completely changed my perspective and I discovered his teaching was anything but random. It was, and continues to be, simply brilliant.

That year, I had a season-ending basketball knee injury. While I was recovering, a friend who knew Frosty suggested I stop playing basketball and try out for the football team. At first, the idea sounded absurd. I mean, who walks-on to play football after a knee injury their junior year?

But that spring, the suggestion began to grow roots. And as Frosty had already taught me, I knew I could either be green and growing, or ripe and rotting. So, I met with the coaching staff and made plans to return to campus early the next fall to be a "Bomber." I ended up playing two years and I eventually got on the field. I even returned a squibbed kickoff in the homecoming game my senior year!

Frosty was a special coach. He was the kind of coach that comes around once in a lifetime. I'm honored to have had the opportunity to experience the "Big Time"—right where I already was.

BONDED BROTHERS

Chris Gant (Pacific Lutheran/1986-91), Physical Therapist

I've been blessed in many ways during my life, but I'd have to give credit to Frosty's teachings and influence that helped build the foundation and planted quite a few seeds (which I wish I had cultivated a little sooner in my life) that created such a fruitful and rich life for me.

I am the man I am today because of the principles and values that Frosty taught, and, of course, consistently modeled for all of us. Though I fail often, I strive to be a humble servant warrior in my career as a physical therapist, as a friend, and certainly as a husband and father.

Regarding friendships, I graduated over 30 years ago and I still have a group of eight other PLU guys that get together regularly throughout the year for guys nights out, annual fly fishing trips, Super Bowls, and family gatherings—quality guys with shared

values that were drawn to come to PLU because of one man. And as a result of Frosty's program, not only did a bunch of boys learn what it takes to become men, but we got to share in some amazing experiences together (both on and off the field) that helped shaped and bonded us forever as "brothers."

Most importantly, because of Frosty, though I often fall short I understand the importance of the role and what it means to be a true father and husband. As the result of Frosty's countless examples and living out his faith in Jesus, the bar has been set high. So I know what it takes when I strive to be my best for my family—to do both the big things and the consistent little things that create an environment of encouragement, love, and trust for my wife and girls to thrive.

Thank you Frosty. I am a better person, with a richer life because of the life you lived.

THE RAINBOW POSTER

Kenny Fagan (Pacific Lutheran/1987-91), Special Education Teacher (29 years), Football Coach (27 years)

I was in my senior year of high school when I suffered a devastating knee injury after playing only two games, I will be honest. I grew up in Federal Way and never heard of PLU even thought it was 20 miles south from where I lived. I was depressed and devastated because I never thought I was going to play again. If it wasn't for my teammate's older brother, I may have never thought of playing football. I would have just gone on with my life.

But Brent Ringenbach's older brother Darin heard of my injury and a couple weeks after my surgery I got this "Rainbow Poster." I saw all these little notes, signatures, pick me ups, etc. I was dumbfounded and confused. What is this all about? Who are these guys? Who is this team? There was no Internet or social media, but I did have a landline and Brent

and I talked about this team in Parkland his brother played for.

My mom hung the poster up downstairs where I spent about five weeks recovering until I was healthy enough to move around with crutches. So every day I read the notes and names of these people. I had no idea who they were or

what would be my next step in my life, but it motivated me to get off my butt and start healing, stop feeling sorry for myself, and make a decision about my future.

We found a doctor and physical therapist that believed I could play again and I started the process of recovery. I read that poster every day! Little did I know that a piece of paper would change my life and give me the opportunity of a lifetime to play football for an amazing man.

My first meeting with Frosty: I was invited to a game late in the season and watched the team play. Afterwards, I went into the locker room, and experienced Afterglow. This was very different. Where was the destroy mentality, anger, and celebration? Instead, it was like walking into a room full of kinship, care, and what was best for all rather than oneself. I left that day with more questions than answers about how a football team like that could be so good.

After the season ended, I started trying to find a school that would allow me to walk on and just have a chance. I still wanted to play football and baseball. In my mind, I really

wanted this more than anything. Education was an opportunity for me to keep playing. I sent VHS tapes of my junior year and the tape of one senior year game to all the schools I could find in Washington, Oregon, and Idaho.

Then one day I got a call to come down and visit PLU and learn about the program. I was in Olson Auditorium, nervous and wandering around, thinking I must have gotten my day and time wrong. Then a player walked up to me and asked if I needed some help. I told him I was here to meet Coach Frosty. "You are in the right spot," he said. "You just need to learn Frosty Time."

Later on, I totally knew what Frosty Time meant.

As I went through the tour, I spent time with some players, having lunch, etc. I was stunned at how they explained the program and what it was like to play for PLU. At the end of the tour, we were led to Frosty's office. There sat this man of stature who greeted the two or three of us from behind his desk. He then proceeded to tell us what it was to play NAIA football, financial aid possibilities, and all the beginnings of what to expect if I was to come here.

The whole time he was drawing a diagram on a sheet of paper with arrows pointing in all directions, acronyms, and highlights of important concepts. Frosty's presence grabbed me. He drew me in, and when he spoke it meant something. To this day I can still hear him talking about being a servant warrior, talking about the "man in the arena" speaking at Sunday meetings, challenging us to give it "our best shot," and sharing incredible tangibles that at that time I maybe didn't appreciate as much as I cherish them now. I was in awe and at a loss for words, but I knew this would be amazing if given the opportunity.

I left there hoping I would have another opportunity to come back again. Now, I waited. I was not sure how long it was, but a few weeks later I received a call from Paul Hoseth who asked me if I would like to come to PLU and play. It was the best gift I was ever given.

About Paul Hoseth: Since I'm a defensive guy, I spent a lot of time with Paul and Craig. They ran our defense and they too had a huge impact on me with the direction they gave to me as a person. As time goes forward, I

realize that I didn't truly appreciate what I had at the time until it was gone. Being able to be around Paul, Craig, and Jeanne (Paul's wife) on Tuesday nights was always a blast. It was our group together learning the game plan, having laughs, and always having some wonderful dessert that Jeanne would cook up for us. She must have spent hours making dessert for a large group of guys every Tuesday.

Paul's directives as a coordinator went far beyond the X's and O's of the game. He led by example and motivated us in his unique way. Paul wanted us to be a punishing defense. He wanted us to take the will out of the offense. I'm almost certain it was the first time I heard the quote, "kick the dog when it's down!" during an intense game. I'm hoping it was Paul who said it, because I have been using that quote for a long time, always saying it to my defenses I've coached over the years.

Paul had a huge influence on my coaching style—holding the vets accountable to work with the younger players, allowing the players to make adjustments on the field, and always having an open door policy to come and talk to him. I took a few of those opportunities and even though at times it may not have been what I wanted to hear, I took his advice and learned from it. It is those moments where you get nuggets that can last a lifetime and help you be a better person. For that I will always be grateful to Paul.

NEVER DULL, EXPECTING ANYTHING

Leif Langlois (Pacific Lutheran/ 1987-91), Commercial Finance

Frosty had a unique way making every moment around him and with the team feel like it was exactly where you needed to be and what you needed to be doing. He had such a presence and persona that you could not help but follow. Whether it was practicing at 11 p.m., in mid-December at Stadium Bowl in 25-degree weather, or a three-hour bus ride to Shenzhen, China, in 90-degree heat with no air conditioning, I treasured every moment. Never dull and expecting anything.

He coached with love and purpose, and commanded your respect and undivided attention. If you were falling out of line or your attention was drifting, you would hear his powerful voice resonate, "Leif, we need ya!" And you would know that was your only warning with Frosty. Even now, 35 years later, I use that one liner in my work life as a way to bring my people back when in a group setting. People work very hard to become strong and effective leaders, and with Frosty it seemed as natural as breathing for him.

As a coach, Frosty knew exactly what the team needed to hear and when they needed to hear it. Whether the team was coming off a poor performance or a huge victory,

Frosty would give us the message we needed to hear. I personally have experienced great success as well as colossal failures in my life, and I've felt like I was better equipped to deal with each end of the spectrum based on what I learned from Frosty's program at PLU. I consider it a gift that I was able to attend PLU and be part of the program while Frosty was there. It provided me with countless amazing experiences, tremendous friendships, and tools that I will carry for the rest of my life. I'm forever grateful.

Frosty built the foundation to the house, but both Paul and Scott were an integral part of completing it. I learned a tremendous amount from both of you as well and, to me, both of you were special parts of my time at PLU. The genius that was Frosty was also contributed by the genius that was Paul and Scott. There are too many skins on the wall for that not to be the case. Thank you to you both as well for your leadership, love, and knowledge you passed on. Again, I am grateful.

THE FROSTY WESTERING TOOL KIT

Brian Larson (Pacific Lutheran/1987-91), ConvergeOne Sales Director, PACNW SLED

I first met Frosty on a recruiting visit during my senior year of high school in 1987. I was immediately struck by his larger-than-life presence. And none of that was ego. He was a whirlwind of energy, and always seemed to be doing a dozen different things or helping a dozen different people all at once. Yet he managed to make each person feel heard and important. You came away with the understanding that Frosty genuinely cared about you as a person.

While I was visiting with Frosty in his office, he started drawing on a huge tablet of paper on his desk. It covered the desk! He had words and clouds around words, and phrases and lines scrawling all over the place. He looked like a street artist creating a masterpiece on a sidewalk. I don't even remember exactly what was on the paper that day or exactly what was shared in our conversations with Frosty and staff, but I do know I came away impressed and wanting to be a part of it.

As I would come to learn, football was the conduit through which Frosty encountered most people, but to him it was always about coaching the game of life. Whether you were a player, a coach, a student, a teacher, a family member, one of the many grade school children we mentored regularly at Lister Elementary, or the waiter at a restaurant during a team trip, they were all treated with the same respect and level of importance. What you got with Frosty from the moment you met him was 100 percent of him. He was completely genuine, and he genuinely cared.

Frosty was the tone setter to this approach and it emanated throughout the PLU program. I became a better, more confident football player because he (and his coaches) removed the fear of failure. You were

encouraged to push the envelope of your physical and mental abilities in your pursuit of "finding a way" to get the job done and get better in the process, and keeping yourself and your teammates positive with the "power of the put-up." We would throw verbal "bouquets" to each other after every game (our Afterglow sessions) or even after practices, or whenever—always focusing on the positives.

On the power of positivity, Frosty's Attaway cheers were legendary! We'd throw these out anywhere, at any time or any setting. It could be for a player, a coach or trainer, the bus driver, a hotel worker or even an inanimate object ("Hey sunshine, Go sunshine, Attaway, Attaway!"). Like so many things, it was a part of the culture. They made people feel good and feel appreciated. And even though they sometimes made us laugh or seemed kind of crazy, they made us feel good as well.

Don't get me wrong, that didn't mean that success didn't matter, but "success" was defined differently. It wasn't necessarily about the scoreboard, but about competing against your best self and continuing to be the best you that you could be. Continuing to raise your bar, and the team's. The scoreboard usu-

ally took care of itself as is evident from his coaching record.

Frosty was truly invested in his players and coaches, and as a result, was never shy about dishing out some tough love when he felt it was warranted. Agree with him or not (and usually he was right), you always knew it came from the right place.

I can remember being on the receiving end of some tough love at least a couple of times. One such instance was right before one of our exhibition games against Evangel College while in China (Yes, China!). Myself and a few of the DB's thought it would be cool to wear bandannas on our heads as they had become a bit of a fashion statement in the NFL at the time, and blare music through our headphones (via our Walkman's—this was 1991!) as we were warming up. Frosty let us know in no uncertain terms that we were not about that, and the rest of the team was able

to hear the message from across the field as well. He reminded us, reminded me, that we had one name on the back of our jerseys— LUTES—and that we "didn't know that we didn't know" the right way to act at that moment. As with most young men, that theme transpired more than once in my late teens and early twenties. Still makes me chuckle.

Speaking of China. I was fortunate enough to take two international trips with the PLU football team during my time there. My freshman year we were invited to play exhibition games and coach football clinics in Australia and New Zealand.

My senior year we were invited to play three exhibition games in China. The reason those governments felt confident in extending those invitations to PLU was because of Frosty and the reputation he had built at PLU. He did this by teaching us and providing the example on how to properly present ourselves and how to

treat others. "Guys, leave it better than when we got here" was a phrase we heard Frosty say as we left every restaurant, every locker room, every charter bus, you name it. I've been saying the same thing to my kids and the youth players I've coached for the last 30 years.

Another phrase that Frosty lived was, "people don't care how much you know, until they know how much you care." I've been trying to live that phrase for just as long.

Frosty was not one to take himself too seriously either. He had a great sense of humor (very PG—he may be the only ex-marine that never swore!) and was quick to laugh at himself. From his beat-up station wagon (The Bomb) that was held together with athletic tape, to his frequent fat-fingers on the bullhorn whistle and alarm buttons, he laughed as hard at himself as anyone. It seemed that 50 percent of the time he was blaring, "Scott! We

gotta go!" over his bullhorn right after five to 10 seconds of an ear piercing, "tweeeeett-brr-rrrrrrpppppppp!" as he was pressing the wrong buttons!

Frosty was part coach, part spiritual leader, and part parent. He devoted his life to giving his players (and any of those fortunate enough to interact with him) the skills and the support to not only be successful tackling challenges on the field, but to be successful in navigating the challenges of life. I can't really put into words how fortunate I was to have ended up at PLU for four and a half years. The friendships and relationships I made there are the most powerful ones in my life. Frosty and his program played a huge part in all of that and it has helped me be a better friend, business leader, husband, and father.

Not a week goes by that I don't pull something from the Frosty Westering tool kit.

AND THE JET TAKES OFF

Del Lofton (Pacific Lutheran/1987-88), PLU Coach (1989-92 and 1996); Colonel, U.S. Air Force, Commander of the 21st Medical Group, Peterson Space Force Base (Colorado, Springs, Colorado)

While playing and coaching under Frosty, I remember hearing about the concept of servant leadership. I also saw it in both his actions as well as those of the entire coaching staff. Additionally, Frosty spoke of love being the best way to motivate people. What I came to realize is that Frosty and the rest of the coaching staff lived out their love through this servant leadership approach, which had a significant impact on me as a developing young adult. Today, I see the concept of servant leadership all over the place. Although it seemed

to be a somewhat unique style back then, it is now everywhere in leadership books and conferences.

Having played at PLU and experienced Frosty's leadership style, I have come to realize that servant leadership truly is the best way to lead any group. As an Air Force officer, I have been given numerous opportunities to lead teams of varying sizes, from just a few to over 500. Leading these teams with a servant's heart is central to how I operate and has been absolutely key to the success I have been blessed with.

As a husband and father, I have tried to set an example for my family by living a servant leadership lifestyle, hoping they will see it as how someone should live and work despite the many contrary influences presented by the world. Simply put, I don't know of a better way to do it. As I continue to lead my teams at work and raise my two sons, I pray that I can have a similar influence on them as Frosty had on me, and so many others. Thank you Frosty!

One of the humorous Frosty memories that often comes to mind is from one of our team meetings. We were sitting in Olson 102 listening to Frosty talk passionately about

something. I can't remember what the topic was, but I think it had something to do with having a sense of urgency. I just remember that he said, "You get in the boat and the jet takes off!" I think everyone in the room heard that and paused, and so did he for a second. You could even see the look on his face that told everyone that he realized what he had said. Then, in classic Frosty style he said, "Well, it was a jet boat!" We all had a good laugh at that and how quickly he was able to flex to cover the comment. EMAL

THE EXPECTATION IS STILL EXPECTED

Rusty Frisch (Pacific Lutheran/1988-92), Teacher and Football Coach (28 years; currently in Birmingham, Alabama)

Frosty's coaching style: Playing for Frosty was one of the best experiences of my life. His philosophy was ahead of its time. Nowadays a big time football coach has coined the term and has talked about "The Process." Well, we were doing the process long before anyone knew what it was. Frosty taught us about the pursuit of excellence everyday. The ability to communicate this philosophy to 18 to 22 year old kids was what made him a genius. It was

so freeing to know you didn't have to be perfect. Mistakes were a part of getting better and this pursuit together with your teammates and coaches was to be enjoyed. I never felt more confident in my teammates and myself than when I played at PLU.

Now that I am in my 50's and having coached football for 28 years, I continually speak his words to my players. It still amazes me that the things we were taught and how we were coached still apply today. So when a player makes a mistake and I tell them to "flush it," they give me a funny look like, "What are you talking about?" I just smile, pat them on the head, and remember my coach, Frosty.

Tough love: Every week during the football season we had to write up our goal sets for the week. I was a red-shirt senior and having done goal sets for four years, I was getting a little tired of doing them. I remember it was a busy school week and I had forgotten to do them. I didn't make it a priority. I remember

thinking, "It's just one goal set. Frosty won't say anything."

Well, Frosty did say something. I was called into his office and we had a talk. I don't remember what was actually said, however, I will never forget how he spoke to me. He didn't get after me like I thought he would because he had every right. Instead, I just remember the principle of our conversation. The expectation is still expected and the standard is to always be upheld no matter who you are.

Travel abroad: In the summer of 1991, we had the opportunity to travel to China for a three week tour and play three exhibition games against Evangel University out of Missouri. What a deal!

After a very long flight, we finally arrived in Beijing and got to our hotel. Next thing I knew we were going to have practice. I figured there was a park or a grass field next door or something. No, we started marching down the sidewalk in our helmets and maybe even shoulder pads. "Where in the world are we going?" I thought. This wasn't a short walk.

Long story short, we end up practicing in Tiananmen Square a year or so after the Tiananmen protests. I thought we were going to start an international incident. It was a great practice but was cut short when people started gathering around to watch and military personnel started coming around. Frosty was all about enjoying the trip and that day was an all-timer.

Practice organization: As football coaches, we are always looking at the latest trends or techniques in order to have an advantage or improve our teams. One of those areas is practice organization. If any coach had visited us to watch practice, they probably would have wondered how in the world did we win any games.

Prepractice

Players showed up and maybe did the monkey bars, others would be fighting with sticks, some guys would be stretching, others might be doing one-on-one moves against each other, punting and receiving punts, throwing and catching, basically waiting until Frosty rolled up in The Bomb. Then it was a team meeting on the bleachers where Frosty spoke to us about the day's focus or any announcements.

Practice

We started with the offense and defense separating and doing a walk-thru—maybe doing five minutes of individual skill work, then to every skill position's favorite, 7-on-7. I loved 7-on-7. Finished with a Team Period, done.

Bill Walsh was a master at practice organization. Individual Period related to the Group

Period, which in turn related to the Team Period. It was the perfect learning format. Today, kids have a hard time seeing the connection from an Individual Period to the Group Period to the Team Period. They get lost and don't see the relationship. This is where Frosty was brilliant. Spending 80 percent of our time in a group or team learning football, it was easier for us to see how our small part fit into the bigger scheme of what was happening. So, when it came time to play, we didn't have to think.

We did no big warm-up routine, no conditioning, no full tackling, and very few practices in full pads. One week we only practiced in helmets. Crazy right? Not to us. It was the 20/80 rule to perfection. Focus 80 percent of your time on the 20 percent that matters in order to be successful. Genius! Frosty was ahead of his time. Over the years, I have listened to football coaches talk about how to be successful. Most of the time, it was something we had already been doing at PLU.

A CULTURE OF JOY

Troy Brost (Pacific Lutheran/1988-92), Asset Manager

Frosty created a culture etched in memory. It

was a culture individuals gravitated toward; eventually discovering what they desired was being part of something bigger than them. Frosty's culture not only permeated throughout his team and Pacific Lutheran University, but extended to friends, families, and fans as well—literally worldwide. It was a culture of trust, best shots, seeking excellence, and joy; unapologetically, a culture of EMALs layered upon his chosen foundation of Christ.

Frosty occasionally quoted Henry Ford, stating, "Guys, "surround yourself with people that know more than you." Initially, young men would not know how to appreciate this statement. What if this quote helped inspire Frosty to trust players and to allow the players to coach each other?

Years later in Frosty's career, this philosophy produced far more fruit than one might have expected. Frosty lived these words by example, surrounding himself with great men in Paul Hoseth, Scott Westering, Craig McCord, Scotty Kessler, John Nelson, Ralph Weekly and exemplary women such as Donna Belle, Dr. Colleen Hacker, and many, many others. Regardless, being trusted and guided by exemplary staff at an impressionable age paid huge dividends in all facets of life both then and now. What an uncommonly genius approach!

Society often focuses on having fun and little more. Having fun is important and unquestionably EMAL style football was fun! Practice, cheering on the women's soccer team during practice, team meetings, games, and trips were indeed fun, yet temporary. One could conclude Frosty's style was exceedingly fun because he created a culture of joy, the intangible experience directly related to being a part of something bigger than you.

Under Frosty, everyone had a role in serving the team, and because the role was important, more so where you as a person. The importance of roles included bus drivers, airline attendants, Mt. Rainier, freshmen Bombers, the band, family, referees, and the list goes on. Frosty gave Attaway cheers to make certain everyone knew (including inanimate objects) of their importance not only to the team, but to him personally. As goofy as giving an Attaway cheer to Mt. Rainier seemed, this type of fun left enduring lifetime impressions of joy. These impressions Frosty created were countless and seemingly daily occurrences. They are cherished and deeply missed. Those he touched are blessed to carry the enduring joy of EMAL!

Giving your best shot was Frosty's expectation, offering freedom from fear of failure and great desire to succeed—a freedom of choice. Tough love from Frosty was firm, always respectful, often requiring no more than, "you are better than that," and he was right.

On the other hand, often times freedom of choice directly resulted in calculated risk and creating significant success. Paraphrasing Jon Rubey, "When playing Cumberland, the QB did not huddle after an offsides and mistakenly ran the same play. When Cumberland

lined back up, Albert Jackson III lined up in a sprinter stance, looked back at me (Jon) and said, 'What is that fool doing? He didn't even huddle. Cover me Rubey, I'm going!' Albert crushed the QB. Judd Benedick scooped and scored."

Looking back, this phenomenal play of Albert is just one of thousands of Frosty's players rooted in a culture of trust, freedom from fear of failure, and freedom of choice. Frosty created the culture of joy individuals collectively bought into it.

TWO DORKS AND A DETOUR

Brian Flattum (Pacific Lutheran/ 1989-93), PLU Coach (1999), High School Coach (1996 to present), Vice President and Chief Operating Officer, YMCA of Pierce and Kitsap Counties

Breakaway: There are so many great memories of Breakaway. I remember sitting in the Bomber van in my first Breakaway. Jon Edmonds was a senior captain and he must have drawn the short stick because he had to drive the freshman. During our drive he said, "Some of the best memories you will ever have will be made in Gearhart, Oregon!" I thought to myself, "What is he talking about? I don't even know where that is!"

He was not wrong—so many great memories.

One year, we all took the trip into Seaside. There was a group of us hanging out and walking around together. As we walked around town, we saw coaches and other players enjoying the sunny day. My group got some ice cream cones, and ended up at the roundabout at the end of Main Street overlooking the beach and ocean. Awesome view, and it was late in the day and the sun was going down. Frosty and Donna were there.

We all started talking and enjoying each other's company. There was lots of laughter and jokes. All of a sudden, a seagull pooped and it landed on Frosty's head! He slapped his head, and said, "nice shot guys" and looked at us! He thought we had thrown ice cream at him! I will always remember the genuine laughter that ensued.

Frosty and Donna always found a way to make people feel included and part of the group. They were genuine people who cared for people and who they were.

The first time I met Frosty: My senior year in high school happened to be the time that Frosty was in Hawaii writing his book. Never

met him in person during the recruitment process. Fast-forward to report date and I still had not met Frosty in person.

Chad Barnett and I showed up together. It was pouring rain. We were both so excited to be on campus as college football players. We decided to go out on the practice field to check it out. As we were standing out on the field, here comes The Bomb around the corner. Of course, we had no clue what this was or who was driving. I for sure thought we were in trouble. I was thinking, "Great, first day and I'm already in trouble!"

Frosty jumped out wearing a polo shirt and shorts and started walking toward us. Huge smile. He says, "Chad Barnett and Brian Flattum! So glad to have you guys here!" And then he gave us the biggest hugs. Again, it was the middle of the field, pouring rain. We talked for a few minutes, and got another hug. Chad and I head toward Olson and Frosty hopped in The Bomb and drove off. He had detoured to see us! He had been on his way to do something else and happened upon us. He saw these two dorks on his field in the rain and made time to come and greet us.

Here is a man who was as accomplished as they come as a coach and greeting two freshmen that he hadn't laid eyes on before

by name on a soaking wet practice field. Talk about feeling included and welcomed!

I tell this story often to staff, players, and others that are building culture. Lots of people can do the X's and O's, but it's how you make people feel that makes all the difference.

US BEING US

Aaron Linerud (Pacific Lutheran/1989-93), Project Manager, Building Materials Industry

"You guys are gonna get killed"

1990, first round playoff game in Mequon Wisconsin, at Concordia University: The day before the game and we were doing our walk through and finalizing on a practice field near the stadium where we were to play the following day. We did not have sideline radio communications or headgear for coaches, so a coach from the competitor school of Concordia let us borrow theirs. As that coach was giving the equipment to Frosty, he marveled at the antics us players were showing.

Frosty had just given us hang loose time, so we were being dorks—playing tag, throwing the ball at each other, just being us.

That coach exclaimed to Frosty, "You don't know who you are playing. Concordia is big, fast, nasty. You guys are gonna get killed." Frosty looked at all us players, smiled and said, "Well that's just what we do, that's us being us." The other coach walked away shaking his head, surely laughing at our impending doom the next day.

The next day after the game was over and we were making our way back to the locker room, we walked through a gate where that same coach from the day before was standing. Frosty shook his hand and thanked him much for letting us borrow the equipment. With a nice smile Frosty asked the coach, "How did we do?" All that coach could do was shake his head, smile and say, "You did pretty good coach, you did just fine." We won the game 37-3.

Frosty—adamant to review a play no matter what

Game at Western Washington University (I think in '91): It was a closely contested game and we were trailing at halftime. In the third quarter, the defense forced a turnover, and

from where the offense was sitting on the bench reviewing a play, most of us could see we now had the ball. So, we shout, "Turnover! Turnover!" and begin to jump up and get out on the field. In those days, the o-line sat in order of position, while the skill guys stood. I remember hearing and seeing QB Marc Weekly heading towards the field (he had the jump on Frosty since he was standing up). I also remember seeing Brian Flattum quickly maneuver around Frosty's left side. But Frosty was not done yet.

Frosty was kneeling near the dry erase board (might have been a magnet board at that time). I was the closest person to him on his left side. As I get up to go, he stiff-arms me back onto the bench, followed by a right forearm shiver to Jeff Douglas right next to me.

Frosty: "Sit down, we are not done with this play!"

Us: "Frosty, we have the ball!" (The defensive players were still yelling, "Turnover! Turnover!")

Frosty: "I don't care if we have the ball! Where's Marc? Marc!" (Now, read that line again but in Frosty's voice.)

Frosty went about drawing lines around the board for a few seconds.

Frosty: "Oh well! Do you guys know how to block this? It is so important you know how to block this play!"

Us: "We know… yes… okay… yeah, we know…" as we took off running onto the field.

While I do not have unsubstantiated proof in front of me, I am 90 to 95 percent sure we took a delay of game penalty. After the game, I gave Frosty a big hug and said, "That was quite a stiff-arm!" He smiled and said, "Yeah,

I shouldn't do that though." I replied, "That's okay. Linemen have a unique bond."

And I am sure we blocked the play correctly. I hope.

Sunday, August 16, 1998

At the airport in Honolulu, my wife Jenna and I were in a packed terminal awaiting our flight to Seattle. We were ending our week long honeymoon, sitting on the floor somewhere near our gate, when I spotted a woman who looked like Donna. Before I could go check, another person moved seats behind her, and a man was sitting next to her that looked like Frosty!

After some surprising hellos, we caught up for a few minutes before boarding. I recall it was a large plane, eight or nine seats wide with two aisles, so I did not think I would be able to visit much on the flight. But as we reached cruising altitude, I noticed Frosty was upfront standing by a divider wall, off the side of one aisle. He had recently had hip surgery and needed to stand to be more comfortable. The reason for their time in Maui was for rest and recovery after the surgery. I can't sleep on airplanes, so I asked Frosty to chat for a few minutes. He told me he would likely stand for a couple of hours, to keep the blood flow in his hip. I was excited for the opportunity.

Five years after my time playing at PLU and I had a chance to have a one-on-one conversation with the man who had so much to give to people in life. As he shared diamonds, the true words of wisdom were perfect timing as we discussed my future marriage. We shared stories for a couple of hours and Frosty had some great ones—memories of his marriage to Donna, the beginnings of his coaching career, to the early days at PLU, hilarious memories of former players, and some serious stories of lessons learned and personal growth we all go through in life. Some stories I had heard before but most of what he shared on that flight was new. It filled my cup and I was blessed to experience that time with him.

Five seasons of EMAL football at PLU—all of the practices, games, road trips, China, Germany, championship games, etc.—but the time spent on that flight and the stories he shared are my favorite memories of Frosty.

SO MUCH MORE THAN FOOTBALL

1993 Captains: Chad Barnett, Judd Benedick, Jeff Douglass, Marc Weekly, Kevin Winder

There are not too many football teams that have had the opportunity to travel to China and Germany and win a national championship. This was a journey of a lifetime that we would never forget.

In 1991, PLU Football was asked to travel with Evangel College of Missouri and participate in three exhibition games in Beijing, Shanghai, and Guangzhou, as a way of introducing the game of football to China. Three weeks in China—visiting the Great Wall, The Forbidden City, practicing on Tiananmen Square (a story of its own), and countless other sites—would prove to build the way for greater things to come.

In 1992, PLU was asked to participate in an exhibition game in Germany against the Hamburg Blue Devils.

In 1993, we started out the season ranked #1 and playing against our rival, the Linfield Wildcats from Oregon, in the Tacoma Dome ending the game in a last second comeback tie. The team in 1993 was characterized by an incredible sense of family. Like many PLU teams from this era, the memories made during diverse experiences made each game,

especially in the playoffs, about having another opportunity to stay together and compete.

Frosty's leadership and learning how to lead others is what impacted us in a profound way. He was the master motivator. He always knew just what we needed. Sometimes we needed tough love, other times we needed to be praised and lifted up. He was sometimes calm and sometimes fiery. Whatever the situation, he knew what buttons to push to motivate our team. As a result, our team had complete confidence to play with Total Release and without the Fear of Failure.

We went undefeated the rest of that season and won the national championship in Portland, Oregon. The camaraderie, the journey, the laughter, and the chemistry were a gift to us all. However, behind this all was our leader Frosty who had the vision and commitment to set it all in motion. We will all carry these memories for life.

ASSUME THE RELATIONSHIP

Jeff Douglass (Pacific Lutheran/1989-93), Gastroenterologist

My first in person meeting with Frosty is one that has left a lasting impression on me over the years. My senior year recruiting process had been somewhat atypical, as Frosty had been taking time away to work on his book. I had visited PLU but Frosty was unavailable at that time and so my first opportunity to meet Frosty was going to be reporting for fall camp before the 1989 season.

I arrived at PLU and made my way to the

fieldhouse in my era appropriate blonde mullet where the team was making preparations for preseason fitness testing. Frosty was in the middle of some other players and I was insecurely aware I only knew one upperclassman when showing up that day. I waited a moment, taking in the scene, and when the activity slowed around Frosty, I approached him.

As I came to his awareness, I reached out to shake hands and he simultaneously focused on me and said, "Oh Jeff, we are so excited you are here" as he bypassed my gestured hand and embraced me with a strong authentic hug. The hug was fitting for long lost friends and lasted beyond my usual expectation where my initial release encountered a warm persistent embrace. It lasted until my initial squirming sensation passed and his affection and care remained. I remember my muscles tensing and then relaxing in that embrace.

I'm not sure what logistics were discussed after my initial greeting but the experience has stayed with me. I have speculated that Frosty had prayed for me prior to my arrival and I was not just another warm body. We heard

the mantra "assume the relationship." I came to know Frosty as someone who valued everyone. It did not matter if someone was a janitor or waitress or bus driver. Frosty made a point to care and celebrate people in all walks of life. His genuine appreciation of people and willingness to go the extra mile to see individuals reflected Christ in a subtle, authentic, and uncommon way.

THE ATTITUDE NOTEBOOK

Chad Barnett (Pacific Lutheran/1989-93), Pharmaceutical Oncology

I grew up about 30 minutes away from Pacific Lutheran University. Football was something I wanted to pursue in college, but I had never really thought about attending PLU until later in high school when I had a substitute teacher named Sue Westering. There was something different about this teacher. There was a passion and energy for life that was so encouraging to me.

This was my first experience in meeting a Westering family member and it would turn out to be a connection that would change my life forever. My senior year, I received a call from a coach named "Frosty" who at that time was in California writing a book called, "Make the Big Time Where You Are." He was going to be home for the weekend and asked to meet with my parents and me. This meeting was something that I had never witnessed in any of my other recruiting visits.

As I had experienced with Frosty's daughter, there was a passion and energy for life that I could not explain. He was drawing out diagrams on his spiral notebook, not about the X's and O's of football, but what

Frosty referred to as the Attitude Notebook. Though I didn't know it then, this notebook would become one of the most valuable tools in my life.

Needless to say, I chose PLU as my home for the next 4 years where I would learn about attitude, goal setting, and leadership (being a servant warrior). As a captain my senior year, I was given the opportunity to soak up Frosty's life lessons firsthand. These lessons have not only shaped my life, but my family's as well.

My two sons Carson and Cody grew up with the Attitude Notebook and attending Lute football games on Saturday. They loved going to say hello to Frosty and the coaching staff and soaking up the post game Afterglows. Though they didn't have a chance to play for Frosty, they both experienced the tradition of playing EMAL Football through Frosty's son, Scott. What a dream come true to watch your kids experience life lessons that go far beyond the football field. They are eternal!

NIGHTMARES, HOPES, AND DREAMS

Andrew Gray (Pacific Lutheran/1990-93),

SIM Global Worker (serving in Niger, West Africa), Marriage and Family Discipleship

I grew up in the confines of PLU and Parkland having attended the Franklin Pierce Schools all my childhood. I attended the 1980 championship in Lincoln Bowl as a nine year old and remember seeing a star defensive back (Scotty Kessler) intercept four passes that day. I remember the joy this dominant team gave to my family and to my heart. What a win!

I remember attending games in the Tacoma Dome, national championships and others. I never dreamt of becoming a Husky, Cougar, or even a Seahawk as a kid. Rather, becoming a Lute and playing for Frosty Westering was my aim.

I played for PLU in the early '90s and didn't realize many of my hopes and dreams; at least not the individual ones. The Lord used these years to train me in different ways, but not so much in personal success. I had a few run-ins with Frosty where I received a bit more tough love than Attaways.

In fact, since that time, I have had a few nightmares each year where in my sleep, I am still playing for Frosty and can't find my shoes or helmet or jersey and he is looking for me and frustrated, wondering about my commitment to the team. Thankfully at 50 years old, I think these nightmares are starting to wane. I am pretty sure I had only one this past year.

Nevertheless, I know Frosty loved and cared about me. I ended my playing days one year early from my Bomber class, very nervous to tell Frosty that I could not go another year; that my passion for football had run dry. And to my amazement, he said some tender things that really touched my heart. This legend of a man really knew me, knew what was important to me, and spoke into those areas during our brief meeting.

I am sure many will say this, but one genius of Frosty was that he knew how to construct a team of unforgettable and inspirational coaches and players and helpers who could and would touch, motivate, and change any life—including mine. I came to know Jesus at an early age through the influence of my dad and mom. But at PLU, I came to understand the need for others to know Him. I participated in something much bigger than myself, and it wasn't just PLU football. It was the Kingdom of God. This wasn't just through the influence of Frosty but so many others—fellow players, coaches, servant warriors, so many. Thank you, Lord!

It's funny that even though I grew up watching Lute football, I really had no idea what I was getting into at that first Breakaway in 1990. I gained so much more. Frosty and his program changed my life and I am forever grateful.

LUNCH AT MARZANO'S

Marc Weekly (Pacific Lutheran/1990-93), Former SEC Coach; Medical Sales, Medtronic (retired)

I have two very loving and instrumental mentors in my life. My father Ralph, who thankfully I get to see each week, and Frosty, my former Coach who invades my mind on a regular basis 30 years

since playing.

Although I enjoyed the food at Marzano's every Wednesday for my one-on-one QB pre-game meeting with Frosty, I needed the time with him more than I needed sustenance. We talked about so many things not related to football. Sure we planned and schemed, but most of that real work was done with Scott. If I had to guess, I do not think Frosty was too concerned about my performance each Saturday. It was just Marc the young man with so many questions who was just trying to navigate every day.

There are not enough pages to tell you what he meant to me. I miss him, I love him, and there are so many days even at 51 that I still need him.

THE BEAT OF A DIFFERENT DRUM

Judd Benedick (Pacific Lutheran/1990-94), Teacher and Coach (15 years a Head Football Coach), Mountain View High School (Meridian, Idaho)

I had the great fortune to play for Frosty from 1990 to 1994 in what I would consider to be an amazing stretch at PLU. During that time,

our class would play in the National Championship three out of five years, winning the championship in 1993. I believe that the program overall had reached it's cultural stride in this particular period. People were completely bought in and definitely drinking the Kool-Aid. Under the leadership of Frosty and his assistant coaches, it felt like the perfect blend of peak performance on the field and the PLU Philosophy working hand in hand.

I have been a teacher and a coach for 26 years upon graduating from PLU. The last 15 years of my career I have held the role of head football coach at Mountain View High School. It is a large 5A school with 2,500 kids in the state of Idaho. During this time, I have done my absolute best to run a program that I think would make Frosty proud. I have made it my version of Frosty's philosophy. It pales in comparison to his version, but you can see his fingerprints all over the program.

To the best of my ability, I have tried to "Make the Big Time Where You Are" a reality. I tell anyone who will listen about Frosty and the profound difference he made in my life. I've been able to shape so many young men over the years thanks to his positive direction.

It is virtually impossible to sum up in words the impact that Frosty had on my life, the lives of my teammates, and the entire community. It was a five-year span that resulted in a lifetime impression. I didn't realize it at the time, but the ripples in the pond would continue to have an impact not only on me, but almost everyone I encounter.

After talking to so many of my colleagues over the years, I now know and understand that the experience we had wasn't like the one anyone else had—not even close. We were

playing the game of football, but it was so much more than that. The philosophy that Frosty shared with us shaped our character, our attitudes, and relationships in ways that are still paying off today.

He was a legend and a psychological genius. He was magnificent, full of integrity, and charisma. Everything he did had purpose. He didn't sell his brand. He lived it. He preached the gospel daily through his actions. Most of the time, we didn't even realize what he was doing, because it was disguised as a game, a team building exercise, or a service project. He was so outside of the box with his methods, those on the outside of the circle couldn't comprehend what he was doing. Those of us lucky enough to be included in the inner circle were transformed and we would never be the same.

I could tell numerous stories about the actual football games we played and the amazing accomplishments on the field, but that wouldn't even begin to reveal the magic that took place with PLU Football. I also could share a hundred additional stories for this book that had much more to do with life. We all could and it still wouldn't sum it all up. The fact is, I find myself subscribing to his philosophy daily. It's evident in the way I teach, the way I coach, the way I raise my family, and the way I treat people. Frosty lives on through all of us who had a chance to play for him and continue his legacy.

We could also print an entire book with "Frostyisms," quotes, and speeches. Like many of you, I can recall countless examples of his love, his lessons, and his greatness. I'm going to focus on a story from the time our team took a trip to China. It was an amazing, once-in-a-lifetime experience that I will never forget. I chose this story from all the others because it demonstrates how unique our entire PLU experience was.

In the summer of 1991, I had just finished my freshman year. It wasn't a normal year for me as I had knee surgery two weeks into the season and missed the entire year. Nevertheless, I was selected as one of the few freshmen that got to go on the trip. I was elated to be selected and excited for the opportunity to see China. The trip was merely the beginning of my PLU experience and for the first time a real peek behind the curtain.

For those of us that got to know Frosty well, we were able to see all the different sides of his personality during our time on campus. He was a bold man. He had complete conviction in the things he believed in. He brought out the best in all of us, his philosophy eventually woven into the very fabric of our being. Because of his confidence in who he was, he wasn't afraid to take chances, which led to some remarkably interesting and sometimes hilarious situations.

When he saw a problem or a challenge, he simply found a way to make it work. To quote him, he often said, "No means maybe," which

was his way of telling us to be persistent and overcome initial obstacles. His way was often times unconventional, but it was one of the many things that made him unique and an attractive leader. To say that we did things differently at PLU under his leadership would be a vast understatement.

China was an unreal experience. We ate weird things, met a variety of people, and saw some of the most amazing places the world has to offer. The most fascinating part of the trip for me happened one day when we decided to adapt and find an alternate place to practice. Beijing has a lot of people, but it doesn't have a lot of room or space to practice the game of football. Frosty had us put on our gear and our street shoes for practice. I don't think any of us really understood where we were going to practice, we just knew it was an open space and it wasn't grass.

So, we walked through downtown Beijing with our helmets and shoulder pads on toward our practice location. Imagine the sight as an entire team of large Americans walked through the streets of China dressed in football gear. Funny stuff in itself, but the kicker is, we were holding practice in Tiananmen Square.

An interesting side note is that a student-led demonstration took place in the square in 1989, about two years prior to our arrival and is known as the Tiananmen Square Massacre. After this event took place, the Chinese were not allowed to gather in the square in groups of people larger than three. It was posted everywhere, but of course none of us knew how to read Chinese. However, I did notice several armed guards dressed in military attire located around the square as we arrived. A perfect place to hold a practice, right?

There might have been some word of caution from our tour director. It didn't matter, though. Frosty had a plan and, if you know Frosty, he is going to make it happen no matter what. So we held practice right in the middle of Tiananmen Square.

On one end of the square was Mao's Tomb, on the other, the gate to The Forbidden City. In the middle of this were 50 plus American football players dressed in gear running a football practice. As you can imagine, this was quite a site for the Chinese, most of which had no idea what football was.

Anyone in the square that day became curious as to what we were doing. A large group started to gather around us to watch. We were having fun and were oblivious to what was about to unfold. As stated before, people are not allowed to gather in the square, so naturally this posed a problem. The locals became fascinated. Pictures were taken and people were trying on helmets.

Eventually the guards, who might have been police, started to take notice and they were not happy with people gathering in groups. At one point it became clear that this could be an absolute disaster if it progressed. The guards became agitated and the locals became nervous. I'm not sure how the panic started (maybe it was like a game of telephone) but people on the team started to learn that this might not be a great idea.

At some point, I think I remember Frosty pointing and yelling, "Let's go guys!" It could've been an overreaction, but I wasn't going to take a

chance. We all took off on a dead sprint from the square and through the streets of Beijing in full gear. I had no idea who was behind me, who was next to me, or exactly where I was going. What I do know is that I was more than a little scared and laughing at the same time. We didn't stop sprinting until we reached the hotel. Now that's a story. PLU Football at its finest!

I ended up with my picture on the front page of the Chicago Times, practicing in Tiananmen Square. Apparently, the event had made quite an impression on the world. I still have that picture framed and it reminds me of the day we made history and possibly avoided something much worse. It also illustrates my point exactly through a simple story. Nothing compares to our unique experience under the larger-than-life figure known as Frosty Westering.

It happened as it so often did with Frosty in control. His way always prevailed and produced some funny results and interesting consequences. That's part of what I loved about the man. He knew exactly who he was. He marched to the beat of a different drum. It's actually a perfect picture of PLU Football and Frosty—a perfect juxtaposition of grace

and tough love; a peculiar blend of football and life lessons; a combination of chaos and efficiency; a mixture of football and philosophy.

Frosty sometimes took on the role of a father, other times a mentor, a leader, maybe a counselor and certainly a coach; impossible to define, unorthodox methods with legendary results. Amidst it all, the underlying theme was Christlike love and relationships. The relationships we built with Frosty, Scott, Paul, Craig and Kess are genuine and will last a lifetime.

He taught us the game of football, but in the meantime, he was impacting and changing our lives in ways that words can't describe. You couldn't go through the program and leave the same person you were when you arrived. We learned that character is our best piece of equipment and that attitude is the one thing we can control and a daily choice we make. We understood that being a servant and putting others above ourselves is the secret sauce to joy and fulfillment. We learned how to face adversity and beat it. He taught us that you could view life as a glass half empty or half full. We were taught how to set goals for ourselves and reach them. I could go on and on and still not capture the impact he made on my life.

I owe a large part of who I am today as a person to Frosty. There isn't a day that goes by where I don't think of him or put into practice something he taught me. He left me with an incredible toolbox to take on the challenges of life. I picked up rocks along the way and they have turned into diamonds. His picture hangs on the wall in my office to remind me of where I came from. I can honestly say that I was blessed by my time spent with him.

Frosty shaped my life at a very influential time, forever changing the kid who was wet behind the ears into the man I am now.

My own dad has played an instrumental part in my life, but I can't imagine my life without Frosty and the other coaches at PLU. God broke the mold when he created Frosty, and I am so glad he did. I will forever be grateful for Frosty and the man he was. When you leave this world, you hope that what you did had some sort of significance in the lives of others. I have no doubt that when Frosty arrived in Heaven the first words spoken were, "Well done good and faithful servant, well done." EMAL #8, Captain 1993, 1994

THE THREE-SIDED COIN

Andrew Hershey (Pacific Lutheran/1990-94), High School Teacher and Coach

[Andrew submitted this story on April 26, 2022, and died on May 12, 2022, at age 50.]

There were so many valuable lessons from Frosty that have stuck with me, but at this point in my life the most meaningful is his three-sided coin metaphor. You can't always be the best, you can't always do your best, but you can always give it your best shot. This has tremendous meaning when you hear the word stage IV rectal cancer.

I was diagnosed about two and a half years ago at the age of 47. I was nowhere near my physical prime, but after constant chemotherapy, three bouts of radiation, and other complications, I am nowhere near my best self. But I wake up every day prepared to give it my best shot. I have so much going for me; a wife and three kids who I love spending time with, EMAL friends to keep in touch with, friends from work and church, and kids I coach and get to be in relationships with.

I sometimes get frustrated that I am not able to do things that were once simple for me, like walk more than half mile, or sit down without being in pain. But I can almost hear Frosty's voice (although at this point Frosty's voice is usually a mix of people doing impersonations of him) telling me to call the flip of the coin and it landing on the edge, and I am reminded to give it my best shot. This helps me to refocus on my situation and change my attitude.

One thing I valued about the program was the Tuesday night meetings—especially Paul and Jeanne opening their home to the defense. There were so many players that couch space was at a premium. Matt Mihelich and I started eating as fast as we could in the cafeteria and arriving at Paul's house 20 to 30 minutes early to make sure we sat on a couch and not the floor.

Eventually a few others caught on and we arrived early only to see the couch seats taken. After that, we would leave the locker room and drive through Frugal's and eat our

dinner on the Hoseth's couch. No one else was willing to make that commitment. Paul and Jeanne would just go about their business pretending like we were not there.

A highlight was Matt asking if he could sit in their hot tub. The next week we arrived early and after eating his dinner, Matt sat in their hot tub for 20 minutes.

The inclusion of the staff's family was something I do not think many other programs across the country had. Growing up in a house without a father, those small glimpses of how Paul treated Jeanne, Mari, and Karl helped shape the father I am today. What a blessing Tuesday nights were!

GRATITUDE

Karl Hoseth (Pacific Lutheran/1990-94), Teacher and Coach, Spanaway Lake High School (17 years); Assistant Principal, Franklin Pierce and Silas High Schools; Principal, Lincoln High School (Tacoma, Washington)

When I wrote the acknowledgment page for my thesis on Relational Leading in 1996, I included a quote from Felix Frankfurter, "Grat-

itude is one of the least articulate emotions, especially when it is deep." Frosty was a big part of that thesis and allowed me to interview him about developing community. He is included in the acknowledgments. I have spent many days and countless hours writing and thinking about what to say about the Westerings. I decided on some bullet-point memories in an attempt at keeping my thoughts brief. At the end I tried to summarize my gratitude, but it isn't as articulate as I'd like.

I was born in 1971. Frosty's first season at PLU was the fall of 1972. I turned one during that first fall and had a chance to watch the PLU football program as a little dork, a ball boy, charting plays for my dad in high school, a quarterback, a part-time assistant coach and a color analyst on the radio. I have so many great memories of PLU football. I feel honored to have loved the program for over 40 years.

Mid-1970s: I used to get so excited driving to Franklin Pierce Stadium with my mom and parking on the baseball field next to the

stadium. I loved watching the Go-Drills and participating in the Go-Tunnel for the team as they ran through the tear-away sign at the base of the stadium stairs. I still get excited hearing the same Go-Drills prior to games—especially hands hitting thigh pads during "1… 2… PLU!"

1977ish: I was at a practice and Brad Westering was quarterback. Frosty wanted to let me catch a pass and score a touchdown. One EMAL let me borrow his helmet. It was way too big. When the swing pass from Brad came my way, I couldn't see a thing because the helmet had slipped down over my eyes. Incomplete pass. Undeterred, Frosty decided I should score via running play on 24 down. I took the hand-off, ran through the line of scrimmage and bounced the play out to the outside. Everyone on the defense was diving and missing me. My dad put on a helmet and started chasing after me down the sideline. As I neared the end zone, my dad dramatically dove and clipped the heel of my foot with his hand. I fell face first into the grass and got a bloody lip because my face slammed into the face mask of the oversized helmet. While washing out my mouth at the water fountain near the tennis courts, John Zamberlin said, "Do you want me to beat up your dad for you?" I declined the offer.

1979: I remember listening to the closing seconds of the game at Moorhead State on the radio with all the coaches' wives and Susan in the basement of our house. MSU had an All-American kicker set to win the game after PLU had led most of the game. I believe Susan had a pillow pulled over her ears, not wanting to listen just prior to the snap. I was incredibly nervous. Then, Scott blocked the kick! Everyone was hugging! It was the first nail-biter I remember hearing on the radio. Donna said she knew Scott was going to block the kick

1980: I went to my first Breakaway. I believe this was the year Frosty made a wager with the team about his weight. A scale was in front of the steps outside Olson Auditorium. He stripped down to his boxer shorts and tipped the scales at 223 pounds. At Breakaway, each Dogpatch team participated in a song competition. The PLU fight song was supposed to be used in the original lyrics. I remember these words from one of the songs:

Our Coach is named Frosty and he's a nice fellow

He always tells us how good we can be
He leads us in practice and makes us our best-est
Bare in his undies at 223

Early 1980s: Frosty's family had a garage sale outside the house. Scott convinced me to buy an O.J. Simpson photograph playing for the Buffalo Bills that was mounted on cardboard. Scott told me, "He's going to be a Hall of Famer." This sold me. I kept that picture above my bed for many years. I occasionally brought it out during U.S. History class when discussing major events of the 20th Century.

1983: I asked my dad if I could be a ball boy. He told me I needed to ask Frosty. At a pre-season coaches meeting on our deck behind our house, it seemed like a good time to ask, but I was really nervous. I approached Frosty and asked him. He was very enthusiastic and excited for me. It made me feel great. I always took my job as ball boy very seriously from '83 to '87, grateful for the opportunity. It was a good experience to be on the Lutes' sideline and the opponent's sideline. However, there are many former players that think my career

as a ball boy lasted much longer than it did. When I run into EMALs from the 1970s, often they will introduce me to their family members and say, "This guy (pointing at me) used to be a ball boy when I played!" I generally don't correct them.

1983: The season opener was with UPS in the Tacoma Dome. PLU and UPS did not play each other the previous three seasons. UPS was dropping down from NCAA Division II to join the NAIA. A UPS player who didn't know what he didn't know said, "We're just going to be pushing over weaker walls."

There were 14,838 people at the game. I was having a hard time getting my butterflies in formation for my inaugural role as ball boy. Brad could see I was nervous and came over and said a prayer with me. It really helped calm me down.

1986: I was playing 9th grade football at WHS and we had an afternoon game on our practice field. PLU players (it might have been just the defense) came over in their practice gear and cheered for us. It was fun to have a big rooting section. I think our crowd quadrupled when the EMALs showed up.

1989: Frosty took his coaching class to scout our WHS football game against Spanaway Lake. It was The News Tribune game of the week (4-1 vs. 5-0). We lost by one point, but it was a great game. After the game Frosty wrote me a nice note about the "double-win" and told me that I had played at a high level and hit .333 for the game. I really appreciated the note.

1991: A million things were amazing in China. The whole trip was unreal. I'm so fortunate I got to go on the trip, especially since I was the last one added to the roster, one week prior to departing (Tom Bomar got a job). In the last game, while on the kickoff team, I tried to bust the wedge and everything went black. At halftime, as Frosty was addressing the team, he looked at me, gave me a thumb's up and said, "Karl's got a concussion. That's just great!" The whole team laughed.

Overseas Trips: How wonderful that Frosty

was able to take teams on four overseas trips from 1985 to 1993. I was lucky enough to go on three of those trips. Now, as someone who has been a head coach and in charge of many events at school, I can appreciate all the planning each trip required and the stress of being in charge of so many college students for multiple days. At the time, I didn't understand all the preparation that goes into a trip. Now, I know they didn't "just happen," but I'm so grateful they did.

1991-94: Drives in EMAL 5 to games at Sparks and nighttime practices were always memorable.

• On I-5 Frosty was discussing the counter criss-cross and started weaving into another lane. All of us in the car started to gasp a little. Frosty said, "That's OK. Del (Lofton also driving on I-5) will block for us!"

• Every time we'd approach the Stadium Way exit, going to Stadium Bowl, Frosty would ask Scott, "Now, which exit is it Scott?" Scott would usually point without saying a word. Once, I asked Scott, "How come you don't drive us?" He said, "Because I like living on the edge."

• I loved when Frosty would put down the light that looked like something a doctor uses to look at your throat from the ceiling of the car and point it in the back seat for better illumination. It wasn't very powerful. Marc Weekly and I would always quietly laugh, as we'd squint while looking at our play sheet.

• Frosty would always turn left on 118th street onto Pacific Avenue. I asked, "Why do you take this way, Frosty?" "Well, Karl," Frosty said, "A lot of people don't know about 118th street. You go down 118th street and a nice window opens up for you."

• Once, while driving, Frosty pronounced, "Turkey is the most popular meat. It just blew past roast beef. Went right by ham."

• One time Frosty asked me, "Karl, how do you feel about the 10-pass?" It was a basic pass and I said, "I feel pretty good about the 10-pass." Frosty then asked Ben Hunt, third string in 1993, "What about you, Guy?" Scott, turned to his left and said, "His name is Ben, Dad." Frosty quickly responded, "I know! I know that," and then continued talking about how the 10-pass might be open.

1990-94: Frosty would tell the team, "You should never have to pay for a high school game. Just wear your PLU hat." I took that to heart and used the "no means maybe" philosophy over the years attempting to get into games.

1992: Andrew Hershey and I were voted "Birthday Song Leaders" as sophomores. At a preseason practice, it was someone's birthday and Frosty wasn't convinced that

Hersh and I were the guys for the job. He decided to lead the birthday song by himself. It was a very choppy rendition. Hersh and I had three-year careers as birthday song leaders, something I'm proud of.

1992ish: At a cold evening practice at Fife High School, we found out it was Cracker Jack's 79th birthday. Frosty wanted to get a picture of Cracker Jack with some of the team in the metal bleachers. I suggested that Cracker Jack wear Ray Kurtz's #79 practice jersey. I don't think Ray or Jack thought it was a good idea, but Frosty did. Soon, Jack had the grass-stained jersey over his brown jacket for the picture. Ray was left without a shirt. Frosty took a Polaroid picture vertically, which just put the large white portion on the side of the square picture. Frosty then served us chocolate cake, wiping the knife clean after each cut with his fingers and licking his fingers clean.

1992: Players switched jerseys at a Stadium Bowl practice. Frosty was in the bleachers with his bullhorn. Captain Brody Loy (cornerback) was wearing Ken Fagan's #99. Brody

tipped a long pass up in the air that a bomber receiver caught. Frosty yelled through the bullhorn, "Whoa! Whoa! You're going to have to better than that #99!" Unquestionably, Frosty didn't know it was Brody wearing #99.

1993: Frosty took Marc Weekly and I to Marzano's for Wednesday lunch quarterback meetings. Once Frosty didn't have his wallet in his pocket. He went out to the car to look for it. When he came back in the restaurant Frosty told the waitress to (with a thumb's up), "Put it on my tab."

1993: When I was helping coach basketball at WHS, one of the varsity players (Joe Canyon) worked at Baskin & Robins. He told me how Frosty came in once wanting a banana split. Joe said, "I'm sorry Frosty. We're all out of bananas." Frosty thought about it then said, "That's okay. Go ahead and make it anyway. I've got some bananas at home."

Summer 1993: Scott asked if I would help light off fireworks for a show commemorating Independence Day. We used flares and wore PLU football helmets. After it was over, we had a Roman candle fight. I received a Roman candle shot from Sue that made a brown burn mark on my white Syracuse sweatshirt.

During the barbecue with the family before (it might have been after) the show, Frosty seemed mellow and relaxed. It was a different side of Frosty and the family than during football season and it was fun to be included.

1993 Championship: All season Frosty would get the play from Scott over the headset and tell me the play on the sideline so I could send in the signals to Marc. After halftime of the National Championship game in Portland, Scott got locked out of the booth. Frosty said into the headset, "Scott? Scott? Well, it looks like it's just you and me Karl." Then Frosty said to me, "Let's get the ball to Barnett." I sent in a spread/iso signal for Chad. Next, he said, "Let's get the ball to Tang." I sent in a spread/iso signal to Aaron. After three plays, we scored a touchdown. It was a great way to start the second half, although I'm sure Scott was stressed out and vigorously combing his hands through his hair.

Our last practice before the championship game we took a team picture. We suggested that Frosty lay down in front of the team on his side. He did it! We all laughed and had a great time during the team picture. It was always great to see how Frosty would help us take something ordinary and make it special and how he would go along with our silly ideas.

1994: Prior to the 1994 season, I was thinking about switching from #15 to #4 and I was getting Scott's approval after a meeting. Frosty seemed to think it was a good

idea, although I don't think he cared as much as Scott how a number looked on a player. Then I said to Frosty,

"But Frosty, Bart Starr wore number 15." Frosty enthusiastically said, "That's right! Don't change!" I did change because we (Scott and I) decided I looked better in #4.

1994: My senior year at Breakaway, I played Frosty in our skit. We got all 10's, except from Jerry Lejeune. It was awesome that Frosty was self-confident enough to allow players to gently poke fun and at him or the program and not get insecure as our leader.

1994: After one late-night practice at Stadium Bowl, Frosty had ordered pizza to be delivered. The pizza came a little early and our practice went a little late. The pizzas were sitting on the cement Stadium Bowl steps and got cold before we ate them. The team was still enthusiastic about eating cold pizza at about 11:30 p.m., but a few guys were jokingly blowing on the slices in their hands as if the pizza was too hot. Then, prior to eating a piece someone slapped a slice across the face of Jon Rubey (I believe), giving him a cheek full of sauce. A few more guys joined in until Frosty yelled, "NO! It's not the Pizza-In-The-Face-Game!" We played that game several

times in the future whenever we had pizza (on our own time).

1994: I've talked with Frosty about how incredible the two Western football games were. The first game against WWU was for the league championship. The defense hadn't given up a touchdown in 10 quarters. We put in the Georgetown offense just that week to save for the second half. We were down 9-7 at the half, then scored four straight times using Georgetown to go up 35-9! I'll never forget the chance to run a quarterback sneak (21) for a two-point conversion right over their big defensive tackle. Then, in the quarterfinal playoff game against Western, we found gold helmets in paper bags prior to going out onto the icy field. It was such an exciting time.

1991-94: I always enjoyed Tuesday night meetings in room 102. I liked strategizing for the upcoming game. I was good at Scott's trivia questions and usually got to eat treats early (trivia winners went first) unless the meeting went long and Frosty starting handing out treats (we always knew Central weeks would go long). Donna's peanut butter bars with chocolate on top were my favorite. Sometimes Frosty would pass out the punch with four cups in one hand and all the fingers on the inside of the cups—pinched together, dipped into the red punch—caused his fingers to turn red.

I liked "Name That Tune" night.

Once, Frosty was dishing out little smokies to everyone on plates as Scott was going over videotape. Dak Jordan declined a scoop of little smokies. I thought it would be helpful or interesting if I informed Frosty that Dak was on a diet. Frosty said, "A diet? Here, have some extra. It will help you with your 21." Dak was not thrilled with me and tried to sneak his little smokies to the offensive linemen.

One Tuesday night meeting fell on Brian Flattum's birthday. Frosty took a piece of chalk and wrote on the blackboard, "Brian's Day" (then underlined it). Andrew Hershey and I still use this as an inside joke when referring to someone's birthday. Example: On Facebook, for his birthday I might type, "Andrew's Day."

1995: l approached Frosty at the golf course coffee shop to see if I could borrow EMAL 5 for my last show hosting Karl's Den on the school's TV station.

Me: "Frosty, Chris Egan has a sports show on KCNS 6."
Frosty: "Yes he does."
Me: "And I have a segment on his show."
Frosty: "Yep, you do."

Then I asked if I might be able to borrow

EMAL 5 for my last show. Frosty got really excited. He said, "You bet! You know all the kids borrowed the car! Stacy did. Holly did. The keys are under the mat." When we were discussing how I would get it back to him, he told me he would just walk home. I got it back in time, but what a fun, selfless example he set. And Chris and I had a good time driving around campus in EMAL 5.

1995: All season long I was on the sidelines and got to send in the signals to Dak Jordan. When the team played at Findlay, Ohio, in the first round of the NAIA playoffs, I came along because I was the only one who could send in the signals. It turned out to be my dad's last game as defensive coordinator. I felt fortunate to be there for that game and I was so proud of the defense after 60 minutes of playing a much bigger team and holding them to 14 points. I shed a few tears on the bus after the game knowing it was probably his last game as a PLU coach after 28 years.

1996: I was working on my thesis for my Master's Degree. I combined Frosty's theories with my personal observations of a junior

high principal after shadowing the principal for five days. I interviewed Frosty at home after he had surgery in April. I came up with five themes on how to become a relational leader. They are: 1) trust, 2) caring, 3) sharing, 4) moral unity/cooperation and, 5) identification/involvement. I then took these themes and turned it into five concepts for EMAL football. It became:

1. Everyone is Important
2. Identification/Involvement
3. Shared Leadership

4. Shared Environment
5. Shared History/Tradition

The name of the thesis became "Relational Leadership: A Middle Level Principal's Role in Creating a Community of Care." At least three people have checked it out at PLU's Mortvedt Library (my mom is one). Doug Lamoreaux (my advisor) found the connections fascinating and wanted to write an article about the process.

1999-2003: I had the privilege to call the games on the radio during the last few years of Frosty's career. The 1999 season (the first for Steve Thomas and I together) was amazing.

2003: I told this story at the Humanitarian Coaches Hall of Fame Induction. When Alison and I went to Hawaii in the summer, I brought along Frosty and Donna's phone number (which I received from my dad). We stopped outside the condo. I called the room. Frosty answered, "Aloha." I said, "Hi, Frosty. This is Karl Hoseth." Frosty said, "Well, Karl Hoseth. An Aloha to you!" I explained that Alison and I were passing by and planning on snorkeling, but we thought we'd say hello.

Frosty encouraged us to go snorkeling and we could eat dinner together that night. We had the best snorkeling experience ever because we swam with dolphins.

That night, Frosty called our place and asked if we had been to Cheeseburger in Paradise. I mentioned we ate there the night before (in Lahaina). Frosty asked, "Well, have you been to the one in Wailea? This one's better!"

Frosty and Donna picked us up. As we got out of the car to go to Cheeseburger in Paradise, we noticed the sprinkler system on the roof of the restaurant was on and flooding the floor so we audibled and went to a rib place (new #1). Everyone greeted Frosty and Donna. They knew the names of everyone that worked at the rib place. A man from Magnolia came up to talk with Frosty. "Magnolia, Minnesota?" Frosty asked.

There was a slight problem with forgetting a cane. Later, Frosty and Donna showed us the new bedspread they had purchased. We had such a fun night. It was wonderful for me to spend leisure time with Frosty, Donna, and Alison.

2003: After Frosty's last game, it was great to see him take the microphone and lead the crowd in fight songs. I was on the air with the radio, but I had to take off my headset and soak it all in. One of my colleagues from Spanaway Lake was at the game. He thought it was an awesome pep rally. It was a perfect way to end 32 years of coaching at PLU.

2004: For Frosty's final Afterglow, I had a chance to speak on behalf of the mid-1990s players. After my short speech, Frosty said, "The real tribute to Karl is he took a team that was just supposed to be average and led them back to the championship game." It was one of the best compliments I could receive.

2004: I had the chance to emcee (with Steve Ridgway) the ceremony for Frosty and Donna's induction into the Humanitarian Coaches Hall of Fame. It was such a privilege to be a part of the night and interview Frosty and Donna on couches. I enjoyed sharing the story of our night in Maui and introducing Dan Hawkins who spoke via video and Rafer Johnson who spoke on behalf of John Wooden. Jim took a picture of Rafer, Alison, and me afterwards. I love the picture and it hangs on our wall. It was a special evening to honor both Frosty and Donna.

2005: Frosty came and spoke to my Leadership class in the spring during WASL testing. He brought a packet to hand out (we didn't get to it), videos, and the small toilet with an audible flush. Afterward, one of my students painted a toilet as a thank you card (for all the class to sign) and wrote, "Frosty, we would never flush you!" I didn't know how Frosty would take it. But when I delivered it to the house to provide feedback, Frosty slapped his knee, laughed and exclaimed, "That's an all-timer, Karl!" At least two occasions on the radio when Steve and I were interviewing Frosty, he mentioned the toilet thank you card.

2004-2012: We had several great interviews on the air during halftime of games. I loved it when Steve said, "Well Frosty, we could probably talk for hours, but our time is up." Frosty often responded, "Just one more thing, Steve."

2011: Late in the school year, my Leadership class made a rainbow sign for Frosty. He wanted to thank each kid in my class and do-

nated a signed book to over 32 kids. He called me and said, "Karl, I'm going to need some help with a few of these names." We went down the entire roster. It was such a generous gift and the kids got so much out of the book. I had them write a personal response to one of Frosty's stories in the book. It was a great way to leave another legacy. I felt a different level of connection to Frosty (even after knowing him my whole life) because he was reaching out to my students and showing his heart to them.

In Closing: I feel like Frosty at our senior banquet. At a certain point he had to cut off the stories. There have been so many great memories throughout my life revolving around PLU football. I would like to thank Frosty for a few specific things:

I appreciate that he helped us "take something ordinary and make it special."

I loved all the singing we did—The Mood (instrumental), Seize the Day, fight songs (even in Tiananmen Square), and the EMAL chant led by Slick, then Ted.

I loved that even if he didn't remember a person's name, he made them feel like they were great friends with a pat on the back, a big smile, and a "Great to see you!"

I appreciate that Frosty created an atmosphere of caring and positivity. It was a wonderful program to grow up around as a kid.

I appreciate that he and my dad worked so well together as a team. He allowed him freedom to run his defense the way he saw fit. He was able to attract, perhaps, a different type of player to be on the defensive side of the ball.

Even if someone on the team wasn't a Blue Car guy, everyone knew the expectations. "That may be like you, but that's not like us."

I love that EMAL means something special

to everyone who played. Others have tried to replicate it. Kansas State uses EMAW. My little league baseball team, the Trinity Trolls coached by my dad, used EBAT (Every Boy A Troll). But being an EMAL truly made you feel a part of something bigger than yourself.

As a leadership teacher at Spanaway Lake, we did the same three birthday songs, used go-tunnels, and passed out bouquets after Homecoming week. As a track coach we had our version of a postgame locker room. All of this was an attempt to build community, which Frosty did in such a masterful way.

I talked with Frosty in 1996 about how a principal would build community in a school. I've been using some of these concepts in the 17 years as a classroom teacher and have been excited to use the things I learned from him in helping build a school-wide community as assistant principal at Franklin Pierce High School, Silas High School, and, as of the summer of 2022, the principal at Lincoln High School in Tacoma.

This was extremely long, but I'm extremely grateful. Thanks for showing me the way.

INK WHAT YOU THINK

Jon Rubey (Pacific Lutheran/1990-94), Vice President, Colliers International

Frosty always taught us to ink what you think if you want to proactively get better at anything. I have been writing down my yearly goals and long-term dreams ever since I played for Frosty. It is amazing how I took it for granted while in college. Using the SMARTER technique is so beneficial in setting realistic and obtainable goals. I still use this technique in my personal life, my professional life, and a little bit with the teams that I coach. Many people pay to get training to learn how to be productive and goal set. We got to live it first hand for five years.

EMAL 5/The Bomb: While walking to Olson during recruiting, I heard one campus safety guy comment to the other rookie officer pointing at EMAL 5. "By the way, you don't touch that car."

Breakaway: While at Breakaway, we always had various games and competitions on the beach. One year when we did the Izzy-Dizzy relay, the players had to run into the waist deep ocean, running around the coach, and then come back. Scott Westering was one of the coaches standing in the ocean for the players to run around. While the relays were in progress, we jokingly made comments that somebody should pretend like they were really dizzy and then tackle Scott into the ocean. Much to our surprise, Big John (don't recall his real name) took it to heart. When Big John ran out into the surf in a somewhat dizzied state, he proceeded to complete a very nice form tackle on Scott. The beach was silent and time seemed to stand still as Scott slowly fell backward into the water with Big John on top of him. Both parties disappeared for a second or two under the crashing surf and then popped up to the surface. The look of complete surprise that was on Scott's face was unforgettable while Big John had a look

of satisfaction on his face. Scott handled the situation with class as Big John helped him out of the water but that look on Big John's face quickly tuned to a look of fear after he realized what he really had done. The ongoing benefit of this incident was it did start a new trend in Scott's hairstyle. Before that day, we never saw Scott with his hair totally slicked back. So Big John not only did something no one else ever dreamed of doing but he also helped inspire a new Steven Segal hairstyle for Scott.

On one of our Breakaway trips, we were hanging out at the roundabout in Seaside where the road ended at the beach. As we were hanging out, just being us, we heard a loud splat. Everyone turned to see what happened and saw that Frosty just got pooped on by a seagull, right on his forehead. Without hesitation, Frosty energetically stated, "Well that was a great shot!" And then he proceeded to give the seagull an Attaway cheer.

Practices: After Judd had his knee surgery, he was always out at practice helping in any way he could. When Frosty called us in together as a team after doing some drills. Judd, being

the Servant Warrior that he was, helped put away the tackling dummies while still in a knee brace and barely able to hobble around. As everyone was now in the bleachers, Frosty was just about to start talking when he looked across the field and saw Judd walking gingerly across the field towards the team. Frosty could not believe the Judd was walking and shouted: "Come on Judd! On the bounce! You are better than that!"

Road Trips: On every bus trip we ever took, I never recall Frosty sitting back in his seat relaxing or sleeping after a long day. No matter what the hour, he would always stay awake and keep talking to the bus driver. I often remember him even standing most of the time in the aisle right next to the driver. If anyone deserved to sit and rest a bit, it was Frosty. I will never forget how he always treated the bus drivers that way. He respected them and always made them feel important.

One season we played Oregon Tech in southern Oregon. It was a long bus ride from Tacoma, which required us driving through some desolate places late in the night. I remembered standing in the aisle talking to Trevor

White when suddenly it felt like the bus was skating on ice, even though it was still summer like weather. The bus slid a little sideways and I recall glancing out the window and seeing a small pickup truck with the back end crushed, spinning in circles then launching off the road. The canopy flew off the back of the truck and a cooler of beer, fried chicken, and potato salad littered the highway.

When the bus finally came to a halt, Frosty quickly stood up and boldly stated "Nobody get off the bus!" Then somebody pointed out, "Slick (Chris Vansligtenhorst) is already off the bus! Look outside!" Everyone looked over and saw Slick running across the road, weaving in and out of the beer cans that were punctured and spraying beer into the air and pieces of chicken and tubs of potato salad and then climbing up into the truck that now was off the road and up against a tree in the woods. Frosty then calmly corrected himself and stated: "Nobody get off the bus expect for Slick." We ended up being stuck in the middle of nowhere for a few hours while we waited for another bus to come transport us the rest of the way. Frosty later gave the bus driver an Attaway cheer stating that he was the best bus driver he had ever seen drive a bus. From that point on, Frosty always requested that bus driver ("the best driver in the fleet") to drive our bus.

Frosty constantly reminded us to, "Leave it better than you found it." He always made sure we picked up our trash and cleaned the locker room before we left. I remember after one away game, I went back to the locker room to check and see if I forgot something. Frosty was in the locker room picking up the smallest piece of athletic tape off the floor to ensure that we did leave the locker room

better than we found it.

The Notebooks: I keep a copy of my football inner game book on my desk. It is amazing how many times I refer back to it. There are so many diamonds in that book. I used it and read from it on numerous occasions that I have spoken at in a business setting, or at a Young Life or FCA talk, or just coaching a team. I have made and distributed a much smaller version of the book for a couple of the lacrosse teams that I have coached as the principles are applicable to any sport. Although some of the players do not initially see the benefit of the notebooks, it is often the parents that really get excited about them. I had a few parents who wanted to know if they could have a notebook and if they could use some of the material with their teams at work. It is fun to share the Blue Car model of thinking with others not only in the sports arena, but in the business arena as well. It is always such a good reminder of the power of what we were taught. We have a responsibility to help share that with others whenever we can.

Nellie (John Nelson): Our senior year, Judd and I held each other accountable to run after each practice. We had a couple different sprint scenarios depending upon how we felt and what needed to improve, but the workout always included slapping the hand of the other guy when we finished our leg going back and forth until our desired goal was met. At one point, Nellie joined our running group. He would push us to do an extra set here and there when we were tired. It also gave us a little longer break now that we had an additional runner/roller in the group. However, depending upon how well charged Nellie's battery was determined how long of an extra break we received. Looking back, it was so special to have a running partner who was in a wheelchair reminding us of the blessing that we had just to be able to run. And Nellie ran with us rain or shine and pushed us to make sure we always finished strong.

Team meetings: We had a Sunday evening team meeting in the classrooms in Olson. I do not recall exactly what the content was that Frosty was communicating to us, but I do remember he was very focused and was filling up all the dry erase boards on the walls of the classroom. After finishing up his point on the last of the clean boards on one of the sidewalls, Frosty moved back to the front of the room and was ready to move forward with his new thoughts. He picked up the dry marker eraser and began wiping, but nothing happened to all the text he had written. He tried again wiping more vigorously with the same unsuccessful results. He then pulled the pen out of his pocket looked at it and stated in a surprised tone: "High impact permanent ink? Oh no!" Then the next words out of his mouth were, "RAAAALPH!!!! We need you!"

Trip To China: While in China, the food was always a challenge. Although we went to some of the nicest restaurants, we were not used to

the food and flavors presented to us. At one of the meals, we were finally excited to see very large Peking ducks cooked to a golden brown and placed on each of our tables. We were so excited to finally eat some protein that we knew would taste good and, more importantly, we knew what it was. The servers came to our tables and then proceeded to cut off the perfectly cooked skin and served that to us. The remaining duck and it juicy perfectly cooked meat was then taken from our tables and never to be seen again.

At the time we visited China, it was still a very closed nation. In Frosty's wisdom and desire to preach the gospel through the game of football, he had every player bring a Bible with them that was in both English and Chinese. That way we could say they were our personal Bibles, and the Chinese Government could not keep us from bringing them into the country. The plan was to give all of the Bibles to a friend that ran an underground

church somewhere in the rural community outside of Beijing. However, upon our arrival, we learned that somehow it became known that we were going to give our Bibles away and our contact was informed that their family would be in danger if they accepted our Bibles.

I do not recall the exact details from that point, but one evening Phil Olufson came into the hotel carrying an old beat-up duffel bag requesting some help. A small number of us proceeded to Phil's room and began wrapping the Bibles in old Chinese newspapers. Those Bible's were then placed in the bottom of the duffel bag with old dirty laundry placed on top. Phil took the bag out of the Beijing Grand Hotel where we were staying and met someone on the street and handed the bag off to him. When Phil came back, we prayed for the Bibles and the person we gave them to. That was the last we heard of the amazing gift that Frosty was able to bring to the followers of Jesus in China.

Post Graduation: A number of years after graduating, I was working in Portland and volunteering as a Young Life leader at a local

high school. I had a meeting with a local business leader named Jim at his office to discuss some potential business opportunities. While waiting for my meeting to begin, Jim came out and introduced me to another businessman that had flown into town from New York City. Jim stated that we worked together with Young Life at a local high school. This businessman got very excited, shook my hand and proceeded to say, "Thank you for your work with Young Life. There are three organizations in this country that have the greatest impact on young people for the Kingdom. They are in this order: Young Life, Pacific Lutheran University Football and…" As you can imagine, I was totally surprised by his comment and don't even recall what the third organization was. What an honor to be a part of two of those organizations.

Assistant coaches: Paul Hoseth was an amazing gift to the team. He also provided an incredible balance to Frosty, which allowed Frosty to be Frosty and created that unique atmosphere that was EMAL football. Without Paul as his wingman, everyone from my Bomber class agrees that Frosty would not have had the impact that he did.

As I was on defense, I was blessed to spend a lot of time with Paul and have a lot of special and fond memories. He knew how to connect with his players and used his sense of humor to strengthen that bond. One memory I will never forget with his pregame speech just before the third national championship game that our class was blessed to play in. We had won the national championship the year before and our class was picked in the preseason to finish seventh in the league. Yet here we were, playing for the national championship once again.

I do not recall all the specific words that he used, but I do know that Paul and many of us players were crying by the time he was done. They were tears of joy as we did something no one else thought we could do, and tears of sadness as we now would no longer be able to keep playing the sport we loved with this amazing group of brothers. I do remember Paul saying: "Okay, that was not the best pre-game speech. Let's get it together, stop crying, and play some football."

Paul also knew how to connect with and coach according to each player's personality. Albert Jackson was the defensive end that I always got to be on the field with. Paul knew he had to communicate with each of us differently. I distinctly remember the worst chewing out that I received from Paul was when he calmly pulled me aside and stated with little emotion, "I am very disappointed in your play right now. You really need to do better." That cut deep and I took it to heart.

In great contrast to that, Paul knew that he needed to communicate with Albert in a much different manner.

One game, he pulled Albert aside and in a very stern and loud voice (some may even say yelling) explained to Albert what he was not doing and that he needed to do much better. When he was done, and after Albert ran back on to the field, Paul looked over with a big smile on his face and said, "Watch this. Albert is going to go out there and hit someone." And he did.

One final memory that I have is his genuine concern for his players. He knew that it was a financial stretch for my family for me to be

attending PLU. I was always doing odd jobs trying to raise extra money. I don't even know if Paul and Jeanne remember this, but they paid me $20 to come and rake the leaves at their house. Although that was such a little thing, it really was a big deal on a number of fronts. Not only did it help me with some extra cash, but it also allowed me to see that he cared about his players on a personal level as well.

The infamous phrase that I always remember Paul saying was, "Keep flyin' around."

Craig McCord was a technical wizard. He watched more game film than anyone I knew. His attention to detail helped me to become the linebacker that I was. Due to his knowledge our team was always in the best possible position to stop the offense before us. In one of our team meetings, I remember him saying the following: "I was watching film from two years ago on this team. After watching this film for the third time I remember thinking, 'really, you watched this three times from two years ago?', I think they may try and do this in the game if they get in this down and distance situation." Therefore, we practiced how

to stop that if it were to happen. On another occasion, he also noted that a slot back would run straight down field if his hand was on top of his thigh and would cut across the field if his hand was on the side of his thigh. That was priceless information that made us all better players.

Scotty Kessler had many roles on our team. Perhaps the most impactful was his spiritual influence on many others and myself. The first time I met him was on the sidelines of the national championship game that we lost to Georgetown College on a very muddy Kentucky field. He was on the sidelines scraping the mud off of everyone's cleats so they could get better traction in the field—the model of a true servant. One quote of his that I often use to this day is, "I'm not saying you're right or wrong. That is your decision." I hated it when he used it on me, but there is so much truth in it.

Scotty led many Bible studies and challenged us in ways that only a person that has earned respect on the football field can. He shared and challenged us in so many ways and gave us tools like the Bible Song and AWCFROG-

ROL that we still use today. He also taught us what it meant to be accountable on the football field, but most importantly off the football field. I had never heard of what an accountability group was until Kess came along. He encouraged us to find some guys and meet together with some regularity and encourage each other and walk through this spiritual journey together.

I also want to note that although technically he ran a football Bible Study, lots of others were welcomed into the group who Frosty graciously referred to as "bubble guys." Hearing about the need for accountability, I was inspired and asked two upper classmen, Todd Green and Jeff Douglass, to be in a group with me. As small of a thing that seems to be, that was a life changing moment in time for all of us. These groups slowly morphed and changed over time. Adding other EM-ALs like Kurtis Bonar as well as other friends like Chris DiCugno. I also want to add that 31-plus years later every Wednesday at 6 a.m., Jeff Douglass and I still meet to encourage each other and grow in our walk with Jesus. Brad Christiansen is now also a part of that group along with a couple other guys. Although they never went to PLU, those two know who Kess is and the role he and EMAL football played in inspiring us to be consistently meeting together as men.

A Few Final Thoughts: I don't recall the platform that I heard this on, but I will never forget the content. Both Frosty and legendary football coach Tom Osborne were sharing about football and life. Tom was sharing how it is a delicate balance of faith, football, and family and how you can keep all those strong and in their separate compartments of life. When Tom was done, Frosty was next and immediately stated something along the lines of, "With all due respect Tom, I don't think you can effectively separate all those things. The true power comes when all those parts of our life work together as one." He then held up his hands with his fingers intertwined. "When that happens, you have more impact and more fun." That's the secret to success right there.

For years we would be asked to sign the Rainbow Signs that were placed on the floor of the entryway to Olson. We always signed them because it was our duty as a team to sign and offer encouragement as others. Then 25 years later, as my mother-in-law was dealing with cancer, I requested a Rainbow Sign to offer some encouragement. It was then and there that I realized how powerful the signs really were. Both my mother and father-in-law could not believe that a group of complete strangers would spend the time to offer such encouragement to them in their time of need.

Some 20-plus years after my playing years, PLU was playing at Lewis & Clark College, not too far from our house. I took my older son Riley to the game. Much to my surprise, Frosty and Donna were both in the stands. I was so glad for Riley to get to meet my coach. What was fascinating to me, Donna immediately recognized me, said hello and

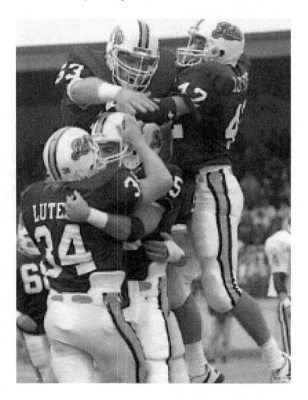

mentioned my name. That is all that it took for Frosty. Although I don't believe he did remember my name, with Donna's help in stating my name, he then energetically went on to state some detailed things about our epic battles on the grid iron that I cannot even remember the details of. He knew the play and the situation, recalled it with no hesitation, and shared it with the energy and excitement that only he can bring.

Football inspired him, motivated him, and allowed him to impact so many people. Such a gift that the Lord gave him to understand and remember a crazy game like football so that he can impact so many people in so many ways.

One of the handouts that Frosty gave us once had a photocopy from a page from his Bible. I am always fascinated by the comments written in someone's personal Bible. The one that I will never forget that was written in the margin: "Touchdown Jesus."

THE .333 HITTER

Albert Jackson III (Pacific Lutheran/ 1990-94), Case Manager and Resource Specialist; Track and Field Coach, Eagle Point High School (Eagle Point, Oregon)

I have been fortunate to have great football coach in my life. Frosty Westering stands out as one of the most influential. He literally left me with notebooks full of knowledge and wisdom about life and competition. Many people have asked me about my experience with Frosty. It was life changing to put it simply. The

man I was when I entered college was forever transformed when I graduated five years later. Although I could write a book on the many things I learned because of him, there is one story that continues to inspire me to this day. It was a long time ago, but it goes something like this. No, it went exactly like this!

The early days as a freshman at Pacific Lutheran University, I was wide-eyed wondering if I had the talent to be a part of such an academically challenging school and accomplished football team. This self-doubt was difficult but did not deter the goal of doing my best. At football practice one day, the team was sitting in the stands waiting patiently for practice to start. Frosty was late, which was common enough that the team understood, from the start of football season to the end, we were on Frosty time. We started when he arrived and we left when he was done.

We all watched as in the distance his old station wagon could be seen coming the down the road. It was so old that many on the team placed bets when it would fall apart (it never did during my tenure). He parked next to the unmarked yet prime space next to the football field. Although nearly every player drove to

practice, no one dared park in it. That was Frosty's spot. This was done out of respect and not fear.

Frosty got out of the car and started making his way towards the field. He hobbled like Humpty Dumpty because of a bum hip but it never slowed him down. He stood before the team and got our attention with a huddle break. He commanded, "Huddle Break are you ready?" "Ready!" we all clapped in unison.

Frosty was a storyteller and one of the best I'd ever listened to. He had one of those voices that was as powerful as a Marine Drill Sargent and as gentle as a grandfather. He would use props and stuffed animals with great effect. On this day, he had a copy of the Tacoma News Tribune. He turned to the sports section and asked, "How many of you watch baseball?" Most athletes raised their hands. "What is the batting average of the best player in the league right now?" One athlete offered up .300 and another said .280. He said, while pointing at the paper, "Edgar Martinez is the best batter in the MLB with a .333 batting average! Do you know what that means?" A

silent pause followed. "It means that he hit the ball about 3 times of 10 at bats. That does not sound very good but if a player retires hitting that well, he is guaranteed to be in the Hall of Fame." As he paced back and forth, he explained that goals and life are not about the successes we achieve, but the journey that we experience with successes along the way. We will have successes and we will have failures but what is important is that we get up to bat no matter what.

The message spoke to me as if Frosty saw all the worries and doubts in my mind. Although it would take me a few years for its deeper meaning to take root, my mindset slowly but surely shifted from what I had done, although that was important, to what I was going to do with each opportunity that I was given. The .333 hitter became one of the most important messages I got from Frosty both in the sports arenas and in the classroom. I learned from the mistakes and endeavored to correct them. I spent most of my mental energy focusing on what I could do better than what I did wrong. It has kept me in the game of life pursuing goals and dreams considering my successes and failures as two sides of the same coin.

As a coach and educator, I teach my young student-athletes the message of the .333 hitter and many others that Frosty shared as my coach. In fact, it was so inspiring to me that I named my non-profit athletic corporation .333 Goal Athletics in honor of Frosty and that message. My answer to the question, "What About Frosty?" does not capture all that he gave, but it is an honor to contribute to what I am sure will be a color collage of memories that honor him as a man who gave so much to this world.

HAPPY BIRTHDAY FROSTY

*Jason Fawcett (Pacific Lutheran/1991-94),
PLU Assistant Coach (1995-97); Owner,
Clutch Players (Beaverton, Oregon); Sports
Consultant*

I was one of the fortunate EMAL's to have
both played for and coached with Frosty. The
number of stories probably coincide with the
number of days spent at PLU over the course
of my seven years, yet one of my most memorable Frosty stories did not happen on the
football field, in the locker room, on a bus, or
in a coaches meeting.

I was in a coaching education class that was
co-taught by Frosty and Colleen Hacker.
There were several athletes in the class from a
variety of sports and even more students who
were not part of an organized athletic team at
PLU. It was a class in early December either
on Frosty's birthday or a day or two after and
as Frosty opened his briefcase and started

to sit down on his trusty stool, someone
offered a "Happy Birthday Frosty!" that was
soon echoed across the room.

Without missing a beat, and seizing the
opportunity, Frosty said, "Well, you know
when you turn 66 your whole life gets
flipped upside down. You feel hungry in
bed and sexy at dinner, but don't you worry,
me and Donna, we got it all figured out!"
As expected the class erupted in laughter,
Colleen looked embarrassed, and Frosty
was smiling ear-to-ear having just reeled in
the entire class like the world-class fisher of
men he was.

I love this story because it was Frosty. His
strengths, gifts, and talents are unques-
tioned, yet what allowed all of those things
to have such a great impact on so many was
his ability to connect in the most genuine way.
Having spent the last 30 years in the coaching
profession, I know so many who have tried
to emulate Frosty in some form or fashion,
yet his genuine humility, servant attitude, and
ability to connect is what has always set him
apart.

A FOUR-HOUR DRIVE

*Kurtis Bonar (Pacific Lutheran/ 1992-94),
Fifth Grade Teacher, Thurston Elementary;
Offensive Line Coach, Thurston High School
(1998 to present); Springfield, Oregon*

Just before my junior year at PLU, I injured
my hamstring while doing some sprints.
I missed the first several games trying to
rehab the injury. Each week the training staff
and I would reevaluate my injury to deter-
mine whether I'd play in that week's game. I
would relay the information to my parents
who would always make a four-hour drive

to watch my games, but if I wasn't playing I didn't expect them to make that effort.

By the fourth week of missing games, I questioned my parents as to why they were still making the long drive to the games when they knew I wasn't going to play. Their response was that they didn't want to miss the Afterglows or spending time with the other families. To them, the drive was worth it for those reasons. It was amazing to hear that my parent's connection to PLU football went beyond just me being on the field on a Saturday afternoon.

At Thurston High School, we were fortunate enough to win two back-to-back state titles during the 2018 and 2019 football seasons, and then play in the title game again in 2021. As an assistant coach at Thurston for the past 25 years, I have continually stressed the importance of focusing on the journey and not the destination to my players.

During those championship seasons, when we were able to extend our seasons as long as possible, that message became clear to the players on the team at that time. After the shine of winning a state championship had worn off, many of the offensive linemen

I coached reflected on the gift of being able to play together for as long as possible. The memories they have of those years go far beyond just one football game. They were able to fully appreciate that even when winning at the highest level on the field, the true value of the season came in the day-to-day work, experiences, and relationships that made up the entirety of their season.

THE NEXT THING TO GOD

Brad Christiansen (Pacific Lutheran/ 1990-94), Senior Vice President, Colliers International

Red Car/Blue Car, Champions Manifesto, Attaway cheers, and Rainbow signs—just a few things that come across my mind when asked about PLU Football.

Frosty was a "one." Yes, he broke the mold. Most importantly, he remained focused on the goal of coaching how he wished he'd been coached. Character of the players was paramount. Developing a culture of success focused on love vs. fear was what made the team and the program different.

I ran into an alum, Jacob Washburn (more than a decade behind me) this past summer and was quickly reminded how unique the "trip" was at PLU. My first visit with Frosty was in that crackerjack box of an office with artificial turf on the floor—Frosty grinning ear to ear with spiked hair and jolly persona. Was this Santa Claus? No. Some crazy clown? No, but unlike any other coach I had ever met.

Our freshman year, many of us revered him, thought he was the next thing to God. He carried himself as the General, but the biggest cheerleader we ever met.

By our junior season, we began to think he was more of a freak of nature only to stumble into his genius our senior year.

Ghandi was extremely intelligent, well spoken, and he pursued a life of purpose. Mother Teresa was the greatest servant who lived on this earth. MacArthur was the General of Generals. And Chris Farley could make anyone laugh (albeit far more crass than Frosty would have approved). Somehow Frosty was a little bit of all of them and demonstrated that to us all at different times.

I'll never forget finishing our last breakfast in Hamburg, Germany. Frosty was moving around the room and sending Attaways and Rainbow Signs to the servers and staff. As I paused to watch the reactions, a number of the staff began to cry and seemed to be humbled and embarrassed as if they had never been seen before.

It was his ability to go from drilling a lineman for not making a block on the field (and he could humble you with his words in a millisecond) to playing the drums in the student band section of the stadium that suggested he must have multiple personalities. But it was all genius—"the real deal" as Kess would often say.

The day he took me for a ride in the EMAL Mobile and waved or honked at everyone along the way and parking 10 feet up on the sidewalk next to Harstad caught my attention. It was like Rodney Dangerfield in "Caddyshack." Everyone liked him. With all his quirks and conjectures, he was the life of the party. He "experienced a joy few people do" everyday.

It wasn't until I was at Breakway for the last

time that I saw the depth of his mystique. It wasn't the games, songs, or even his rendition of the Izzy Dizzy on the beach.

I became the truck driver. I'd hauled boats and equipment, and driven RV's—big rigs from the time I'd turned 16. I became the volunteer to haul the gear back and forth to Breakaway by my junior year. You see a lot more from behind the scenes and, likely, this was the best of EMAL. I was able to arrive a bit early and a few coaches and wives were already there. What I learned that day is that the families make it their mission to love and serve these boys. We were a bunch of young, mostly immature men needing to be humbled. We were "green and growing!"

The real genius was the supporting cast of EMAL Football and Frosty's system was the whatever-it-takes attitude that everyone had. If it were unloading gear, everyone including would jump in to help. Glenna's ranger cookies, massive efforts to wash dishes or clean up after us on road trips was status quo. Whether overseas, on playoff runs, or across town against Puget Sound, the entire Westering family was involved. I totally took for granted that Chad Johnson was the ball boy in our era. Frosty's son-in-law was helping out on the sidelines every week too. Chad played on his own national championship team 10 years later.

It was infectious. Granted, not all teams had the same success, but the attitude of serving one another was a priority each and every year. I'm so grateful for the model Frosty and his family displayed. I'm beyond thankful to have gotten behind the scenes. I'm forever indebted to Frosty, the Westering family, and the entire staff. Becoming an EMAL was transformational for many others and my-

self, because the real goal was to demonstrate a love for God and to learn to love others. Thank you!

Brad "CHEETO #9" Christiansen, Centennial Bomber

Year	Record	Postseason
1990	9-2	NAIA Division II Second Round (1-1)
1991	11-2	NAIA Division II National Runner-Up (3-1)
1992	9-2	NAIA Division II Second Round (1-1)
1993	12-0-1	NAIA Division II National Champions (4-0)
1994	11-2	NAIA Division II National Runner-Up (3-1)

CHAPTER 6

THE 1990's PART II

[1995 - 1999]

AN EMAL-STYLE HEART

Corey Bray (Pacific Lutheran/1991-95),
Athletic Director, Oklahoma City University

I had a typical high school athletics experience for my era—old school coaches that motivated through yelling and negativity. When my high school career was over, I knew I wanted a different experience, something better. I just didn't know what that was exactly.

I was being recruited by a few small schools in the region, but one caught my attention because one of my good high school friends, Jon Rubey was a student-athlete in Parkland, Washington, at Pacific Lutheran University. During my campus visit, I got a taste for the Blue Car model of athletics. I didn't quite understand it yet. I just knew PLU and EMAL football was the place for me. It was one of the best decisions of my life.

When I became an EMAL, I began a journey on the success road that opened my eyes to the art of coaching (the psychology of sport and student-athlete development). The father in Frosty taught us how to become young men of character (our best piece of equipment) while the sport psychologist in Frosty taught us how to excel in sports through love (which is desperately needed with today's student-athletes as they cope with mental health challenges).

From our inner-game playbooks, he taught us about things like leadership styles, the potential performance gap, goal setting, the put-up game, the attitude games, servant leadership, feedback (the breakfast of champions), the mind's eye, tough-minded optimism, MAGIC, total release, the inner circle,

the double win, the parable of choice, and how to hunger for excellence. But most of all, he taught us how to make the Big Time where we are!

My entire career has been in intercollegiate athletics and there is not a day that goes by that I don't use a lesson from Frosty as I lead coaches and student-athletes. When I interview coaching and athletic administrator candidates for open positions, I look for indications that they lead with an EMAL-style heart. But, unfortunately, the Blue Car leadership style is not as prevalent as this world needs. When my career is over, I hope that I have taught a few student-athletes and administrators along the way about the blue car model of athletics. EMAL!

PERHAPS JUST ONE

Ryker Labbee (Pacific Lutheran/1991-96),
Co-founder and Director, Zomia SPC
(American social purpose corporation providing fair and affordable higher education loans in Southeast Asia; most students come from Myanmar)

The summer before I settled into an aging room at Foss Hall, Frosty took his team to China. Although I would only catch glimpses of the adventure on video months later, I recall being dumbfounded to see my future teammates running through plays on Tiananmen Square.

Prior to that, all I'd known about the iconic Beijing square involved the 1989 student-led uprising that culminated in a bloody standoff between Chinese citizens and the military. A photograph of "Tank Man" staring down a column of imposing tanks on a corner of Tiananmen Square would become one of the most recognizable images of the 20th century.

And yet, just two years after these events, Frosty had his players running around in shorts and shoulder pads in the shadow of the Gate of Heavenly Peace, first built in 1420. Outwardly oblivious to any concern about whether holding practice on Tiananmen Square might raise eyebrows, my hunch is that inwardly, he was making a point. He usually was.

Times were changing and nothing bolstered the desire of a long-supplicant people to have some say in how they're governed like having American athletes hoist footballs into the sky beneath an ever-watchful Chairman Mao.

Frosty's magic was in flaunting conventional wisdom and dancing to his own chaotic rhythms. How many teams gave Attaways to a mountain, or a sunset, or a flight crew? How many paused practice for popsicle breaks or heated rounds of Izzy Dizzy?

How many college football coaches would, two years removed from the fall of the Berlin Wall and a violent uprising in Beijing, schedule a carefree practice on a sunny day at the

symbolic heart of Communist China?

Very few, perhaps just one.

UNHINGED LAUGHTER

Josh Arnold (Pacific Lutheran/ 1992-96), Science Teacher, Canadian International School of Hong Kong

I've spent a lot of time recently sorting through my PLU memories, which have become, of course, increasingly fragmented over the years. As this vast treasure chest of memories flash before my mind's eye, a theme quickly emerges: Unhinged laughter. Tears streaming down your face, sore stomach muscles the next day, kind of laughter. Of all those images, my favorite is of Nellie laughing so hard that his entire body shakes like there's an 8.0 earthquake happening inside him!

Everyone who has known John is better for it. Frosty could see that early on I'm sure. Assisting John with all aspects of daily life imprinted on me what Frosty meant when he talked about being a servant warrior. Frosty lived it and modeled it for us, but it wasn't until I had the privilege of bringing John to my hometown for Thanksgiving that it truly resonated. That opportunity changed how I viewed myself and what I believed to be important. This was the first gift that John gave me.

The second gift from John I have yet to receive. Whenever I start feeling sorry for myself, I think of Nelle and how tough he was. I'm 48 now and have managed to cruise through life relatively unscathed. I've had enough laughs for several lifetimes and so far I've avoided more pain and loss than many of us in the PLU family. My time is coming however, and I'll be honest, the transition from caregiver to care receiver is terrifying. However, I have a role model in John Nelson who has shown all of us that when your body betrays you, carrying on with grace, courage, and frequent fits of laughter allows us to meet life's inevitable challenges.

THE BETTER WE GET

Curt Mulder (Pacific Lutheran 1992-96), Mental Health Counselor

One of the most interesting things I experienced was Frosty's take on winning and losing. In the five years I played for Frosty, I never once heard him refer to us winning a game, or needing to go out and win, nor even losing for that matter. Instead he employed euphemisms like "meeting the challenge" or "pursuing excellence" or if we lost he would say, "we didn't lose, we just ran out of time."

When Frosty did use the word "win" it was to educate about different perspectives on winning. Any talk about beating a team was always from the other team's perspective with sayings like, "Some teams come to *beat* us, we come to *be* us." This was a revelation for me.

Coming from a traditional public high school that won about half our games, winning was something we focused on and celebrated. I remember as a freshman at PLU being bewildered and impressed that after several wins there was never a celebration, but an enjoyment that was calmer, longer lasting, as the talk was about performance and excellence. Success felt so routine that early on I even felt a little bad for the team because no one seemed too excited after a win.

With time I came to internalize and appreciate the fact that pursuing excellence is a higher calling, by far, than pursuing victory. Winning was just a probable by-product of the enthusiastic pursuit of athletic perfection. Later in life I have cherished these lessons and incorporated them into my brief career as a college football coach, my longer career as a mental health counselor, and my seven years coaching my sons and their friends in elementary flag football. Those kids learned quickly that every week we were "playing our best selves" and that the answer to "the longer we play" is "the better we get!"

JUMP IN THE WHEEL-BARROW

Brian Walker (Pacific Lutheran/1992-96), Teacher, Coach, Athletic Director, Assistant Principal, Boise State District (25 years); Area Director, Timberlake Quadrant

How I Met Frosty

For many years I have reflected on my first encounter with Frosty and the impact it had on my life by essentially changing the path I was on. Every day of my life I

praise God for how He used Frosty in my life. We all have the ability to look back and see how God works in our lives. Some moments are easy to explain, yet, other moments are unexplainable. For me, this was one of those unexplainable moments of God's faithfulness and love for me. The story goes something like this. No, it goes exactly like this:

Following my senior football season in high school, I visited multiple schools like Linfield, Willamette, UPS, and PLU. In January, I went on visits to all the schools for football except PLU. I only visited PLU as a student. When I visited PLU, I dropped off a tape with the Assistant AD Larry Marshall. About a week later I get the tape back in the mail—just the tape, nothing else. I thought, "Well I guess they are not interested."

A couple of days later I received a call from Craig McCord to set up another visit. It was during my senior baseball season and so I had to do a quick up and back trip. I left at 3 a.m., for the eight-hour drive in early April. When I arrived, I met my host Judd Benedick (one of my greatest lifelong friends) for the first time. Frosty was out of town the day I visited and so I just met with Craig.

I will never forget being in the conference room in Olson Auditorium listening to Craig's pitch for the program. I was so tired from the early morning drive that I was nodding off throughout the meeting and Judd had to keep elbowing me. In truth, Craig did an amazing job of presenting PLU football to me. It was clear to me it was not something you get, but something you become. I left that visit knowing that was what I wanted.

From there I never heard another word from PLU. Crickets. I finished out my senior year,

moved to McCall, Idaho, where I lived at our family cabin and was working at a lumberyard. I remember being depressed and stressed about the path I was on. I spent many nights in tears praying for God to rescue me from the path I was on.

Then it happened. The last weekend of July I was sitting in our cabin after work. The phone rings. It's Frosty. I was thinking, "How in the world did he get my phone number up at our cabin?" He quickly introduced himself, "Hi Brian, this is Frosty Westering from PLU," and then he followed with, "So are you coming?" It was a jump in the wheelbarrow moment for me. I had no idea of the adventure he was offering me, yet I knew this was God answering my prayers. I said yes! It was the most impactful yes I have ever said in my lifetime outside of marriage.

Three weeks later, I showed up at PLU for preseason practice. I was there a day early in Foss Hall all by myself. I don't think there was another person on campus. I remember walking the campus (it was a ghost town) and then walking into Olson Auditorium for the first time. You could hear a pin drop it was so quiet as I stood in the lobby looking around.

Then all of a sudden I heard a door open and close from around the corner from the locker room. Frosty comes walking out from around the corner and before I could even introduce myself he said, "Brian it is so great to meet you" and he came over and gave me a giant bear hug. Later that night as I sat in the Foss lounge I wondered, "How did he know my name?" He had never met me in person and never had access to any photos of me. It was unexplainable. It was God working in one of the most mysterious ways I have ever seen in my life.

Frosty never messed up my name in all the years I knew him. God used Frosty to show me how much He loves me. What followed over the next five years was a life changing and magical experience. It reset the foundation for the person I am today. The inner game and love that Frosty, Paul, Scott W., Craig, Scott K., and other coaches built into us is still with me to this day. I am forever grateful for that phone call I received at the last hour from Frosty.

Reflections From Four Years at PLU

When I showed up at PLU, I was expecting something similar to what I experienced in high school. In high school we had three-a-day practices and truly beat ourselves up during preseason. When I got to PLU, I was blown away. To be honest, I was concerned and doubted our practice plan. I spent my first two weeks at practice without pads. It was crazy! In my mind I expected full gear and full tilt from day one—the dog days of August. Not the case. This was my first real understanding of something different going on. If I was at a preseason practice anywhere else in the nation, it probably would have been in line with my expectations out of high school. Frosty was different.

I will never forget that first team meeting in August of 1992. It was at the time of the Summer Olympics in Madrid, Spain. Frosty showed us a video clip of the archer lighting the caldron. It was an amazing moment—one shot, one arrow, and one caldron. It was a great example of the "Difference of One Degree." Peak performance at it's best. As a new EMAL, this session left an impression on me. It was one of the most amazing coachable and teachable moments I had ever experienced. It showed me that what lay ahead was going to be transformational. Frosty nailed it!

Looking back at the perfect combination of inner game and talent we had at that time, I realize just how special the 1990's were for PLU football. A lifetime of work and ideas being put together by Frosty that went to highs unseen to this day. It was a time where the inner game and talent rose to levels not seen and created a platform for many things none of us can explain today.

My Bomber year in 1992 was a tough one for me. I blew out my ankle in an early scrimmage and missed most of the season. I was bummed. Anyone that has experienced a severe injury that forces you to miss a significant amount of time knows how hard it is on you mentally and emotionally. It was through this that I experienced early examples of love in the PLU program. The tradition of the Rainbow Sign was so amazing to me. It is actually one of my artifacts that I cherish the most. To see the notes of encouragement from players and coaches was truly life changing. The fact that so many people took the time to write me a note of encouragement blew me away. It was humbling.

The other thing that helped me get through my injury was Frosty's "Nut In The Jar." Such a cool illustration of how you can't keep a good person down. Later in the season I had the opportunity to plug back in and serve on the Bombers and prep the Gold Team for the playoffs. I remember giving my best to serve the defense and prepare them for postseason contests. My experiences through my injury early on helped shape my mindset to give my best every day for all of my teammates and coaches for the love they had shown me when I was down.

This was the beauty and the science behind the program that Frosty built. You can't make sense of the logic behind it all, but all of it was beautifully connected to not only teach us how to be good teammates and care about one another, but much more than that. Through each experience, whatever it was, it was teaching us how to navigate life in a way that models the love God has for each one of

us. Frosty was a genius!

Following my Bomber season, there was much anticipation and rumors that the PLU Football team would be taking another international trip. As winter rolled on, that international trip became a reality. We were headed to Germany! As a young Bomber who missed most of the season, I did not expect to be included in the roster for Germany. When I heard that I was included it was very humbling for me. My classmates Josh Requa, Josh Arnold, Jon Roberts, Mark Givens, and I had the opportunity to experience a once in a lifetime amazing experience.

The 1999 team brags about the road show they went on with Frosty, but I would have to say going international with Frosty was the most incredible and unique experience. It was a true road show. I remember Frosty getting into the car with Axel, giving the thumbs up, and Axel screeching the tires as they rode off to wherever. I will never forget Frosty's taste in music and having us listen to Lee Greenwood's "Proud To Be An American" before going out on the field. It was perfect!

Following the game, the promoters had an event set up for us to attend. After climbing 40 flights of stairs and finding ourselves in a crazy place, Frosty got us out of there. We ended up at Burger King to finish off the night. It was truly an unforgettable, amazing adventure. I was fortunate that my dad was on a trip to Europe and happened to be in Hamburg the day of the game. I keep a photo of my dad and me in my office from that game.

All of us that have had the opportunity to venture through life with Frosty are incredibly lucky. He was unique and a joy to experience life with. I would be more than happy to go back to Germany and take 50 more team photos with Frosty and the EMALs. We didn't know how good we had it.

1993: Coaches Among Coaches

The 1993 season was an incredible journey for all of us that were part of it. It was where I was introduced to another building block of Frosty's program. Frosty taught us the concept of being "coaches among coaches." It was a freeing concept. Traditional programs are set up with position coaches that everything runs through. They are the people that you look to for guidance and feedback. Not so much at PLU. In fact, during my time I don't know if there was ever an official offensive line coach. Frosty

taught us to coach each other.

At the start of 1993, I knew very little about the X's and O's of the PLU offense because as a Bomber you spend all your time running the opponent's offense. Right away the upperclassmen took the younger players under their wing and taught the offense to us. I will never forget Brian Flatuum, Jeff Douglas, and Aaron Lenerud. They were all conference players from the year before, yet they had very little ego and cared about helping guys like me learn. It was a priority to them. This is extraordinary in our world. Most people just care about themselves. Frosty taught us how important it was to care about each other and that by making each other better we can reach heights we could never reach on our own.

Playing at a high level, which we did, occurred out of this "coaches among coaches" model. It was incredible. In fact, I think if you changed the model and provided position coaches, our performance would have dropped off. It wasn't an accident that the 1993 team achieved at the level it did. It was the perfect blend of talent and incredible inner game buy-in.

"Coaches among coaches" is a life skill and

concept that I have maintained throughout my professional career as an administrator in public education. I have been blessed to be part of some successful leadership opportunities and in each of them I have made a point to have "coaches among coaches" one of the foundational values.

As incredible as the 1993 journey was to be part of, the 1994 journey is one I will never forget. Not because of the success we achieved, but because I really feel like it was in this season that the inner game and all of Frosty's teachings shined the brightest. We still had talent but it was not at the level from the year before. The inner game exponentially increased our performance that allowed us to return to the National Championship stage.

Final Thoughts

Frosty and PLU Football had a significant impact on my life during my precious five years in the program. I was a mess when I got there and I was a mess when I left. The difference is I left with tools that would guide me in my journey of life.

I will never forget my last game at PLU and the talk in the locker room after the game. We were up at Western Washington and had just lost a crushing overtime game on the last play in the playoffs. They scored and kicked the extra point. We scored on a last gasped effort on 4th and 10. We went for two. We called a play that had been good to us all year—Spread Right Halfback Draw Pass Right. I remember pulling around and seeing three defenders at the goal line. It was one on three. I threw my body horizontal and took out two of the guys. The third guy stuffed us at the half-yard line. Game over.

I replay that play in my mind still to this day.

What I could have done differently to get a different result? The reality is I got the result I needed. Although we didn't win the game, I knew that for the rest of my life I needed to have the courage to throw that body block over and over again. Sometimes it worked and sometimes I would fall short. The key is I needed to throw the block. In the locker room following the game, I remember Frosty and Scott talking about the pain we were feeling. I remember them telling us that the pain we experienced in this game of football would help us know how to respond to pain we experience in life. That moment has stuck with me throughout my life.

Throughout my life I have experienced much pain at different times. Whether it's been a struggling relationship with my parents, failures as a husband and father, or coming up short as a friend. Life is hard. What I am most proud of is I have never stopped using my tools I learned from Frosty and PLU Football. Over and over again in my life I have had to rely on being a tough-minded optimist, a .333 hitter, to ride in the Blue Car, jump in the wheelbarrow, meditate on Psalm 23, be the Man In the Arena, pack my own chute, be a Servant Warrior, Total Release, and all the other inner game tools we received from

Frosty. It is a way of life and something that I am proud of in living my life using these tools.

I have struggled, I have thrived, and I have grown as a person and with my relationship with Jesus. I have an amazing wife and kids who love me no matter how imperfect I am. I struggle in my relationship with God at times, but one thing I never struggle with is my endless pursuit of knowing God and having a personal relationship with Jesus. I credit that to the impact Frosty, the coaches, and my EMAL brothers had on my life. I know I can handle what comes at me because Frosty gave me the tools for living life and I know the love that we shared at PLU never goes away. It will be with all of us until the day we die. God is good!

We have all been blessed to be part of something that was not from this world. Frosty was an amazing witness to all of us and showed each of us God's love. As a 47 year-old man, I still thank God every day for how he used Frosty and PLU Football in my life. It changed me!

COMMUNION

Jon Roberts (Pacific Lutheran/1992-96), Firefighter and EMT

When asked about my memories of Frosty there are many that come to mind. The one that immediately jumps out and is most meaningful has nothing to do with football. The ironic thing is that even though this is probably my best memory, I can only remember a few of the details.

It was during one of our annual Breakaways. Frosty had invited all of us to participate in communion. I remember it was a decent size group of people that decided to show up. It was late afternoon/early evening after all of our daily activities. We met down on the beach and the coaches read scripture, players spoke, we prayed, and then we all walked out into the ocean together.

As a Christian who had only recently been baptized and given my life to Christ, this was somewhat of a new experience for me that didn't fit into the traditional style of communion I had experienced. But as we stood in

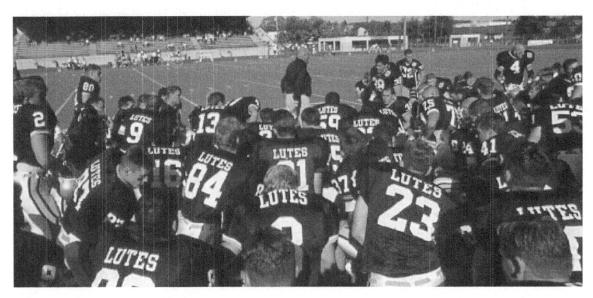

the cold water holding hands looking out at all of God's magnificent creation, it felt perfect. It was one of the few times in my life that I felt like I was surrounded by a bunch of guys that truly cared about me. At that moment as we shared in communion, I felt an amazing presence of God.

I realized how lucky I was to have ended up playing for a man like Frosty and his staff. You see, I wasn't supposed to go to PLU. During my senior year of high school, I was all set to go to a different school. The plan was for me to go out of state, play football and do track, and essentially only have to pay for books and a small portion of tuition. Then, later in my senior year, the coaches at that school decided they only wanted me to do one sport. I decided I didn't like that idea, but then I didn't know where I was going to go.

Then one day during a high school pep assembly, I listened to this football coach they called Frosty talk about Red Cars and

Blue Cars, a nut in the jar, and a completely new way of thinking about competition. After that pep assembly I went down and introduced myself to Frosty.

Later during my track season, I was able to build relationships with the track coaches from PLU and one thing led to another and I ended up going there. Looking back, it is simply amazing to me how that whole process worked out.

I was truly blessed to have played for Frosty. I often wished I could play on the offensive side of the ball just so I could spend more time with him, but then my defensive teammates would remind me of how long the offensive meetings were. And even though he often got my name confused with couple of other EMALS (there were three of us that were all about the same size, height and build and all had crew cuts and he could never keep our names straight), and I may have been the only EMAL to get into a car accident with Frosty (he ran into my truck in front of Olson), I knew that he truly cared about me as a player, as a student, as a Christian, and simply as a person.

That's a great memory.

THE BEST YEARS OF MY LIFE

Rob McIlraith (Pacific Lutheran/1992-96), History Teacher, Eatonville Middle School

Next to the birth of my children and my marriage to my wife, playing for Frosty and his Lutes coaching staff were the best years of my life. I cherish every memory the PLU football program provided me. Frosty and his assistant coaches will always have a place in my heart, and I am so thankful for the invaluable experience the football program allowed me to have.

IMPACT ON A DAD

Marc Elliott (Pacific Lutheran/ 1992-97), Chief Information Officer, Olympia School District

While I have countless memories and stories about the five years I was fortunate enough to spend playing football for Frosty at PLU, the one I find myself explaining most to people was his ability to influence myself and others.

It's important to set the stage for my experience. I was raised in Newberg, Oregon, which is 15 minutes from Linfield University. My grandparents taught there, my dad played football and ran track there (and was also adjunct faculty), and my sister played tennis there. My senior year I was pretty much locked in to play football for them.

My high school football coach played on the 1980 PLU National Championship team and took a few of us up to meet Frosty our senior year. I immediately made my decision that PLU was the place for me. I delivered the news to my parents, and needless to say, my dad looked a little heartbroken. Nevertheless, they supported my decision and off I went for my first year as a Bomber.

After the first home game, my parents were in attendance and came to their first Afterglow, where they really got to start soaking in the principles that Frosty was imparting to us. Sometime during my first red-shirt season my dad told me that I absolutely made the right decision in choosing PLU over Linfield.

This was about thirty years into my dad's career as the Newberg High School band director. He was always fairly successful in that time, often qualifying for the state band competitions and doing well. I don't know that I noticed it at the time, but he started taking much of the lessons, philosophy, and drive for personal growth and success to his own teaching.

After I graduated from PLU it became apparent that his interaction as a parent with Frosty was shaping the way he planned, interacted, and supported the students in his band program. They became incredibly successful for the remaining 10-plus years of his time at Newberg, often placing highly at the state competition.

[Side note: He brought the Newberg High School Pep Band to play at both the 1993 and 1994 National Championship games in Portland!]

My dad worked with 70 to 80 students individually and coached them to strive for their own personal excellence. He was teaching them to know that they were their own strongest critics and to be proud of a performance in which they played their best even if the end result wasn't the most desirable. This was the most "Frosty" thing I could think of—striving for excellence, encouraging each other, and enjoying personal and group success as a by-product.

While I owe so much of my career success to what I learned and experienced while playing for Frosty, I'm most proud of the impact it had on my dad.

OUTSIDE THE BOX THINKER

Josh Johnston (Pacific Lutheran/ 1993-97), Orthopaedic Surgeon

Frosty was an outside the box thinker.

He had a radically unconventional coaching philosophy: EMAL, make the big time where you are, the Blue Car model of winning, give it your best shot, Attaways, make it a great day, the edge, cast your bread, nut in the jar, flush it, put-ups, mental playbooks, goal setting, models of learning, visualization, the secret of the geese, good day drills, popsicle breaks, tough love.

He implemented creatively unconven-

tional football strategies: spread offenses, no back sets, bubble screens, bunch formations, "special" plays, passing on first down, "GO" (get open) routes, aggressively going for it on fourth down, odd numbers to the right.

He lived in many ways an unconventional personal life: married for over 60 years to his grade school sweetheart, stayed at the same job for over 40 years, practitioner of "-ish" time, wore colorful stocking caps, creative station wagon parker, mixed Kool-Aid by hand without utensils.

I loved road games: taking the show on the road with your brothers, no distractions, heading into a hostile environment, those old-school all white, yellow striped uniforms. I think Frosty loved road games as well. On the bus ride to the game, Frosty would stand in the stairwell and enthusiastically sermonize to the bus driver about his coaching (and life) philosophy and invariably won a fan of the program for life. I'm sure the free tee shirts didn't hurt either. In the dark ages before cell phones and GPS, Frosty would also helpfully, whether the bus driver needed it or not, provide driving directions.

One away game at Simon Fraser, Frosty led

the bus driver on a "short cut" through campus. The route may indeed have been a short cut for a wooden paneled station wagon but it turned out to be a long cut for a bus. As the bus driver attempted to negotiate a tight turn in a campus parking lot, he became stuck. Like stuck—stuck, like Austin Powers in a golf cart, couldn't go forward or back, and the driver lost it like Cougar in Top Gun.

We were in real risk of not making kickoff. We may have been still there to this day if not for Frosty's outside the box thinking. From the front of the bus, with a sly grin and a twinkle in his eye, he raised a finger and the yelled, "All-Black offensive line!" Being a 165-pound safety and holder, I watched from my seat as the All-Black offensive line carefully picked up and moved several cars allowing the bus driver to complete the turn and then just as carefully replace the cars back into their parking spaces. I don't remember anything from that particular game, but I will always remember that look on Frosty's face.

THE SUCCESS ROAD

Jarrad Mock (Pacific Lutheran/1994-98),
Compliance Manager

What stands out most about my time playing for Frosty is that the man was fun and committed to making memories along the journey. Some examples:

On an overnight trip down to Oregon, we stopped for dinner at Saylor's Old Country Kitchen in Portland, a steakhouse known for its 75-ounce steak challenge. No one from the team took on the challenge (I was hoping Scott would give it a shot), but the steakhouse atmosphere, guys eating good steaks together, Attawaying the staff, and other shenanigans that come with every PLU Football trip made for a loud, hilarious memory.

Another year, driving down the freeway to our hotel for a game against St. John's in Minnesota, Frosty spotted a sign for the exit to the Mall of America and I think spontaneously

said to himself "let's do it!" and made the bus driver take us to the Mall for a couple of hours, just for the fun of it.

And the ultimate example during the years I was there happened on a trip to play Cal Lutheran down in Thousand Oaks. I barely remember the game, but what I will always remember was staying an extra night and going to Disneyland the next day. Fifty-plus EMALs unleashed on the Magic Kingdom was one of my favorite memories from my PLU days.

Twenty something years later, now that I have a family and have helped operate businesses, projects, etc., and gained a real understanding of budgets and limited resources, I have a much greater appreciation of Frosty's willingness to prioritize time and money to build a treasure chest of memories for his teams.

Frosty understood it wasn't the final destination that mattered most, but the journey itself. He lived not on the road to success, but on the "Success Road."

GOOD RESULTS

Wai Tim Petersen (Pacific Lutheran/ 1994-98), Logistics Manager, Manson Growers (Lake Chelan, Washington)

Frosty made a huge impact on my life. Throughout my time with him and being around the program, he taught me numerous principles and another way to operate and thrive in this world.

I'm a huge advocate and love the power of the inner game. The very first thing I remember Frosty writing on the chalkboard was, "When I feel good about myself, I produce good results." I remember as an incoming freshman sitting there in my chair thinking, "Hmm, this could be interesting but I think I'll like it here."

That very principle was a never-ending cycle of increasing the esteem regulator to then achieve and perform better than I thought I ever could. But not only for myself, but also to brings others along in that journey. It became an addiction of tapping into the personal esteem to then produce good, which in turn, perpetuated the esteem again and the cycle continued.

Because of his influence and me being so much impacted by what he wrote on the chalkboard that warm autumn day, I went on to further my education in Sports Psychology and apply these inner game principles everyday to make the most out of everything. The power of the inner game has helped me to appreciate the process, which leads to the results, and certainly makes "The Big Time" where I'm at.

There are so many other memories and top

drawer accounts that I can recall. Above all, he was always serving us and was following his ultimate coach and Savior's example, Jesus Christ. And as a result of his servanthood and knowing the needs of his players, he saw the greatness in us before we ever achieved it. Thank you Frosty!

A REAL LIFE YODA

Kurt Kalbrener (Pacific Lutheran/1994-98), Aegis Integrated Pest Management

Frosty Westering was the most caring, genuine, and authentic leader that ever existed, without a doubt, period! He was a real life Yoda. Of course, I took this for granted as a player.

Frosty has accumulated countless mementos in his years at PLU, and his office is a shrine to the people he has played and worked with.

EMAL= EVERY MAN A LUTE

Frosty taught everyone to believe in themselves and others. The bond created amongst the players, coaches, and EMAL family is indescribable and timeless. I am honored and grateful to have experienced the master storyteller and king of the powerful one-liners first hand. The philosophy of Red Car vs. Blue Car and the four-psych games have helped guide me through the often-challenging journey of life.

Frosty used to tell a story about an eagle in a chicken coop. The story is also in his first book. Psychologically, after leaving PLU, I eventually went back to the coop. I reached a low point in 2015 when I became physically ill and was on my deathbed. Thank God for Frosty and my EMAL brothers. Rather than give up, I chose to fight and focus my attention on getting healthy. By implementing the principles and tools given to me by Frosty and following the examples of some others from the program, I made a complete recovery and even miraculously avoided surgery.

Frosty used to say that the lessons he taught would hit different people at different times. He was right. After getting healthy, I no longer count the days, but make the days count. I now run my own business and use goal setting and visualization as well as my old football notebooks to keep me accountable.

I always look forward to seeing my EMAL brothers and miss the coaches who created a magical environment. I miss Donna and the whole Westering family who I got to know well over the years. I intend to continue to practice the principles taught by Frosty and keep on keeping on. I will forever remain a tough-minded optimist who packs his own shoot. I try to make everything I do a "want to" rather than a "have to" and I believe in the power of the V.

Thank you Frosty, Donna, and the PLU coaching staff for making a strong family man out of me. I appreciate and love each of you.

WIT AND WISDOM

Jeremy Johnston (Pacific Lutheran/ 1995-99), Attorney, Evergreen Injury Counsel (18 years); Assistant High School Football Coach (since 2009); Transitioning to become a Teacher

I played for Frosty at PLU from 1995 to 1999 and was one of five captains from the 1999 National Championship team. During the 1999 season, the captains often met with Frosty. I cherish the memories of those meetings—both the wit and wisdom of Frosty.

At one mid-season meeting, Frosty talked about the need to have good player and coach communication, particularly in the later part of the season. At the end of the meeting the five captains (Judd Hunter, Anthony Hicks, John Eussen, Andrew Finstuen, and myself) huddled into a circle. As was typical, Frosty concluded with a prayer. He finished by saying: "And Lord we thank you for Judd, Anthony, Jeremy, Andrew, and uh . . . uh, and, uh, and. . . ." Realizing that Frosty needed help, John whispered, "John" and with no hesitation, Frosty said, "Thank you Lord! John.

Amen." Frosty had great wit.

I recall another captain's meeting where Frosty talked about disappointment and losing, which seemed rare at PLU. That meeting helped me immediately recall one game during my junior season in 1998. That year, defensive coordinator Craig McCord had installed a zone blitzing 3-4 scheme, which at the time was extremely innovative. The season began with a nail-biting overtime win at Sparks Stadium against California Lutheran. That game was followed up by what is likely one of the worst defensive performances in PLU history—a 58-21 loss at Southern Oregon. Southern Oregon's running back rushed for nearly 350 yards!

Most coaches would have been irate postgame, but not Frosty. Instead, Frosty displayed perfect sportsmanship in his congratulation of Southern Oregon's play and the performance of their running back. More than that, he displayed overwhelming restraint at the post-game Afterglow. Sure, we had lost, but we left Southern Oregon without feeling defeated. In fact, we were excited to get back on the field and give it another try. After losing to Southern Oregon, we went on a seven-game winning streak before finally losing in the playoffs to a good St. John's team in Collegeville, Minnesota.

What Frosty said at the captain's meeting in 1999 mirrored what Frosty did after our 1998 loss to Southern Oregon. Frosty said that as a coach and as a leader, no matter how frustrated or disappointed you might be, you should never show your frustration or disappointment immediately after the game. As he put it, the emotions are just too high and the time is just not right.

Frosty was right. Without question, our 1998 loss to Southern Oregon and the post-game experience was a catalyst to what would come in 1999. It allowed us to build trust and cohesion, particularly on the defensive side where so much was new. In the end, the 1999 season finished with a national championship win against Rowan University in the Stagg Bowl. And, while Frosty may say stats are for losers, there is one stat that helps tell this story. Rowan University finished that game with minus 63 rushing yards, a Stagg bowl record to this day. And, we were playing that same 3-4 defense Craig McCord first installed in 1998. Frosty had great wisdom.

A SELFLESS, UNPRE-DICTABLE, UNSTOPPABLE FORCE

Kevin Lint (Pacific Lutheran/1995-99), Software Engineer

At a spring football meeting in 1998 (the type where you show up and are made to watch "Cool Hand Luke" on an old 80's TV/VCR setup strapped to a rolling cart) I added my name to a list of players who needed a summer job. I forgot about the list. A few weeks later I got a call from Frosty. He was requesting or possibly demanding that I come to his house because he had "something for me." I had no idea what it was about.

As I arrived at his house, I half expected to find other players, but it was just me. I was welcomed at the front door by Donna who ushered me into the living room where Frosty lay on a gurney having just undergone a double hip replacement. Now I was really confused. What was this all about?

As soon as he saw me he hopped up and hustled over to a table and began rummaging through a random stack of papers. He still had on a hospital gown and his backside was laid bare for the whole world to see. Donna wasn't having any of it and Frosty wasn't having any of her not having it. Dismissing Donna's disapproval with a few hand waves, he finally found what he was looking for. With his giant hands, and in true Frosty penmanship (left handed, all caps, with flare), he wrote down a name and a number for a summer landscaping job (which I ended up doing).

After that I made my way back to my car. As I drove I began to ask myself why couldn't he have just given me the contact info over the phone? And did I just watch him shuffle around his living room with his bare butt hanging out? And why is he bothering himself with this stuff when he's trying to heal up from a major surgery? And, why would he take the time to help me with such a small thing?

Everybody who knows Frosty most likely knows the answers to these questions. He was a selfless, unpredictable, unstoppable force to

be reckoned with. He was a man of true faith who touched many souls. I take comfort in knowing he's home with the Lord now and I'm sure his hips are doing just fine.

STRAIGHT TO THE POINT

Dave Raney (Pacific Lutheran/1995-98), EVP and Chief Banking Officer, Sound Community Bank

When I first met Frosty, he told me that he coached because it was the best platform he'd found to help young men become better brothers, fathers, husbands, etc. That initial meeting has stuck with me to this day and I think of it often. A man that had at that point (1994) accomplished a great deal by conventional means of measuring a collegiate coaches success, however he didn't spend any time boasting of wins, facilities, or prestige. Rather, he cut straight to the point, unapologetically stating what the program was all about.

I played a very tiny role in out team's storied history, but the program left me forever

changed. In business, I'm afraid that an increasingly small percentage of boardrooms believe that it is possible to run a values-based organization while simultaneously delivering excellent returns to stakeholders. Thanks to Frosty, this concept is not foreign to me, and is something I aspire to on a daily basis. I will forever be grateful for my time with him. EMAL

THE SUCCESS ROAD

Luke Balash (Pacific Lutheran/1997-99), P.E. and Health Teacher, Head Football Coach since 2016, Lathrop High School (Fairbanks, Alaska)

I arrived at PLU in 1997 as a transfer player from a D2 program in Colorado. At 5'5" and 160 pounds, I was not your prototypical college football player. I also was not your typical EMAL candidate as a blue-collar kid from Alaska that was an avowed atheist.

I did not make the team that 1997 season and instead watched from the stands and longed to play. In 1998 I made the team as a special teamer and depth guy. Playing for Frosty changed my life's course. I was privileged to play on the 1999 National Championship Team, but that wasn't the best part.

As I enjoyed the journey with the EMALs I tried to learn and integrate everything I could as fast as possible. Two seasons is not enough to fully integrate all that Frosty offered, but I worked hard to change and learn and grow into the kind of man I needed to be. I experienced one Breakaway, two playoff runs, countless meetings, Donna's treats, visits with Alumni, Afterglows, FCA meetings, home visits, inner circles, goal sets, and worship

times. The Lord used these experiences to change my heart and massively influence the way I coach today.

If you dropped into a season at Lathrop Football in Fairbanks, Alaska, right now you would see EMAL on the practice jerseys in a season that starts with a Breakaway. You'd see players memorizing sports psychology cues like The Best Shot and Eager Beaver Mindset. You'd see a coaching staff and team who love each other and play for something more than victories.

And if that season were 2021, you'd watch us win the first state title in the history of the city of Fairbanks. Not because it was the goal, but it was simply a by-product of pursuing excellence on the Success Road.

Year	Record	Postseason
1995	6-3-1	NAIA Division II First Round (0-1)
1996	7-3	NAIA Division II First Round (0-1)
1997	7-2	
1998	8-2	NAIA Division III First Round (0-1)
1999	13-1	NAIA Division III National Champions (5-0)

CHAPTER 7

THE 2000's

[2000 - 2003]

LIFE CHANGING MOMENTS

Benji Sonnichsen (Pacific Lutheran/ 1997-2001), High School P.E. Teacher and Head Football Coach (Mt. Vernon, Prosser and Mead)

Frosty Westering. Wow, talk about a person comfortable in his own skin! He made me want to be around PLU Football. He helped me think differently than I had ever thought before—Red Car vs. Blue Car.

During 1997 to 2001, Frosty's bomb was Brian Fulker's car. Frosty ended up borrowing Brian's car. I don't know if Brian ever got it back. Frosty would race through campus with it. Amazing.

During the 1999, 2000, and 2001 seasons, I recorded many of Frosty's Inner Game talks and still have them on mini cassette tapes. I also got to spend time with the Spani's and when I married before my fifth-year season, my wife and I talked with them in depth about shaping our family structures. We still use some of those structures to this day. Yearly birthday purposes (based on biblical scripture) and birthday celebrations was one of the structures.

Breakaway, preseason, practices, game day and the locker room Afterglow were all great experiences. I have tried to mimic them and didn't have the same success. I have found different success, but wow was PLU's special. I used to study the inner game religiously along with my Bible on a daily basis. I took goal setting seriously. Our involvement with the Lister and McIlveigh schools was also a great experience.

One of my favorite Frostyisms is "Pop the top" (meaning take off your hat). My very good friend Jonathan Carlson used to go around to all of us during Monday inner game meetings and say, "Poppy the top!"

Nellie was life changing. I was one of his caretakers at PLU. Wow, how this shaped us young men. I still show his tribute in Health Class to this day. He was in my wedding and my older brother's wedding. We took him home during holidays and vacations many times to my parents' house. Our family had a deep love for Nellie.

Our team meetings were life changing. Frosty pushed us out of our comfort zones and into deep thinking. I recorded so many of them. I have shared many with my teams over the years.

Frosty's tough love was such a great balance. I was about to propose to a girl that I dated between the 1999 and 2000 season. We ended the relationship because her dad told me no. I called Frosty and we met in his office. He listened to my story and then told me something I have retold many times to many different young people over the years.

"Benji, you are up against the trees and you don't know where to go. You need to go back and climb up the hill and look out and see the whole forest. Then you will be able to see where to go. Right now you can't see anything because it feels too overwhelming." Then he prayed for me and held my hand. Frosty took 30 minutes with me, calmed my heart, and gave me the courage to keep trusting in God, which led me to the beautiful wife he had right around the corner for me. Donna was also life changing for my wife and me.

After graduation I went into teaching and coaching immediately because of my PLU football experience. I've hired many coaches during my career and I can't say I've ever had a staff like PLU's from 1997 to 2001. They were special men.

Frosty also influenced the way I coach the game. I've attempted at times to take PLU football to the high school level. I even installed parts of the Georgetown offensive package in the 2021 season with my son as quarterback. At Mount Vernon we used EMAB. At Prosser we already had STANGS. At Mead we used EMAP. These have been team favorites.

SPEED STICK AND GOAL SETS

Chuck Woodard (Pacific Lutheran/ 1997-2001), Power Line Contractor

The year escapes me, but it was a Monday following a tough game. The entire team was sitting in the lobby waiting for Frosty to make his appearance on a typical light duty day. With his rolling gait, he entered the lobby, briefcase dangling below his loose watch-band while barking for the team's attention. After briefing the team on the plan for the day, Frosty informed the Gold and All-Black offensive lineman to muster at one of the PE classrooms. This was totally against the well-rehearsed Monday script. Something was up.

Upon entering the classroom Frosty calmly placed a Speed Stick deodorant on the front desk as he sat on a stool. With a mysterious new tone to his voice he asked, "Guys, why did I bring deodorant?" It was plainly obvious he was baiting us into a verbal response. Absent all defensive and skill players, the room sat silent. Each player sat without movement or emotion. We all knew one word would bring a preplanned verbal attack from an extremely agitated Frosty.

After roughly 30 seconds, he grabbed the Speed Stick slammed it down, leaned forward and belted, "Because you all stink!" It then turned into a five-minute session where we received detailed examples of our transgressions from the previous Saturday.

Frosty masterfully moved between guilt and insult to drag us to the emotional bottom. He then slowly started to build us up with a call to action and a lengthy list of tasks for our weekly goal sets. The O-Line did not get Donna's treats that week. Good times and amazing memories.

THERE IS STILL ROOM IN THE INN

Chris Inverso (Pacific Lutheran/1997-2001), CEO, Rainier Industries

Making the Cut

In the fall of 1997, I tried out for the PLU football team but didn't make the cut. Truthfully, my athletic abilities didn't compare favorably to those of my peers and it was the right call. Still, I didn't give up and I wrote Frosty a letter and left him a voicemail message asking for another opportunity to try out. After the first game, Frosty called and asked me to meet him the next day—Monday at 8 p.m., in the lobby of Olson Auditorium.

When I arrived, I saw another PLU student, Jake Allan ('01), who had tried out and been cut like I had. Little did I know at that time, but Jake would become my college roommate for two and a half years, a groomsman in my wedding (and I in his), and a close, lifelong friend.

When Frosty arrived, walking quickly with his tottering gate, he was fashionably late. This was my first

introduction to "Ish Time." Frosty enthusiastically waved Jake and I into his office, which was filled with PLU Football memorabilia collected over the preceding three decades. I was struck by the amount of energy he had at 8 p.m., in the evening—more than any other man I'd met in his mid-70s.

Then Frosty spoke eight words that Jake and I will never forget, "Guys, there is still room in the inn."

The next day, before practice, Scott Westering issued us our gear and we began our Bomber year at PLU. This started a journey that continues to this day—a journey to love and honor Christ with my thoughts, words, and actions; to experience the Double Win by bringing out the best in myself and others; to strive for excellence and compete with my best self; and to make the "Big Time Where I Am."

Missing Goal Sheets

Frosty used weekly goal sheets to help us set "SMARTER" goals in four categories which directly related to our in-game performance as PLU football players. To this day, I use a process like this to set

personal and professional goals in my life. The resulting impact has been profoundly positive.

The process for completing these goal sheets and submitting them for review was a well-oiled machine by the late 1990's. Every Tuesday they were to be turned in before practice. There were two boxes, one for offense and one for defense. Frosty reviewed the offensive goal sheets and Craig McCord, our defensive coordinator, reviewed the defensive ones.

One sunny Tuesday, Frosty was in the mood to provide some tough love. He found his opportunity on the way to practice when he found the offensive box full and the defensive box nearly empty. Thinking quickly, he grabbed a roster and compared it against the names on goal sheets.

Before practice began, he began calling player's names in alphabetical order, by last name. Without any explanation, Frosty gave A's to all players that had turned in goal sheets and F's to all the players that hadn't. It quickly became clear that offensive players were getting

THE CARPET SQUARE

Trevor Roberts (Pacific Lutheran/1998-2002), Assistant Coach, PLU (2002-06 and 2010-17); Midwest Regional Sales Manager, Riddell

A's and defensive players were getting F's, but no one knew what was going on.

It all came to a screeching halt when Frosty got to one of his favorite players, Michael Mauss, who was a defensive player. Frosty simply couldn't accept that Michael didn't turn in his goal sheet. It turns out that Frosty was right, Craig McCord had grabbed most of the defensive goal sheets before Frosty walked by. As we turned to look at Craig, he was laughing so hard that his whole body was shaking. Soon the whole team was overcome by laughter, including Frosty.

I work for the global leader in football head protection and protective athletic equipment and my office overlooks an operations plant that produces helmets for every level of football. In my office is one of my most valued possessions, a 5x7 framed piece of green AstroTurf carpet from Frosty Westering's office at Pacific Lutheran University.

Looking at this carpet square always brings me right back to Frosty's office. I imagine him busily working, but always finding the time to give his attention and love. He had an innate ability to build someone up and set them straight simultaneously. Frosty had an incredible sense of humor, and I think he got a kick out of showing his scar from his hip surgeries.

Most notably in that PLU office is where Frosty changed my life. I had the honor of playing for and coaching with the legend. He accepted me as a transfer student and at the end of my playing career asked me to stay on and coach with him. I spent 16 years in the program and I consider myself one of the lucky ones.

This piece of nostalgia in my office means more to me than a great conversation starter. It gives me daily direction, reminds me to strive for excellence, and inspires me to always help others. In my current position, that

5x7 piece of carpet serves as a reminder to make a positive impact on those around me, the game of football, and the driving force to ensure his legacy lives on.

I bring up Frosty and PLU any chance I get. Recently, I met a coach from the Midwest, and it just so happened he was an NCAA host rep for the playoffs in 1999. He recalled that on a conference call a week before the game, the only concern Frosty had was whether the campus bookstore would be open because he planned to bring his team in to buy some gear. Frosty didn't ask about locker rooms or a game day set up. He just wanted to know the hours of the bookstore.

I have always been curious to know how much money was spent at a playoff opponent's campus bookstore. I know I dropped some of my parent's cash at several of them. I have two storage tubs full of shirts and hats from our 1998 to 2001 playoff runs and I can't get rid of them. My kids even wear some of them to bed. I mean, how many Johnny Shirts does a guy need? You know the Lutes are in town when a bus pulls up to your bookstore.

Some of my most memorable Frostyisms are:

"Who's ready for some cake guys?" (To the team after serving cake with his hands and licking his fingers.)

"Scott! Run 08-09!"

"You smell like B.O., and you don't even know it" (In an O-Line position meeting that was not going well.)

"You can take your hamstring and eat it!" (To a player that was struggling with a hamstring injury.)

WORKOUTS, MAGNETS, AND GETTING BACK UP

Todd McDevitt (Pacific Lutheran/1999-2001), Pear Orchardist, Leavenworth Mountain Pears

Workouts: College football programs are not generally known as choose-your-own-workout type operations. Most, if not all, have strength and conditioning coaches and very rigid mandatory workouts all school year long. I had heard PLU was a little different in that regard.

However, on my recruiting trip, a coach showed me around and brought me by the weight room and told me about the 6 a.m., workouts that would be starting the following year. This information brought on a certain amount of confusion and not a little consternation as I had been told the opposite was the case. Although I love to compete, people who know me would not exactly refer to me as a workout warrior.

Later in the recruiting trip I was brought over to Frosty's office in Olson and introduced to him. He brought me out to his red Astro van and wanted to show me what upper campus was like, so naturally instead of taking the road, he took the red brick walking trails. I remember his window was down and he was yelling a hearty greeting and thank you to the grounds staff when he swerved off course and flattened a freshly planted sapling.

I chimed in, "Frosty, I'm not big into weight lifting but I want to be prepared to play my best for the team. Do I need to do all the stuff they are saying I should do?" He looked over at me and said "No, no, no. You don't need to do all that stuff. Just do 10 pushups, 10 sit-ups, and 10 pull-ups a day and you'll be fine!" Needless to say, I was about as surprised as that sapling must have been.

Magnets: We were getting ready for a big home game against Linfield and Chad Johnson, Frosty's grandson, went down hard on Tuesday afternoon while practicing at Sparks Stadium. He had severely sprained his ankle and had to be helped off the field. Things were not looking good for his playing chances that Saturday. He went right to the sideline and

iced immediately. Then back at Olson he got the complete treatment and was told to keep icing and rest it.

Chad was a roommate of mine and as college students are prone to do, we stayed up late dorking around. I woke up the next morning and heard voices in the living room. I didn't think much of it until I got downstairs and heard that one of those voices belonged to Frosty. Apparently somehow he had gotten a hold of a magnets expert/salesman and got him over to the house at seven in the morning. However, the salesman was sitting there on the couch like a child next to Chad listening to Frosty talk about the incredible healing powers of magnets.

I was invited by Frosty to sit down and join in the clinic next to my other roommates and a small entourage that had been conscripted by Frosty to learn about magnets and fix Chad's ankle. Apparently the magnets worked because sure enough Chad was ready to play that Saturday.

Japanese Mother: Going to Frosty and Donna's House was a special experience. He and Donna made you feel so special and at home. Being an EMAL was much more than just being on the team. They really did bring you right into the family. One of the things that I loved was that every time I would leave the house, after hugs and goodbyes Donna would wait by the door as you walked to the car and say "Japanese mother." She would then stand by the door and no matter how long you took getting your keys out and seatbelt buckled and situated to drive out she would wait there and watch you drive off, waving the entire time.

Later on at the end of Frosty's life when he was in hospice and didn't have much time left, I went to visit him and Donna. It was a sad but amazing time. They loved each other very much and it always spilled over into their love for others. They asked about my wife Jodi,

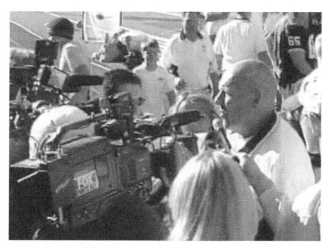

whom they remembered by name, and about my kids and our life. We prayed and hugged and it was my last time seeing them until glory. As I walked out and down the hallway of the care center I turned around and there was Donna waving and she said, "Japanese mother." I don't know what that was but it meant so much to me. Now we always wave people out and say "Japanese mother."

Get Back Up: I was teaching and coaching in Redmond, Oregon, where my wife Jodi and I were raising our two kids at the time, Elsey and Tom. My phone rang and it was Frosty letting me know that he and Donna would be coming through town and wanted us to join them for lunch at Izzy's. Frosty always loved All-You-Can-Eat (dessert first). Of course I said, "Yes! We will see you there!"

We met Frosty and Donna in the parking lot and the gals and the kids went on ahead of us. We had stayed in the parking lot because Frosty had something he couldn't wait to show me. He had been retired for five years or so but he was still working on updating his Inner Game book and had a new idea to show me. As he was excitely telling me about the changes he slowly started changing colors and swaying around in circles a bit. I could tell he was lightheaded and about to fall. I ran around back and as he collapsed I caught him, breaking his fall, and laying him down on the asphalt parking lot next to some pizza pepper packets. I was paralyzed and scared with no idea what to do. I just froze and looked at him, wondering what to do for about 20 seconds.

All of a sudden, BINK! His eyes popped open and he said with a smile and a twinkle, "Life will do that to you Todd. It will knock you on your butt. When you get knocked down you have to get back up." And he rolled over, got on his knees, and got back up. Then we went into Izzy's and ate dessert first. Apparently he had become lightheaded because of some medication he was taking. But that was Frosty, genuine to the core. He didn't just say it. He lived it.

DONE

Tyler Teeple (Pacific Lutheran/1999-2002), Owner and COO, Pursuit Distilling Co.

There are many stories that I could write, as I'm sure many of you could as well. But the one that brought everything together, the experience that put into perspective what being an EMAL was all about happened on a beautiful October day.

It was the Fall of 2002. I had been chosen to be one of the captains for my senior season during one of the final years of Frosty's Hall of Fame career. I was a transfer from a D1 school and now the starting quarterback.

It was a home game again Eastern Oregon. As we were driving early in the second quarter deep in Eastern Oregon territory, OC Scott Westering called a pass play. As I came to the line to read the defense, I immediately noticed the defense preparing to blitz. The ball was snapped and as I delivered the ball over the middle, two defenders from opposite sides simultaneously hit my throwing arm. The pain was immediately excruciating. At that moment, four games into my senior year, I was DONE. My arm was broken. My senior season was cut far shorter than I could have imagined. There were no preparations for this type of ending. It was just DONE.

As I came to the sidelines, I sat with the trainers and doctors, as they looked my arm over, only again to confirm the worst. The pain was excruciating both physically and emotionally. The freshman quarterback was inserted into the game. It was at this point where Frosty did something only he would ever do. In the very middle of the game, during the next offensive drive, he took off his headset, handed it to the coach standing next to him and walked over

to sit down beside me. He put his arm around me as I wept on the bench. He didn't say much for those first couple of minutes. He just sat with me and held me.

What high profile college football coach of his stature leaves his responsibilities to do what he did…for me? Well, that would be Frosty! When I was finally, for the time being, able to get past the emotions of the moment, Frosty leaned over and spoke, "Now, I need you to get up, go over to the sidelines, help Dusty (the freshman quarterback), and be the leader I know you to be."

In those moments it was reinforced that I had great value to that man, but also, that I was no more important than anyone else. He reached inside of me and pulled character to the forefront and basically called upon me to lead and not go dark or retreat into myself. As difficult as it was to no longer perform on the field, he was reminding me that there could be a greater fulfillment in serving others and in helping them to be successful.

THE BEST DECISIONS

Ryan Borde (Pacific Lutheran/2000-02), COO, Carcraft Auto Appearance Center, Carcraft Chevron

I vividly remember the first time I spoke with Frosty. It was June 2000 and I was getting ready to transfer from a community college to PLU to play baseball. I hadn't played football since high school and I thought I would give it a shot so I called him. He wasn't very enthusiastic about me playing and mentioned something about the joining the Bombers. Rather discouraged, I shelved the idea.

When I was moving into Foss in late August, a football player named Josh Parsons introduced himself and told me about walk-on try-outs. That night I tried out and the next day I was one of nine guys given pads. From the very first practice the next day, I was drawn to Frosty's leadership and the way he went about things. There was just something about him. And he drove a beat up yellow Ford Festiva. I mean c'mon, that's pretty cool!

After a few weeks of being around Frosty and

his grandson, Chad Johnson, I accepted the Lord into my life. Attending PLU and accepting Christ were the best decisions of my life. In 2016, I was named the head softball coach at West Albany High School in Albany, Oregon, and my first order of business was introducing the players to the Success Road Notebook. It was such a joy teaching others about Frosty's way of looking at sports and life, and giving Attaway cheers to so many different people over my six years as head coach.

Next to my father, no one has impacted my life the way Frosty has. His legacy and way of doing things have been with me since 2000 and will continue to be every day moving forward.

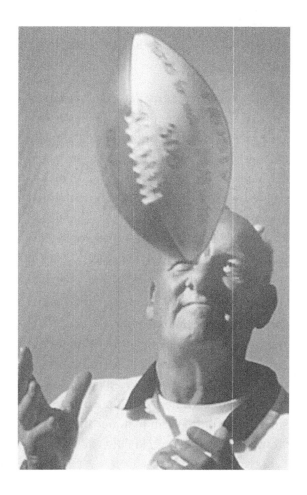

THE LONG STRAW, FROST-ED FINGERS, AND BLINKING RED LIGHTS

Josh Parsons (Pacific Lutheran/1998-2003), Instructional Designer

Frosty was the most gracious coach when it came to having some fun. He didn't encourage pranks, but he also didn't condone them. During one particular game day team breakfast, a few of the players took more than 50 straws from the university dining center and brought them onto the team bus. The idea was to create one long straw that would start from the back of the bus and work its way up to the front where the coaches sat.

As straws were pushed into each other and inched forward, this one long straw would rest on the shoulders of players sitting in the aisle seat as it moved up to the front. A few times Frosty turned around and stood up in his seat to direct a new song for everyone to sing, but he didn't seem to notice the giant straw taking formation. Finally, the straw

reached the seat directly behind Frosty, occupied by his son Scott. Seamlessly, Scott supported it with his hand, until it was long enough to find its final resting spot on top of Frosty's head.

We all watched with baited breath as the straw touched Frosty's head and sat there, unwavering, for what seemed like an eternity. Finally, Frosty reached up and felt the straw, broke out in a grin, then turned around and bellowed out "You guys got me!" followed by his trademark thumbs-up. The whole bus broke out in laughter, followed by an Attaway cheer for Frosty being such a good sport.

To this day, I am sure he saw the long straw forming, but he was probably curious as to what mischief his players were up to, and true to his nature wanted his players to have some natural fun. For most football teams, bus rides on game day are supposed to be serious, a time for getting ready, but PLU football bus rides were just the opposite. Some of my favorite PLU football memories were created on the bus, and this time at the expense of Frosty.

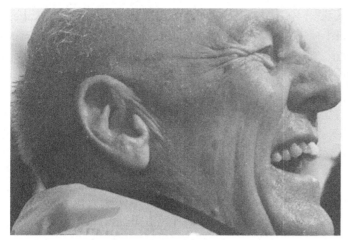

Team meetings were always a super fun time, especially when they involved food. The whole team would gather in the Olson Auditorium foyer. Most players would sit on the floor engaged in some sort of lively conversation as if we hadn't seen each other for a month. Sometimes Frosty would emerge with some sort of large sheet cake. We had no idea where it came from.

He would start cutting pieces, and while he was putting them on small plates he would bellow out "come get some cake, guys!" Then Frosty would resume cutting the cake, but by now he had frosting on his fingers, so he did what any sensible server would do: he started licking his fingers, and then continued to put more pieces on plates. This was followed by another summons to the team to come get some cake, because, "in the Marine Corps, food never went to waste!" Players would now saunter up to the table to get cake, and Frosty would continue cutting pieces and licking his fingers.

Sometimes, however, he would forget to lick the frosting off his fingers and instead scratch his head. So now he had frosting on his head while he continued to cut pieces and lick his fingers, thus admirably upholding his name,

Frosty. Understandably, many pieces of cake discreetly ended up in trash bins inside the Olson foyer!

Midweek night practices at Stadium Bowl or Lincoln Bowl were always a great time because players would pile into cars and take different routes to the site like it was some sort of big race. Sometimes, there would be a Frosty sighting on the drive over. That two-door Ford Festiva he drove was unmistakable.

One night, Frosty turned just ahead of us at an intersection, so we followed him. As we approached the next intersection, a four-way stop with blinking red lights, we slowed down. Frosty, however, didn't. He cruised through that intersection as if it had blinking yellow lights. We all laughed. Maybe he just had a senior moment.

We continued to follow him, and as we approached the next four-way intersection, we thought for sure he would adhere to the blinking red lights. Again, he coasted right through. We continued to follow him and noticed a trend: Frosty would stop at intersections with solid red lights, but at intersections with blinking red lights he would slow down a bit to make sure there weren't any cars on his left or right waiting to go, and then just continue right through the intersection.

After that night, we always looked behind us on our drive over to Stadium and Lincoln bowl to make sure Frosty wasn't behind us!

FROSTY'S ASSISTANT

Matt Ferguson (Pacific Lutheran/2000-03), Assistant Athletic Director, Bonney Lake High School

1. It was my freshman year, 2000, and it was our first road trip to play Whitworth. I had just finished loading the buses with all our travel gear and football bags. We were waiting to leave from the bus drop off by the outside stairs of Olson Auditorium. The guys had just about finished loading. Frosty, Scott, and a couple other coaches were talking and trying to figure out an issue. Frosty called me over and says, "Matt, we need you to drive one of the vans to Whitworth and we will have another guy ride too."

I was only 19 at the time but was pretty sure I was old enough to drive the rental van over. Frosty told Scott the plan, which Scott wasn't completely happy about due to my age. However, there weren't many other options. So, Scott handed me the keys and told me to just follow the bus the whole way. That's when Frosty came over to me and told me I was driving Donna Belle and Glenna. I proceeded to follow the buses all the way to Wenatchee where we did walk-throughs and a team meal at the Madison's home. I then continued to

drive all the way to the team hotel in Spokane. My player and co-pilot was supposed to share driving duties but slept the whole time.

2. During one of our pre-Breakaway team/family dinners at Spanaway Lake Park, we had just finished serving everyone the catered Italian food when Frosty approached me and said, "Matt I have an idea for a new game to play here after we are done with the meal. I need you to go to Toys 'R Us and buy 12 Nerf glow-in-the-dark footballs and get them back to the park before everyone heads back to Olson." Needless to say, I quickly ate and then had to book it to the Tacoma Mall, grab the footballs, and hustle back to the park. Never in my wildest dream would I have thought I would be getting toys for a college football team.

3. During the 2001 season, Scott and the other coaches wanted sideline film at practice for film study. The year before there had been a very questionable scaffolding. Frosty came up to me and said, "Matt, I have a new idea to film practice from the sideline. It will

even let you follow the ball up and down the field during offense vs. defense. We will a use an old maintenance school van with a roof rack that you can stand on while another guy drives." A.J. Jefferies ended up as my driver. For the whole season we would get the van from maintenance and then use it at practice. The van, however, had a mind of it's own. There were times where A.J. would drive me down, even with the line of scrimmage, and stop the van, yet the van kept running! If we needed to film and it was raining, another guy would come to the top with me and hold an umbrella. Sometimes the van ran really bumpy, but Frosty always said, "Matt, you have the best ride for practice!"

4. In 2001, we went to Fargo, North Dakota, to play the St. John Johnnies in the playoffs. The game was moved to Fargo from St. John's due to a major snowstorm. The day before the game we had our normal team dinner.

Our hotel was across the street from a truck stop diner. Nellie asked Frosty if he could walk over with some football guys instead of riding the bus, to which Frosty said okay. So, Nellie, myself, and two other EMALs started the cross the street while the rest of the team loaded onto the bus.

As we walked out of the hotel parking lot, we soon realized the sidewalks were covered in four feet of snow. We improvised and instead walked in the street to get there. After the dinner, the four of us started walking back. Again, we had to walk in the street. We had to stop at the stoplight and as we waited for it to turn green, we realized we had three big rig trucks lined up behind us. We all couldn't believe that three college guys and Nellie were standing there with all the trucks. Needless to say we got a lot of happy honks from the truck drivers who thought it was the funniest thing ever. Once everyone got back to the hotel, Frosty came over and said, "Nellie, we might need to upgrade your chair."

5. During Frosty's Farewell Locker Room, Frosty shared the story of how Nellie came to be a part of PLU Football. As he went about telling the story, he brought up Nellie and his #39. Frosty went on to tell the crowd that I had pulled the jersey for him and helped Nellie get all stocked up. I will never forget the majority of the crowd turning and looking at me where I was sitting in the bleachers. After Frosty had finished, I had about 20 older EMALs questioning me on how I got Nellie all hooked up with PLU Football. I told them in 1989, when Nellie first appeared at PLU, I was eight years old!

6. We were getting ready to head to California for a road trip. We loaded the bus and as

we were getting close to the airport, Frosty reminded everyone to make sure they had their IDs ready to get through the airport and to the plane. Once we were at the airport and starting to have each guy check in, Frosty realized he didn't have his ID. A bit of panic mode set in until Donna Belle looked in Frosty's briefcase. Just by luck, she found a magazine in his briefcase featuring a story on him. They took the article up to the airline staff member and showed them the magazine, and for whatever the reason, they said that was good enough and Frosty was all set to go.

A FULL DOSE OF CULTURE

Bo Winnberg (Pacific Lutheran/2000-03), Personal Trainer, Self-Employed

Frosty directly influenced me—especially through the atmosphere he built and the teammates I had. I don't really think anyone really knows how much. I am pretty sure I might be one of the few if not the first Swedish player in PLU football history. Yes, I am not American, although I hope to become a citizen in the near future. I have spent close to 20 years in the USA. My amazing, beautiful wife and wild wonderful kids are all American.

I have a deep love for the USA, the culture, and its people. And it all started when I was selected as a walk on my sophomore year in college. In fact, I tried out with two other fellow Swedes that had some rugby and amateur football experience like me. We had all come from Sweden to pursue a college degree and experience American culture. I got selected to be an EMAL and it changed my life.

Boy did I get a full dose of culture. I got swept into the warm loving blanket of EMAL football and my roommate's family became my surrogate parents. I got to fly and travel across the country, and play and practice with amazing friends. All that birthed a deep love for the USA in a way that I don't think any of my fellow foreign students experienced.

I got to live not only as a student-athlete but also as an EMAL. I still have the playbook full of quotes and affirmations. I know that whatever comes my way I can make it a great day. My closest teammates are still my brothers and family. I got to be a part of something really special and unique—all thanks to Frosty and the atmosphere he built.

Thank you Frosty, Donna, and PLU.

Year	Record	Postseason
2000	9-2	NCAA Division III Second Round (1-1)
2001	8-3	NCAA Division III Third Round (2-1)
2002	5-4	
2003	6-3	

CHAPTER 8

ENDURING LEGACY

[STORIES OF TIMELESS IMPACT]

WIZARD OF THE NORTH

Don Hartmann (Lea College/1968-72),
Former Director of Admissions, Lea College

I first met Frosty when I played freshman
football at Parsons College in the fall of 1960.
Even though I didn't play beyond that first
year, as a physical education major, I took
several classes from Frosty over the following
years and got to know and admire him more
than any other professor at Parsons.

In 1968 I accepted the position as Director
of Admissions at Lea College and one of
the greatest benefits of that position was the
opportunity to work closely with Frosty in
recruiting football players from the Chicago
area. Together we managed to recruit some
of the most outstanding athletes who went
on to become a big part of the success that
the Lea Lancers enjoyed on the football field;
players like Mike Hemerich, Bob Swanson,
Phil Klek, Jerry Anderson, and Bill Sosnowski, just to name a few. I often marveled at
how easily Frosty was able to really connect

with high school seniors and instantly win
their respect.

There are so many things that made Frosty
special, but one that immediately comes to
mind was his eagerness to help the ladies in
Albert Lea, Minnesota, learn more about the
intricacies of the game. As Frosty liked to explain to them, football is a lot more complex
than the quarterback handing the ball off to
a running back or completing a pass to a receiver. So, Frosty conducted a class for local
women every week and during that class he
would diagram a particular play and then
explain the role that each player, regardless
of his position, played in the success of that
play.

For example, Frosty would explain the
critical role that one or both pulling guards
needed to perform in a certain play and then
he would tell the ladies that during the next
home game, he would wave a towel over his
head right before they were going to run that
particular play, and that meant he wanted
them to watch the guards instead of the
quarterback. The ladies absolutely loved it
and they all became much more
sophisticated football fans as a
result.

Another fond memory is the
night, shortly after I became
engaged to my future wife, Trish,
that Frosty and Donna took the
two of us to dinner. They informed us that they had both been
very involved in counseling young
couples in their church about
what true love was and the four
stages that every successful marriage would ultimately go through
before they discovered what true

love was all about. Trish and I went through all four of those phases during our 44 years of marriage and by the time I lost her to ovarian cancer in 2013, we had become closer than we ever could have imagined.

We stayed in touch with the Westerings after they moved to PLU in Tacoma where we visited them several times. Over those years apart, we would often find ourselves calling the Westering household when we would be at a party and would find ourselves playing a game called the Wizard of The North. It was a card trick wherein you could have someone pick any card out of a 52-card deck and then tell them that you were going to place a long-distance phone call to the Wizard who would be able to tell them (from over a thousand miles away) exactly which card they had chosen. It didn't matter which member of the Westering family answered the call, because they all knew exactly how to respond, and it blew the person's mind when the Wizard always picked the correct card.

Finally, one of the greatest lessons I learned from Frosty was something I was able to carry over into 27 years of coaching my three sons in youth football, YMCA basketball, and little league baseball. That was the philosophy that whether we won or lost a game, what really mattered is that if we won, we won with dignity, always respecting the effort put forth by our opponent, and if we lost, we lost with pride, pride in the fact that we had done our very best throughout the entire game. That is a lesson I have passed on to hundreds of young athletes, some of whom are now wearing Super Bowl rings or went on to play major league baseball.

They often say that the mark of a truly great person is how long they are remembered and admired after they have left this earth. In that regard, Frosty will always be right at the top!

IN THE BEGINNING

David Olson (Pacific Lutheran/1962-96), Dean, School of Physical Education; Director of Athletics

My initial contact with Frosty was in the '60s when we both were coaching in Iowa—he at Parsons College and I at Wartburg College. I had numerous contacts with Frosty at conference meetings and many athletic events. It was very clear that he knew how to coach football. We never beat Parsons! More importantly, however, it was obvious he understood the word team. Frosty had the ability to mobilize each person as they contributed to a common goal while enjoying the trip. He knew how to make it meaningful for both participants and spectators.

Frosty and family moved on to Lea College in Minnesota and I was appointed Dean and Director of Athletics at Pacific Lutheran University. Frosty made a contact with us indicating he was looking for a football coaching position. At the same time, we had a football coaching vacancy. The interview went well—even the bean in the jar demo. There was unanimity with the search committee and the university administration to hire Frosty. It proved to be an excellent decision. Now you know "the rest of the story."

A SPORTS PUBLICIST'S DREAM

Jim Kittilsby (Pacific Lutheran/1972-93), Sports Information Director, Baseball Coach, Assistant Athletic Director

It was a sheer contrast from my last Sea Tac Airport drive representing the Pilots to my first chauffeur assignment for PLU. In baseball, I went to pick up the crass and turbulent Billy Martin, a candidate for the managers job. He didn't get it. At PLU, I was sent to pick up Frosty coming to be interviewed for head coach for the football team. Having no idea what he looked like I searched the arrivals. Charisma prevailed. Frosty always stood out in a crowd.

In one of his first days on the job, Frosty sent memos to the athletic director and to me signed off with EMAL. Dr. Olson scurried into my office and we together pseudo-intellectually guessed that EMAL could have some deep spiritual significance in either Greek or Hebrew similar to the INRI inscribed on Jesus' cross. Soon EMAL became a readily recognized acronym—Every Man A Lute.

Frosty's wife Donna frequently hosted potlucks for the athletic staff. The delicious offerings were varied each month until one event in particular where, after enjoying Dorothy Tobiason's lasagna and Donna's carrot cake as well as other favorite contributions, it became a mandate that these marvelous cooks should always bring the same dishes every time they met to eat together.

Frosty soon became a favorite Seattle personality. One year the football team opened its season in the Tacoma Dome. The major Seattle networks KOMO, KING, and KIRO broadcast their dinnertime sports news from the spacious Tacoma Dome press box. At halftime they fed over 150 working press. Frosty's favorite line rang true: The Big Time is wherever you make it! The Big Time is right here, right now!

Frosty was a sports publicist's dream. He often took breaks during practice sessions on campus to accommodate the media. On one occasion Bruce King, sports director for KOMO-TV, and his film crew came down to shoot some footage. Without any prompting, Frosty walked over to the cameraman with a heads-up. The next play from scrimmage would be a pass to a "phantom" receiver. Captured on film and featured on that evening's sports show was Bruce King making the catch.

AN AWESOME SERVANT LEADER

Joe Broeker (Pacific Lutheran/1966-77), Assistant Football Coach; Baylor University (1977-79); University of Richmond (1980-82); Willamette University, Head Football Coach (1982-92); Fellowship of Christian Athletes (1997-2012)

Very special people supported Frosty so very well during his tenure at PLU. The first person would be Frosty's wife Donna—such a special person and wife of a coach. They were a team in whatever was accomplished. Donna served and welcomed each player and coach to the PLU family. At games you could always hear Donna. She was a terrific cheerleader for the Lutes. My wife Sharon and I and continued to meet with Donna after Frosty passed away. What neat times those were—so many memories!

I was a coach and teacher before Frosty arrived at PLU. A few years later Dave Olson came as AD followed by Paul Hoseth. Then Dave hired Frosty as the new head football coach. Dave and Paul made a significant impact in the physical education department. They were noticed by their colleagues because of their professionalism, passion and care in their work and service to the PLU students. They were behind the scenes supporting Frosty in so many ways and served PLU with excellence over the years. Dave gave such good leadership to PLU athletics, including supporting the football program. Paul succeeded Dave as the Dean of Physical Education and Athletic

Director and served both Frosty and Scott as an assistant football coach as well.

Behind any servant leader you will find special people deeply committed to the mission set by the leader. Donna, Dave, and Paul respected, loved, served, and supported Frosty so well.

Breakaway: The beginning of a new PLU football season began with welcoming the new team back in a special way. Two or three days of two-a-day practices were committed to teambuilding and building relationships with one another.

Breakaway Lodge in Oregon was a Young Life property utilized for many years for this focus. My wife and I discovered Breakaway when we used this property for a special Christmas gathering with our family and other families who were meeting weekly in a Bible study.

In August, athletes and coaches traveled several miles to Breakaway, which was located in Gearhart, Oregon, on the Pacific Ocean. Breakaway was filled to the max with athletes using all the bedrooms and beds. Support folks came to prepare the meals, which was a huge job. We all ate well.

Awesome activities included FCA's dog patch Olympics, teambuilding by Frosty, captains, and coaches; Team Huddle time for sharing devotions, and sharing Jesus in a variety of ways with minimum emphasis on football X's and O's. This getaway set the tone for our entire season. It was always a highlight for the beginning of football season.

Saylor's: Frosty and I enjoyed a good steak dinner. It was so good! Sharon and I took Frosty and Donna to a Saylor's Steak House in Portland. The meal and fellowship were terrific.

Then, when a PLU football season was ending, Frosty would plan to have the seniors and their families and football staff join Donna and him at Saylor's after a game in Oregon. Sharon and I joined them for one of these dinners. As you came into the entrance, you saw at both sides of the counter pictures of various youth programs Saylor's was sponsoring. You also saw a picture of Frosty, a PLU football, a Frosty bobblehead, and a few comments.

During and after dinner, Frosty was so complimentary to the servers. This always happened with Frosty when he was eating out. In addition, he would ask to go to the kitchen where he also complimented the chefs. He was a master in expressing his appreciation for others.

An awesome servant leader: I've seen many leaders in my time—some that were great leaders and some that were weak. However, I've never met a weak servant leader. When servant is added to leader, it takes us to a deeper and higher level. Frosty was such a special servant leader. He served others so very well. He modeled servanthood.

After completing a night football game with Western Washington, we needed to make a 3-plus hour trip back to Parkland. I was the trip coordinator and had taken roll of our players and coaches. One person was missing—Frosty.

I checked to see if he was talking to the press. That wasn't the case. I found Frosty in the locker room picking up the tape and garbage off the floor. I commented that our team was ready to go except for him. Also I shared that the custodian would take care of cleaning the locker room.

Wrong. Frosty proceeded to tell me that the custodian had an important job to do and didn't need extra work from our team. The locker room was left with nothing on the floor. He modeled an example of servant leadership. The next game, there were two people cleaning up the locker room. By the end of the season, athletes and coaches had joined

Frosty leaving the locker room in great shape for the custodian.

Total Release: Alongside such terrific coaches like John Wooden and Tom Landry, Wes Neal (Total Release) and Bruce Brown (Proactive Coaching), Frosty was a pioneer in the coaching profession with his passion and commitment to being a coach who radically lived out coaching for significance with winning being a by-product. Total Release was based on Colossians 3:23: "[Coach] heartily unto to the Lord not man." That was Frosty's commitment to Jesus, to his family, to his players, and his coaches. He walked his talk and his talk was right on.

He made The Big Time where he was at and was always stressing to others the value that one could make in serving others. Frosty also introduced Double Win—and awesome focus on competitions—and Blue Car/Red Car, which were comparisons of coaching styles (others vs. self). He was the master of being an other-centered person.

Many wonderful ministries to coaches (Jeff Duke's 3D Coaching and FCA's 360 Degree coaching training) are now available for coaches to examine as they develop as servant leaders with their players and coaches. Frosty was modeling these concepts throughout his coaching career and deeply impacted so many coaches.

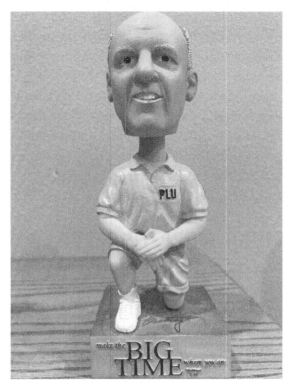

As Frosty always said, "People don't care how much you know until they know how much you care." He lived this concept out daily in his relationship with others.

A note from my wife Sharon: Donna Westering made a huge impression on me as a young mother of three and coach's wife. Thinking back on those years, I realize I was not overly confident and looked up to the head coach's wife for an example. From her I learned how to support my husband in the good and the hard times.

I remember the wives would meet before the home game. Our theme was "we need each other." It was a great time of bonding, sharing, and caring. For the athletes, Donna was always ready with a plate of brownies or peanut butter crispy bars. The guys looked forward to her huge plate of goodies. Her warm welcoming personality made everyone feel included and valued.

She was always interested in others and easily extended words of encouragement. Even after Frosty was gone and she was alone, every time we were in the area we would take her out to lunch. She inquired about our grandkids and especially our youngest that was a huge Eagles fan. Donna's interest in others continued. As a young wife, I was fortunate to have her example. For 28 years, I modeled what I had seen and heard those early years.

MUCH MORE TO OFFER

Paul Hoseth (Pacific Lutheran/1968-2005), Professor, Assistant Coach, Dean of School of Physical Education, and Director of Athletics

In the fall of 1963, I was a sophomore at Concordia College in Moorhead, Minnesota. Our first football game that season was in Fairfield, Iowa, vs. Parsons College, which was coached by Frosty Westering. I injured my knee in that game was unable to play much for the remainder of that season. The following year, Concordia won a National Championship. Frosty left Parsons to complete his doctorate in Colorado.

Jeanne and I were married in 1967. We both had jobs in Bemidji, Minnesota. I was teaching and coaching football and gymnastics at Bemidji State College and Jeanne was teaching first grade at a nearby elementary school. We left Bemidji after one year to travel west to Tacoma, Washington. Jeanne was able to secure an elementary teaching position in the Franklin Pierce District at a school close to Pacific Lutheran University and our home. I accepted a teaching and coaching position at PLU in 1968 after meeting with Dave Olson who would be the new Physical Education Department Chair and Athletic Director.

In 1972, I was on the search committee to look for a new football coach. When Frosty came to campus, he had several weeks of material in his briefcase for two days of interviews. One afternoon, Joe Broeker, the other assistant football coach, and I met with Frosty in a classroom. Frosty went to the backboard to describe his cross-blocking system and how he combined the 5-2 and 4-3 defenses. I remember saying, "Frosty, there are many good offenses and defenses. We're flexible and can work with whatever you want. Let's just sit down and talk about the players." That was the beginning of a love affair.

After one home game in 1972, the first year Frosty coached at PLU, we ended up in Olson Auditorium with the team and parents. The post-game session was called Locker Room and later was changed to Afterglow. At one point in the Locker Room I remember holding one-year old Karl in my arms and saying to the players and parents, "I'm not sure yet what is happening here, but I hope Frosty stays around long enough for Karl to play here if he wants to play football." Karl's last year playing football was 1994 and PLU was runner-up to the National Champion.

A few years later, Joe Broeker left for a sabbatical to complete his doctorate. We had an interesting group of coaches. Frosty, Joe, and I each completed doctoral degrees and were coaching football. That was not a common occurrence. I became defensive coordinator and was allowed the freedom to experiment and try many different ideas. Frosty was supportive in almost everything, but one thing he particularly liked was to get pressure on the quarterback. That was fine with me.

Jeanne came from a background where the important part of a football game was half-time when the band played. I was trying to figure out how to help her understand the game, but also the time commitment involved in coaching. I thought it might be more helpful if she got to know some of the players rather than trying to learn about the X's and O's of football.

Early on, we began to invite players to our home. The offense would meet in Olson Auditorium for the Tuesday night meeting and the defense would

meet at our home. We had 25 to 30 large humans in one room. We would watch film and talk about the upcoming game. This may have been as or more important than what happened on the practice field.

As youngsters, Karl and our daughter Mari always looked forward to Tuesday nights during the season. Some of these players were their babysitters. The other important part of the meeting was that Jeanne always made desserts. Sometimes she would bake pies, ice cream chocolate chip cookie sandwiches, or brownies a la mode for the group. There was always a special treat. The order for determining who got to eat first was by answering a trivia question. Answer first. Eat first. It's amazing how competitive some people can be when food is involved.

We often had part-time assistant coaches who were former players. In many ways, I thought it was more important for assistant coaches to understand who Frosty was and how he operated than it was to have a great understanding of the technical aspects of the game. Former players could often make those transitions easier. Scott Westering joined the

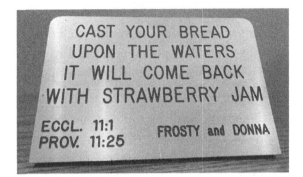

CAST YOUR BREAD
UPON THE WATERS
IT WILL COME BACK
WITH STRAWBERRY JAM

ECCL. 11:1
PROV. 11:25

FROSTY and DONNA

coaching staff shortly after his graduation. The explosive offensive combination of Frosty and Scott provided opportunities to combine the old and the new. Craig McCord came in the later '80s and provided special assistance to the defense.

We won many games, traveled to France, Australia, New Zealand, China, and Germany with Frosty-led teams. We played in numerous postseason games and won four national championships. I remember relatively little about the football part of the journey.

Frosty was not about winning and losing on the scoreboard. His goal was much bigger. He was trying to use the game of football to teach life skills. Many people will look to the wins and losses as a measure of success. From that criterion, Frosty was successful. Many people in Elkader and Fairfield, Iowa, or at Parsons College, Lea College, and Pacific Lutheran University would agree that Frosty had so much more to offer. Football was only the vehicle to accomplish his goal of helping others to be the best they could be.

Frosty had a strong Christian faith, but it came through mostly in his actions. And none of this would have happened had it not been for Donna Belle. She was the glue that kept things going and the ship afloat. Thank you, Frosty. Thank you, Donna.

DONNA BELLE

Jeanne Hoseth, Elementary Teacher, Franklin Pierce School District (27 years); Alternate "Mother" To Hundreds of Football Players

Donna and Frosty decided to share copies of his book "The Strange Secret of the Big Time" with students in our son Karl's leadership class when he taught at Spanaway Lake High School. Students read the book and wrote reflections on how one of Frosty's chapters related to their own life.

In early June 2013 (just two months after Frosty died), Donna, Paul, and I went to Karl's class to hear his students share their stories. They openly spoke of the joys and challenges they were facing, not just the difficulties of growing up, but their struggles with having been abandoned, neglected, and bullied. They told how Frosty's words had inspired and empowered them to hope and take more control over that which they could control.

At the end of class, Donna responded to what they had shared and so genuinely told about her own early life. They were spellbound. When the bell rung, the class stayed put. Staying put was not a normal behavior for high school students when the bell was signaling the end of the day. They honored Donna with respect and affection by continuing to listen and then lined up to give her hugs. Every student got a kiss on the cheek before they left the room. It was a very special day. Karl said it was the favorite day of his teaching career.

Donna Belle's faith in God, faith in young people, generosity, openness, love, and acceptance were special treasures to all of us who knew her.

WHAT HAVE I GOTTEN MY-SELF INTO?

Reid Katzung (Pacific Lutheran/1967-80), Sports and Entertainment Industry; U.S. Olympic Committee (1996-2006)

It was the fall of 1967 and I was excited for the flag football season (actually, we substituted the flags for 18-inch pieces of rope secured under the belts of our play pants, i.e. jeans). My Hawthorne Elementary team in Albert Lea, Minnesota, was playing Oakwood Elementary. They had one player, their quarterback, who stood out. Today, one might say he had some swagger. He was a new kid in town and his dad was the football coach at the local college, Lea College. His name was Brad Westering.

We actually lived quite close to each other and eventually ended up playing various sports at the same neighborhood park—younger brother usually was part of the fun. We spent many, many days over the next four years just playing.

Frosty was head football coach at Lea College and the Westering family made me a part of it in so many ways. Fifty-plus years later, I realize now that EMAL was born at Lea College—Every Man A Lancer!

When the Westering's made the move to PLU in 1972, little did I know that I would not see them again until the fall of 1979. We stayed in touch via mail and an occasional long distance phone call. I had graduated from Gustavus Adolphus College and was finishing up a master's degree program at the University of Michigan in Ann Arbor. Meanwhile, Brad was leading the Lutes to the NAIA national playoffs. He alerted me that they would be playing in Findlay, Ohio. I had to be there!

I had no car, but borrowed my roommate's AMC Gremlin and hit the road. My memories of that trip: it was like I had never been apart from the Westering's, it was a cold, snowy day, the Lutes lost, a Gremlin is not a good winter vehicle, and I experienced my first Locker Room. Long story just a bit shorter, we also discussed the immediate future, and eight months later I was on the campus of PLU. Frosty offered me a job with his Lute football program.

From my playing days, my football memories of preseason practices were of two-a-days, film sessions, being exhausted, etc. I was more than overwhelmed with the perceived responsibilities I would likely have with the Lutes. I was relieved a little when I was told the team's first few days would be spent at something called Breakaway down on the Oregon coast. My understanding was this was a no-pads weekend of primarily team building. Regardless, I convinced myself to be ready for X's and O's, position meetings, film, and conditioning.

I maintained those expectations right up to the morning we left for Seaside, Oregon. I would keep my mouth shut and do as I was told—taking the "I'm the new guy" approach. We were to meet out front of Olson Auditorium and depart from there. As I recall, there was no bus, so there were lots of vehicles lined up for departure. It was my introduction to Frosty Time as he was nowhere in sight.

He eventually made his entrance driving what I believe was a white, '65 Chevy station wagon. To this day, I don't know if it was The Bomb that Frosty drove back in Albert Lea. It was identical, but there was no way that car could have made the journey from Minnesota. Puffing blue smoke with much of its exterior rusted out, Frosty pulled up and got out of the car to the roaring applause of the team.

Frosty was carrying a bathroom scale, which he sat down in the middle of the street. He stripped down to his tighty whities, t-shirt, and socks. I was looking for answers to what was going on! One of the players then told me Frosty made some kind of bet that he would lose at least so many pounds before leaving

for Breakaway. Frosty's weigh-in was successful, he quickly dressed, and concluded the festivities with a few choruses of "Hey Lutes!" and "Are You Ready, Ready, Break!" cheers. We hit the road, likely stopping at one of the Westering boys' favorite eateries (the Maid-Rite outside of Portland) on both legs of the trip.

This team won the 1980 NAIA national championship.

Frosty and I share the same birthdate, December 5th. Every year we made a point of visiting on the phone with each other. Since his passing, I celebrate that annual treasure by talking to his son Brad.

FROSTY'S GREATEST SUCCESS

Jerry LeJeune (Pacific Lutheran/1972-2000), Psychology Professor

Frosty and I had a different relationship. We both came to PLU the same year. One afternoon I decided to go and watch a PLU football practice. Frosty's enthusiasm and joy of

life really attracted me. I became a Lute. I felt more like a friend than a colleague to Frosty. I did not have the responsibility of helping him with the nuts and bolts of being the successful coach he was.

Friendship has its rewards, and from my privileged standpoint of just being with Frosty without having coaching responsibilities, I was allowed to see through the energy and optimism that he exuded, to the gentle, human person he was.

Many knew Frosty the successful football coach, and that was well deserved, but I was able to see a warmth and vulnerability that made him Frosty, the compassionate man. I saw a legend that treasured his family, was humble, and was not afraid to listen and admit his mistakes. Frosty was not immune to pain and conflict, but his steadfast belief in God and the goodness of man brought him and all who knew him endless joy. That indeed was his greatest success. Attaway!

THE GIFT OF TIME

Lauralee Hagen (Pacific Lutheran/ 1972-2013), Alum, Senior Gift Planner, Administrator, Friend of Frosty

I played for Frosty—just not in the same way

as most contributors to this book!

When the Westering family pulled into Parkland in 1972, I was a student. I loved PLU athletics and many of my friends played football, so I loved attending games and what later became known as Afterglow while seated practically atop one another in the hallway that led into the Franklin Pierce High School locker room.

As a PLU administrator (Residential Life and Alumni and Constituent Relations), Frosty and I forged a partnership that was mutually beneficial. I clearly benefited the most! We established the move-in-day program, which continues to this day. On that day, most of the PLU football team wait outside the residence halls ready to help students and parents carry all their worldly possessions from the car to their new campus home.

Dog Patch Olympics, led by Frosty and the Lutes, became a part of Orientation Week and helped build community amongst our student body. Frosty was a regular speaker at Family Weekend and Homecoming pregame tailgates. And, for 10 years, I was the cheerleader advisor and our collaborations are too numerous to list.

If ever a big project needed big help, Frosty was my go to! Almost before asking, twice as many Lutes as requested were present with a smile on their face, a spring in their step, and a heart ready to serve. They literally whistled while they worked and made any task fun!

Frosty gave me many gifts and handwritten notes over the years, but the greatest gift he gave me was his time. I will never forget a moment of the hundreds of hours in his office, my office, his house while eating tacos with the family (also a gift), on the practice field, over lunch at Paradise Bowl or the Gateway Cottage, and more than one hospital room.

After our last lunch, I wrote: "As we drove home from the Gateway Cottage, we agreed to do this more often. Frosty pulled in, turned off the car and then the 80-something sage coach that could not walk without pain escorted me to the door. I had barely made my way back to my desk before there was a voicemail thanking me for lunch and the great conversation."

Today, I write to represent the thousands of Lutes that didn't play football but benefited from Frosty's presence in the PLU community.

AN IRRESISTIBLE FORCE

Steve Thomas (Pacific Lutheran/1978-82, 1999-present), Football Broadcaster; Seattle Seahawks Play-By-Play Broadcaster (1992-97)

Frosty was an irresistible force. Not in the disciplined, regimented way I expected a former Marine drill sergeant to be when I first met him in 1978. He had high expectations for himself and his players because he wanted everyone to compete against their "best self and be better than you think you are."

He was a great teacher of life lessons: "Football is life not a war game." I've been fortunate to interview many of the best college and pro football coaches around the country over 50 years in broadcasting and without question Frosty was the best I've ever met in sports psychology. I know so many of his former players remember the terms "play without fear," "red car, blue car," "double win," "eager mindset," and so many others.

Whenever he spoke to a crowd or one-on-one, his focus was right on top of you, not always about winning, because "you don't always win the prize but love the challenge," and "winning is a byproduct of bringing out the best in others."

How many times over the years have I thought about giving it my best shot to reach my peak performance and if it didn't work out to flush it and bounce back? Wow, what an influence he was in my life to try and be a better husband, dad, and broadcaster—that if you are good at the details, you'll gain confidence and perform better.

He had his quirks, like the yellow sweatpants. Frosty Time had me waiting quite often later than scheduled for our weekly Friday night pregame interview, but worth it, as when he got there he always dropped some knowledge that was unexpected. And how about his car, The Bomb? Being invited for a trip across campus, you wondered if this old station wagon would even make it across campus without breaking down. When you stopped, would the doors just fly open? A son of the Midwest he liked his eggs fried, his bacon crispy, and his toast, toasted—not light and soggy. He could poke fun at himself (and as I'm now in my later years I can relate): "I had a crew cut but the crew bailed out," but, "grass never grows on a busy street."

In post-season playoff runs on the road in 1979 and 1999, PLU teams embraced the challenges: "iron sharpens iron," and "the longer we play the better we get." In the cramped Afterglow locker room in Findlay, Ohio, in '79, I was standing directly under a leaking overhead pipe and had to wipe away the water from my face, but as I looked around it appeared others, not under the pipe, were having the same issue—disappointed in finally losing but happy for the opportunity and the way the players picked each other up.

In '99, the road warriors under Frosty's calm leadership proved it's somehow possible to win five straight playoff road games and a national championship, and have a great time with your teammates doing it. Can you say, "steamroller?"

He did have the best of helpers. Could there have been any better combination than Frosty and Scott Westering calling the offensive plays, and Paul Hoseth and Craig McCord leading the defense? They were outstanding and all men of character.

I was so lucky to know and be influenced by Frosty, Donna, Scott, and all the tremendous young men that the PLU Lute football program produced. I won't forget that they had one of the best teachers of how to navigate life, ever. Attaway Frosty!

FROSTY THE SHOWMAN

Kirk Isakson (Pacific Lutheran/ 1977-2013), University Communications

I was hired by Pacific Lutheran University in September 1977 to work in the Office of Radio and Television Services (ORTS changed to University Communications, 1982). My title changed over the years, but I was the "Video Guy." The position covered everything related to television production—studio lighting, sets, engineering, writing, camera work, editing, and teaching. It wasn't a job. It was a hobby. I held that position for 39 years (the last five in phased retirement).

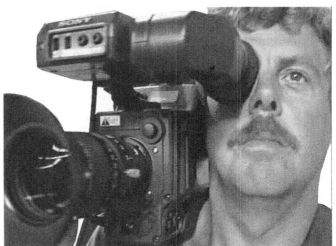

Off the Field

New student orientation for the start of the academic year would meet on Red Square where Frosty shared his philosophy on Red Car vs. Blue Car and the Nut in the Jar. He would explain adjusting to life in a new environment, meeting new people, and services available to help them through the process.

In 1972, Frosty developed PHD (Pride, Heart and Determination) to combat negative attitudes and build self-esteem at Lister Elementary. Players and cheer staff spent eight weeks in the fall volunteering at the community outreach program. The team tackled every classroom to inspire the kids to "work together, care for other, and do their very best." Eventually, the program expanded to include McIlveigh Middle School.

In 2002, the PHD program earned honors at the Tacoma City of Destiny Awards for Young Adult Group for their involvement at Lister and McIlveigh. The football team and cheer staff fostered a positive and winning attitude and the "Big-Five" concept—attitude, caring, challenge, confidence, and comparison—that evolved into the Double Win philosophy.

In 1976, a group of five football players organized a singing group called the Non-Lettermen. It was composed of Mark Reiman (guard), Kris Morris (linebacker), Marc Accimus (fullback), Mike Catron (tackle), and Phil Early (defensive end). Their fame was a vocal performance on the NBC program "The Gong Show" hosted by Chuck Berry on April 18, 1978 where they performed the song "Young Blood." The panel (Pat McCormick, the Unknown Comic, and Jaye P. Morgan) gave them 26 points out of 30 without a gong.

Another musical success was Michael Peterson (offensive tackle) who played on the 1980 national championship football team. He wrote songs for Denise Williams and The Imperials and performed contemporary Christian songs. He found his way to Nashville, Tennessee, writing and singing country. In 1997, Michael was named Best Male Artist of the Year by Billboard magazine.

The Sidelines

Before the games, Frosty would work with the cheer staff to get the crowd excited and cheer the team. He made sure the pep band was loaded with marching songs to keep the spectators on their feet. After every touchdown, the band played "When the Saints Go Marching In," but Frosty renamed the song "When the Lutes Go Marching In."

On September 20, 2003, Frosty reached the pinnacle of his PLU career with 300 collegiate wins in football. The defeat of Chapman University brought the PLU crowd to its feet in the final seconds of the game as they realized that Frosty was one of 10 college coaches to reach this milestone. He was the second winningest coach in Division III history. Frosty finished out the season with five additional wins on the board. He retired from coaching at the end of the 2003 season.

For 20 years, John "Nellie" Nelson drove the sidelines in his motorized wheelchair. The team and coaching staff adopted John into the program and he became one of the volunteer assistant coaches. John had a disease that locked all of his joints from the neck down, but that didn't stop him from being active with the team. Where we go one, we go all. Sadly, John passed away on August 30, 2009.

International Travel

Frosty was not a coach that sat and waited for things to happen. He made things happen. With the football team being nationally recognized, there were numerous opportunities over the years to engage in foreign travel to share the meaning and success of American college football.

France: In July 1985, I was provided the opportunity to travel to the French Riviera with the team. PLU

was the first U.S. college football team to play in France. They played three exhibition games against the French team (Paris Blue Angels) led by promoter, captain and player Jacques Accambray. Frosty and the team provided some learning moments for the Blue Angels. Frosty shared about PLU's style and the spirit behind playing football—that the scoreboard doesn't represent the outcome of a game, but it's about doing your best in striving to be the best.

The team traveled into Nice one sunny afternoon to explore the city. In the walk about town, Frosty discovered a large fountain pool. Figuring the guys needed cooling off from the beating sun, he looked at the fountain as an opportunity to take a dip. The locals wondered what was going on and watched. The players performed laps, exercises, and a final plunge into the water. The crowd applauded their efforts.

Later that evening, there was a large floral parade on the promenade with floats, bands, and various groups. Somehow the team became part of the parade. They tossed out small footballs and flowers. They then lined up for a play and provided an Attaway cheer to the crowd.

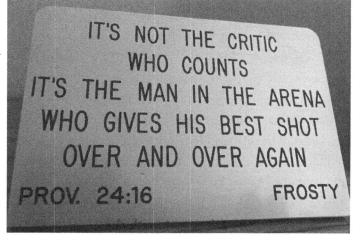

China: Another travel adventure occurred in June of 1991. PLU football was offered the unique experience to travel to China and play three exhibition games in Beijing, Guangzhou, and Shanghai. A travel group in Florida handled all the travel arrangements, which included five-star hotels, transportation, meals, game sites, and excursions.

Before our departure, Wei Hua, a PLU faculty member in the language department, provided a tutorial about China. She shared information about the culture, food, and expectations. Wei also indicated there was no Chinese word for football, so they called it "gǎn lǎn qiú," or olive ball.

Our first stop was Beijing, several days before the two-year anniversary of the Tiananmen Square Massacre. Our arrival at the airport was greeted by security. They noticed I had a video camera larger than the home version and thought I would be a threat by taping footage at Tiananmen Square that would reflect a negative image. Our China support team worked with the officials to indicate I was with the university and there to document the team travels. The Chinese government security reviewed the request and released my equipment three days later.

The travel group assigned us an interpreter by the name of Tony. He provided his knowledge about China, walked the team through travel protocol and entertained the team.

When we arrived at the hotel, the team had been cramped since the start of their travels. Frosty asked the hotel staff about a place where the team could stretch out and pass the ball. A park 45 minutes away was offered. He indicated that was too far and asked for something closer. Getting directions, we all headed out the door and down the sidewalk. The players were wearing their jersey tops and helmets and a few of the players had footballs tucked under their arms. We came upon an underground walkway that opened to Tiananmen Square.

The first game in Beijing was played in humid

Someone on the bus yelled out to put in the music tape and play the song that Tony taught them. "Yiddi-Ya" was cued and cranked. Tony sang in sync with the lyrics and the team provided the chorus. The bus was alive; the driver's head bounced to the beat, and people on the sidewalk appreciated the entertainment. It's the small things that have the most impact. The song was reprised on our last day before heading to the airport. Tony led both teams through the chorus.

In Guangzhou, we had a dinner cruise on the Pearl River, which included a live band. During one of the breaks, Frosty, following the beat of Gene Krupa, found his way behind the drum set and kicked out a solo that had the boat rocking. Tony also entertained the crowd singing his version of "Edelweiss," complete with disco ball and colored lights.

Meals were a new experience for the team. Chinese cuisine was uncharted territory. Food was placed on a Lazy Susan and a chopstick was placed between two dishes and spun. The chopstick pointed to an individual who had to take the first bite. At one of the dinner sittings, Frosty was chanted into eating an eel head. As he held the chopsticks squeezing the eel, the mouth was moving, reluctantly the eel went down (but came back later). At one of the meal stops, a cook brought out a small jar of peanut butter and a spoon. It looked like a player shark attack.

The last game in Shanghai was Pacific Northwest wet. It poured rain the entire game; the crowd was thin and the field was soup. The

conditions. Most of the Chinese in attendance paid the price of a week's salary. Both teams entered the field and the crowd cheered. Tony announced the game with help from the team assistants. American football was not known in China. The action was swift. The teams moved both directions on the field.

Halftime arrived and the players headed for the locker room. Most of the spectators thought the game was over and started exiting. Tony quickly explained that the teams were taking a short break and would return. When the second half played out, it looked much like the first half and the crowd was getting restless. There was a section with Marines, hooting and cheering above all the others. They started "the wave." It soon caught on and the Chinese were more involved with the wave than the game.

Following the game, the PLU players interacted with the remaining crowd. They threw out small footballs and gave high fives.

As the PLU team headed through town, Tony used a microphone to explain the sites.

field was ripe for mud sliding. Frosty led the way and players from both teams joined in the muck. PLU won all three games.

Our closing ceremony included a farewell dinner and a group of kids that performed a variety of amazing acrobatics. Susan Westering sang a song in both American and Chinese. The audience appreciated her ability to master the tune in their language with a beautiful voice. It was an evening that provided the perfect closure to an incredible adventure.

One thing that Frosty stressed to the players from the beginning: respect the people, appreciate the Chinese culture, listen to the people, and thank them for sharing their story and history. Never did I hear anyone ask how long will it take to get there, how long before we leave, or criticism about the people or places to go. I Ding Hau!

Germany: The football team had their final international road trip to Hamburg, Germany, in 1993. PLU brought along current and past football players to play in the UNICEF Charity Bowl against one of Europe's top teams, the Hamburg Blue Devils.

Events

Frosty was a showman. He was comfortable on or off the camera. He enjoyed spreading the gospel of the PLU football program, share the Double Win, and highlight individuals that made a difference. Over the years, Frosty has been involved in numerous university programs.

For several years, the music department put on a musical spoof called "Music You Hate to Love" created by music professor Richard Farner. The showcase features faculty and staff performing classical music. Frosty participated in 1991. His part was to play a drum.

In 2000, Frosty and the players loaded a bus headed for the Olympia Capitol. John Bley met the team upon arrival. Governor Gary Locke also met with the group, which included Nellie, Ted Johnson, and students from Lister and McIlveigh. The Governor read a proclamation, "I, Gary Locke, Governor of the State of Washington, do proclaim March 3rd, the year 2000 as PLU Football Team Recognition Day throughout the State of Washington and urge all our citizens to join in this special observance and celebration."

The team was also invited into the House Chamber while it was in session. Players were recognized for their national championships and from the podium Frosty talked about "the power to choose, from the left and the right," followed by a few small footballs tossed into the crowd and an Attaway cheer to a standing ovation.

After 32 years of coaching

PLU football, Frosty played his final season in 2003. Team members across the years assembled in Olson Auditorium to celebrate his successes and an end of an era to Frosty's brand of football.

Every fall, the athletic department recognizes players, coaches, and community members at the PLU Athletic Hall of Fame. In 2004, Frosty was honored for his years on the gridiron and shaping the lives of so many students.

Each year, the governor recognizes individuals for their service and commitment to the community. In 2010, Frosty was presented the Washingtonian of the Year award.

Happy Trails

This story allowed me to travel back in time and relive the times I spent videotaping Frosty. For all of us, it seems like yesterday. We all have our memories, but for me it might be a bit different. I can throw in a tape and listen to our interviews going back 30 years plus and think how it could be re-edited into a new story. Reviewing the Frosty tapes shows his energy and spirit. The message was the same from the first show to the last, maybe a bit more fine-tuned over the years.

We had a good run and it was an honor and pleasure to be associated with Frosty Westering for 34 years. I knew most of his stories and jokes, but watching new players hang on his every word was like listening to new material. The power he instilled in his players and students gave them self-esteem, confidence, appreciation, and renewed spirit on how they view themselves, others, and the world.

After his retirement, he wasn't finished sharing his vision. We met several times a year editing his show for a new generation of view-

ers. His scripts were usually written with lines and arrows along with a handful of VHS tapes to capture a clip to assemble a new presentation. He said his people were still out there and they're interested in hearing his tales one more time.

Frosty and Donna invested in a condo on Maui about a half-mile from our unit. My wife Pam and I would get together in the spring with them for breakfast or lunch at the north end of the island. Most of the people working the restaurants and businesses knew them by name. Frosty was slowing down, but it didn't stop him from giving them a signed mini ball or an Attaway. Frosty was a true showman—yesterday, today and tomorrow. Make it a great day! Happy trails.

THE FOOT FIGHT

Craig "Mac" McCord (Pacific Lutheran/ 1979-2003), Assistant Football Coach (33 years)

Frosty, Paul, Jerry and I finished the final check at Breakaway Lodge, leaving it better than we found it. I was a rookie with EMAL Football, serving as an undergrad gopher. God had blessed me with the chance to be around Frosty and Paul. We were really running late to get back to PLU for a special Donna return from Breakaway celebration (this was before the ladies joined us at Breakaway).

Frosty let us know he was going to be in the doghouse and we had to get back ASAP. Much to my surprise Frosty tossed me the keys to drive The Bomb back. Soon after we embarked on our journey, Frosty started "encouraging" me to speed it up and go faster. Due to my severe aversion to speeding tickets, I wouldn't go over the speed limit. His verbal affirmations did not have the desired effect.

Shockingly, I felt a foot bump mine off the gas pedal and floor it. Thus began my foot fight with Frosty for control of the gas pedal. Since I had to block Frosty's foot, we quickly lost speed. Frosty realized this loss of speed was putting him deeper in the doghouse, so the infamous foot fight came to an end. A few miles down the road I was asked to pull over and I was relieved of my duty. I thought my time with EMAL Football might be short lived.

You see, since I was an 8th grader, I knew I wanted to be a coach. I started studying them to find out what made coaches successful. Frosty shattered my mold. He redefined my definition of success. The "foot fight" and many treasure chest experiences confirmed to me that Frosty marched to the beat of a different drummer. That drummer was Jesus Christ. Frosty was committed to excellence and Total Release. He let the Spirit drive him to be the best he could be. Frosty was moti-

vated by love (including tough love) and a heart to serve.

That's true success.

THE 12TH PLAYER

Colleen Hacker (Pacific Lutheran/ 1980-2003), Professor, Department of Kinesiology, Sport Performance Psychology

I have often joked, although it's not really a joke, that PLU Football and PLU Women's Soccer produced more marriages than any other group pairing in PLU history. And, it's true.

I believe there's a good reason for that fact. Our teams were both coached with a unique blend of high standards and expectations coupled with a high degree of love, caring, and support. Both groups were relentlessly positive and relentlessly successful. We understood each other. We respected each other. We felt fortunate, grateful, and distinct.

One of our favorite traditions occurred during home games. No matter the opponent, month, or time of day, if PLU Women's Soccer had a game, we knew we could count on and expect a visit from the football team. Now, this visit was not your typical, sit in the stands, clap on occasion, or begrudgingly cheer for fellow student-athletes. Not if Frosty had a say, and trust me, Frosty always had a say. He would send the entire football team over to our field, interrupting the middle of his practice and have the guys, more than 100 strong, surround the entire soccer field.

If PLU players touched the ball, the guys yelled, loud and strong, "Yes!" If the opposing team touched the ball, they groaned equally loudly "No!" On and on and on it went like that with every single touch of the ball, lifting us up and unnerving our opponents. Teams often highlight the value of the "The 12th Player." Well, PLU Women's Soccer had a 12th

Player all right—the entire PLU Football team!

Then, before they left to head back to practice, we always received the familiar Frosty led "Hey Lutes!" cheer. We all knew they had to leave but we never wanted them to go.

Thank you, Frosty! Thank you, PLU Football!

A LEGACY THAT MAY NEVER BE MATCHED

Bruce Haroldson (Pacific Lutheran/ 1983-2002), Head Basketball Coach; Personal Basketball Trainer; Basketball Radio Analyst

I met Frosty for the first time in 1983 when I was being interviewed for the head basketball coaching and teaching positions at PLU. We had lunch at the golf shop café. My first impression of Frosty was that he was totally concerned about the "hire" and that it fit the PLU mission at the time.

After I was hired, I began to realize how significant Frosty was in promoting the image of PLU through his coaching philosophy: "Make The Big Time where you are." This made a favorable impression on me as I had recently had Division I head coaching experience.

All the while that I was at PLU, with the exception of mandatory staff meetings, we were coaches who passed in the night. We were two people who respected one another, but were busy with our own programs and had little time for chitchat.

Football was the driving force of sport conversation around campus and deservedly so. Under Frosty's leadership, his players were

instrumental in helping new students get settled on campus. His Afterglow gatherings following each home game were unique to his program and very impressive.

The success of Frosty's football program brought many students to PLU and the school enjoyed national recognition that may not have happened otherwise. Pacific Lutheran University football under Frosty Westering is a legacy that may never be matched.

EXPERIENCES AND RELATIONSHIPS

Mari Hoseth Lysne (Pacific Lutheran/ 1974-1997), Coach's Kid; Middle School Counselor, Teacher, and Coach, Bonney Lake, Washington

When I reminisce about Frosty and the PLU football program, it is rarely the actual football games that I think about (even though I would guess there are only a handful of people who have attended more games than I have). What I remember vividly are the experiences and the relationships.

Family and Donna: Frosty was intentional about involving family with his football program. Families participated in more ways than just cheering in the stands. Defensive players came to our house each Tuesday night. My mom made countless desserts to feed the players each week and I know Frosty's wife, Donna, also made treats weekly. This connection of sharing treats and meals made relationships with players personal for us. The coaches' families knew them, cheered for them, and cared about them.

I can't think about Frosty without thinking about Donna. She had a similar tough handed but tenderhearted quality as Frosty. Her tough handedness was usually directed at those officiating the game and some members of the opposing team and her tenderheartedness was shown to everyone else, especially Frosty, who was her lifelong love.

Travel: Frosty brought some amazing opportunities for travel to PLU Football. Whether it was a new adventure in a different country or one of the many times a very large group had to wait around for the next step, Frosty had the ability to lead others to find joy, fun, and sometimes craziness in every situation.

I was able to go along to France, Germany, and many Breakaways on the Oregon coast with the team. Just a few highlights I remember include:

In France, the team did go-drills standing inside a large public water feature in Nice and participated in a parade where we walked next to ladies on floats who were not wearing what I would consider tops.

In Germany, we waited a long time to go to a nightclub after the football game only to

"microphones" and laughter. Again, it was a way to actively involve families and create connections with players that made us feel like an important part of the program.

I also recall some hilarious skits where players often took on the role of impersonating Frosty (my brother Karl, who knew him for a lifetime, was an amazing Frosty impersonator) and all the games and competitions on the beach that helped build and forge not only teammates, but also friends.

Afterglow: As a school counselor, looking back on the Afterglow meeting time after every game, I love that Frosty asked players to reflect on the experience they just had and share how they were feeling. They acknowledged and looked for the good in others and came together no matter what the outcome of the game. This event was shared with friends, family, and anyone who wanted to show up.

have Frosty tell us this is, "not our scene!" and leaving immediately. We visited the last remaining part of the Berlin wall and felt very moved by that piece of history. We also caught unprepared in a summer downpour of rain. Matt Mihelich pretended to take a shower, Donna used a found piece of a cardboard box to cover her head, and we all ended up laughing while getting soaked at the beginning of a long day trip. It's nice to face bumps in the road with people who can choose to laugh about it.

Breakaways: The wives, daughters, and friends of the coaches were recruited to do the cooking for the team when financial restrictions called for a creative solution. Donna, Sue, Susan, Jeanne, and Glenna could take a monumental and potentially exhausting task and make it fun. What I remember most from the kitchen work was lots of singing into whisk

And of course, there was some zany fun with a crazy rendition of the birthday song complete with music directors and lots of cheers. There was also prayer and a sharing of faith, which was foundational to who Frosty was and what he hoped to share with those around him.

THE ADVENTURE OF THE BIG TIME

Chris Egan (Pacific Lutheran/1991-95), TV Sports Anchor and Reporter, King 5 TV in Seattle, Washington

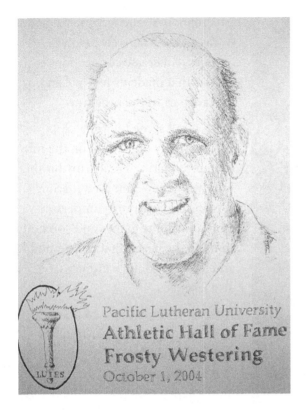

Pacific Lutheran University
Athletic Hall of Fame
Frosty Westering
October 1, 2004

My name is Chris Egan, a sports anchor and reporter at King 5 TV in Seattle. I've been in the TV business since 1995 and in the Seattle market since 2000 and have been honored to win 10 Emmy awards, three Edward R Murrow Awards, and Sportscaster of the Year awards. I've covered three Super Bowls, five Olympics, and three MLS Cups. I've interviewed thousands of athletes, and my broadcasting career started the first year I met Frosty in 1991.

I never played for Frosty, but I covered the PLU football team as a student at Pacific Lutheran University from 1991 to 1995. At PLU, I told Frosty I wanted to be an anchor in Seattle, and he constantly reminded me to, "Make the Big Time where you are."

Thanks to Frosty I treated my work at KCNS 6 at PLU like ESPN. When I got my first job in the small market of Klamath Falls, I reminded myself daily of Frosty's words. It was his motivation that helped carry me from Parkland to Klamath Falls to Medford to Boise to Seattle and my dream station King 5. In 1991, he signed his book to me writing, "Chris, enjoy the adventure of the Big Time." So simple, yet such a strong message that I carry with me every single day.

As a media member, I loved Frosty because he loved to always have fun with the media at practice or at games. One of my favorite stories about Frosty happened when the Lutes were playing Central Washington in 1993. I was running a camera on the sidelines and remember in the fourth quarter with the game very close Frosty yelling out, "Egan, come here!" For a second, I thought he wanted me to go in the game, but then I realized he wanted me to help pump up the packed crowd at Sparks Stadium.

Frosty and I went in front of the students, and he said, "Egan, point your camera at the crowd." I said, "Frosty, I'm sorry but my battery died in the third quarter. I have no batteries left. My camera doesn't work." He smiled, looked at me, and said, "They don't know that. Just point your camera at them and let me do the rest." It was the fourth quarter, his Lutes were in a dogfight with CWU, and Frosty was with me in front of the student section. As I pointed my camera at the stands, Frosty got on his megaphone and told the crowd, "Get on your feet, you're live and we need you up."

Within seconds the entire PLU section was on their feet and they never sat down the rest of the game. The Lutes won a thriller that day 49-48 and went on to win a National Championship that same season. Frosty was also named the national coach of the year. I never played for Frosty, but maybe I did, and maybe I had a very small part in a national title run as the master motivator Frosty worked his magic on a beautiful football fall day in 1993.

Thirty years later his book remains in my office, his Frosty plaques remain on my work desk, and as I broadcast, as I coach youth sports, and as I father, I always enjoy the adventure of the Big Time and I constantly remind people to "Make the Big Time where you are!

EPILOGUE

I ACTUALLY CHOSE NOT TO PLAY FOR FROSTY

The book is aptly titled "I Played For Frosty" since it contains many memories and stories from those who played, coached or were associated with him during his 50 plus years of coaching football. Ironically, as his youngest son, I actually chose not to play for Frosty—at least not initially.

On the night of February 15, 1977, the day before National Letter of Intent Signing Day, my brother Brad (who at the time was playing quarterback for dad at PLU) and I were going out to get a pizza. I was prepared to tell him of my decision to accept a full scholarship to UCLA. As I was walking out of the house, I turned to my dad and mom who were sitting on the couch and flippantly said, "We're going to get something to eat but I want you to know I'm going to sign with UCLA tomorrow. I believe that's the best place for me." Then I walked out the door.

I never really stopped to think about sitting down with them and walking through one of the biggest decisions at that point in my life. I still have regrets about how I handled it. I believe my mom was excited for me, and the adventure it would hold, but looking back at that moment, I know dad was hurt—especially because I never even really considered talking to him about playing football at PLU.

After the last game of my freshman season, we had just lost to USC with a chance to go to the Rose Bowl, I was sitting in the locker room and came to realize that very few teammates really cared about anyone but themselves. I reflected about how I was raised and that at the end of the day, relationships were the most important thing in life. I thought about my dad, the man and coach that he was.

Deep feelings really started churning in me.

I'll never forget the night sitting in my dorm room when I came to my decision to leave UCLA. I called home to talk to dad. I told him I was coming home and that I wanted to play for him. It was silent for a moment. I don't remember exactly what he said, but I'll hold on tightly to the memory of that joyful sound in his unrestrained excitement. It was a cherished memory between him and I—father and son and soon to be coach and player.

For the next three years, I played for Frosty, two of those years being amazingly unique, playing with my brother while playing for our dad. His distinctive coaching style and approach to the game by not worrying about the scoreboard but, "giving it your best shot" and "enjoying the trip" made it all the more validating of my decision to transfer back home. My senior year, I was blessed to be one of five captains on the 1980 team, which ended up winning the first of four National Championships dad coached while at PLU.

For the next 22 years, I had the honor and privilege to coach alongside my dad. Working closely with him most every day enabled us to become almost best friends as I got a front row seat to see how he was so unique and special in almost every aspect of coaching.

Many people forget that dad had his Doctorate in Education degree as well—something very rare for a college football coach. He was using sports psychology in coaching and teaching long before it was a common practice. He was one of the earliest coaches to teach about peak performance while also being a great scientist of all facets of the game. Dad had a creative and innovative football mind, rare instincts, and a sense for how to approach and play the game.

You don't win over 300 games, become an inductee of the College Football Hall of Fame, and retire as the ninth winningest coach in the history of college football without being committed to your convictions. Dad's style and approach was very different than how most successful coaches do it. His art of coaching created purposeful understanding, a genuinely positive outlook, and a deeply caring culture along with his great science which translated to what one sportswriter once described this way: "Frosty had the ability to make average players good, good players really good, really good players great, and great players consistently great."

One of the greatest memories of coaching with my dad was not during a game, but in the pre-game warm up. It was during the 1999 NCAA Division III National Championship game versus Rowan University, loaded with talent, size and a bunch of Division I transfers. We weren't given much of a chance by any of the national sports writers or even the ESPN broadcast crew.

Dad gathered the players in the end zone and lifted his head to the sky. He then raised his hands and began praying for focus on the game about to begin and surrender to the Lord's purpose in how He wanted to use the PLU football team that day. Dad's mindset correlated with one of his favorite Bible verses. Matthew 5:16 states: "Let your light so shine before men that they may see your good works and glorify your Father in Heaven." We ended up playing pretty well and won 42-13. It was a microcosm of everything dad was about.

Whether a former player, a former coach, or someone who was impacted by crossing paths with him (a janitor, waitress, bus driver, pilot, hotel desk worker, camera man, store clerk, etc.), I hope you continue to be inspired as you remember the qualities, character, and faith by which Frosty coached and truly lived. ~ Scott Westering

UNIQUELY MEMORABLE

His players implored him to bellyflop into a California hotel pool, and he complied -- at age 75. He once took a running plunge into the mud during a soppy game in Oregon. He adored when players pulled pranks on him, insisted players use his first name -- Frosty! --and corrected them if they used "Coach."

He sometimes halted practice to have players spend five minutes gazing beyond the giant evergreens to Mount Rainier. He sometimes halted practice to have players go to other sporting fields and cheer on, say, the soccer team. He always halted two-a-day practices in August and instructed players to go help freshmen move into dormitories.

He believed deeply in singing. His players sang before games, after games. Sometimes they sang to the mock direction of the coach's cane. Always they learned to sing without embarrassment, for it had become uncool to refrain from the refrains. For his 300th win in September 2003, an offensive lineman led the team in James Taylor's "Steamroller." During warmups for the NCAA Division III national championship game in December 1999, right there on the field in Virginia, his players sang "The Twelve Days of Christmas," then, proceeded to win 42-13.

Can you imagine warming up on the other side, then losing 42-13 to that?

During three of the best days of my career -- those in his company, in Tacoma, Wash., in 2003 -- he requested that I join his players for supper in their dining hall. Three of them drove me, in a pickup truck, back to my car. Along the way, they sang "Leaving on a Jet Plane."

"Why singing?" I asked the coach.

"When you sing," he said, "your consciousness is raised."

And lest you think this guy some Left Coast flake, let me hurl at you this biographical detail: former drill instructor, United States Marine Corps.

Did you know one of the most remarkable American coaches died on Friday? Did you know that Frosty Westering, who had 32 seasons at Pacific Lutheran without a losing record in any, who never mentioned playoffs or titles to his players but won four national championships and four runner-up finishes on two levels, died at 85 surrounded by his considerable family? Please know. Please, please know.

An airline pilot wrote to the university president. He wrote because the Pacific Lutheran presence on his airplane had taken a routine day and whipped it up into memorable. He wrote because Westering insisted his players respect other people's work. He wrote because that respect included rapt attention to the flight attendants, which in turn included a phenomenal sound that came when the players clicked their seat belts in unison.

He wrote because at the destination gate, the college football players had held back and lined up on two sides in a "go" tunnel so they could give high-fives to disembarking crew.

A janitor wrote to the university president. He wrote because when he came upon Pacific Lutheran's visiting locker room one postgame in Portland, he found the chairs lined up in impeccable order. He wrote because he found the floors and lockers completely free of the normal detritus. He found the place just about spotless.

He wrote because, when he arrived in the room, he found a note on the whiteboard suggesting he go home and join his wife by the Christmas tree.

A man in a wheelchair came to the "Afterglow," a Westering postgame concoction where a few hundred players, coaches and fans would gather in the bleachers. They might discuss the game. Players might thank the fans for support. Fans might thank the players for inspiration. Everyone would sing "Happy Birthday" to anyone with a birthday nigh. The "Afterglow" would happen after wins, but -- oh yes -- the "Afterglow" would happen also after losses, because in Westering's mind, losing meant you had just completed the privilege of playing.

On a weekday after the "Afterglow," Westering happened upon the man in the wheelchair and invited him to practice. Soon after that, he made the man an assistant coach, and so John Nelson, a quadriplegic Singaporean-American born with a debilitating condition and spinal-cord problems, came to head up the freshmen players. And they, in turn, had to take on responsibilities for his care: dressing him, helping him eat, helping him go to the bathroom. Do you suppose that taught them anything?

By 2003, Nelson had lost count of the times he had appeared as a groomsman in the weddings of former players, reckoning the number beyond 10. He told of a road trip stop at Disneyland when the players determined he should take a ride, so one player hugged him all the way through. During those three days I spent with the team in 2003 Nelson said to me, "There's a reason for this, a reason for the guys coming out to this program, to see somebody who's different. Hopefully, it inspires them. If someone in public needs help, I'm sure they will be comfortable with helping them."

Doctors thought Nelson would have trouble making 30. By 2003, he had made 38. By his death in 2009, he had made 44. At his memorial service, Frosty placed a jersey on his wheelchair.

Westering had such stern rules. His players had to help up opponents during games on the premise that the privilege of playing could not occur without opponents. Troublemakers didn't have to run sprints; no, they were denied the "honor" of running. He knew fear could motivate but thought love could motivate for longer, so players badly in need of upbraiding -- of putdowns -- would receive what Frosty called "put-ups," and he mandated six put-ups per day.

One put-up, "Attaway" -- a configuration of "That a way" -- became a staple. He had players use it prolifically, including toward hotel clerks, short-order cooks, fast-food clerks, custodial staffs, flight crews. They used it one day at practice after Frosty had some women's volleyball players address the team about their recent and difficult victory over Puget Sound.

In a football world chockablock with practices planned to the minute if not the second, Frosty's practices carried a decided imprecision. His son and coaching successor Scott said that, to his knowledge, his father had never written a practice plan. One day he had me address the team, impromptu. Sometimes he'd serve popsicles, with root beer one flavor during my visit. Wet days might enable frolicsome sliding contests. Meetings never started on time, and Frosty's penchant for hazy punctuality proved so entrenched that Donna, his wife and the mother of their five children, found an "ish" clock with the suffix "ish" beside each number and placed it on their kitchen wall.

Said Donna, one day on the phone, "In fact, it's five after 2-ish right now."

Players never wore full gear until game days, then would suit up on Saturdays, sing (of course), maybe even listen to some music professor Frosty had invited to play drums for them on an upside-down bowl and plastic pitcher. Then the whistle would blow, the kickoff would go up, and players would tell of this astonishing transformation into hard, hard hitting -- replete with helping up the people they'd hit.

Then again, one day in September 2003 the quarterback came to the sideline on fourth-and-12 and said, "Let's go for it," whereupon Frosty said, "You're kidding," whereupon a small gaggle of players agreed with the quarterback, whereupon Frosty said, "Let's do it, then," whereupon Pacific Lutheran converted the first.

Seasons would begin with a three-day getaway in which players bonded, played games but not football, apologized for any insufficient effort the prior season and sang, sang, sang, the freshmen standing on chairs and singing their high school fight songs unless they could not remember them, in which case they got stuck with "Twinkle, Twinkle Little Star." Seasons would end the way almost all seasons everywhere end, with a loss, but with a way almost no seasons end, with an "Afterglow." Or they ended with a win and an "Afterglow."

And when PLU careers ended, the graduates sprinkled over much of the Northwest, some in coaching. One helped run a car dealership where they took time to behold Mount Rainier and they declined an applicant after a job interview in which the applicant told of being a No. 1 salesman, because they thought he had missed the point of it all.

Their former coach always bought used cars, so he drove me to the dining hall in his 1993 blue Oldsmobile. When he left one day for a speaking engagement, he offered me the use of his small office, which surely meant he wasn't cheating. And when I returned to New York, a dear friend who does not follow college football but who read my story said something simple, but said it with an inflection that made it ring in my head for good.

"He's a great man," my friend said. A great man died on Friday. A great man also lived from 1927 until Friday, and while he lived, oh boy, was he alive. ~ Chuck Culpepper

[Editor's Note: This article originally appeared in Sports On Earth, April 16, 2013.]

PHOTO SECTION ONE

YOUNG FROSTY

FROSTY AND DONNA

FROSTY AND DONNA'S STORY

Known by so many yet their history familiar to few, Frosty and Donna were both born in 1927 in Missouri Valley, Iowa, population under 4,000. Frosty grew up as an only child and Donna with three brothers. They attended every school together in their formative years. As early as second grade, Donna knew who the man of her life would be when she wrote on her pencil box about a classmate, "Donna loves Frosty." They both pursued and participated in a myriad of activities ranging from multiple sports to school clubs to civic leadership groups to being drummers in the marching band together. The rumor that Frosty wheeled Donna to their senior prom in a wheelbarrow is true with his car having broken down prior to the event. Each of them was sought after by many, yet they had their sights set only for each other.

After graduating from high school, Frosty entered the Marines for a three-year commitment and Donna began her pursuit of a college degree from the University of Iowa. While beginning these separate directions, they decided to still stay in contact yet with "no strings attached." In the course of that time, there was a line forming to date Donna. Once Frosty heard this news via letters while stationed in China, he quickly moved to writing love poems and long letters to Donna who waited for her Prince Frosty. Donna graduated from college while Frosty continued to finish his undergraduate studies. He started his college years playing football at Northwestern University and then transferred to the University of Nebraska at Omaha due to his father having cancer, where he received his bachelor's degree.

Married in 1951, the two began a trek that would span over six decades, deeply touching multiple communities through the vehicle of coaching football, accompanied by their presence to have a positive impact on others. Frosty would continue his college education receiving a master's and doctorate degree from Colorado State College (renamed the University of Northern Colorado). Life and football brought them to Elkader, Iowa (coaching Elkader H.S. football, basketball, baseball, teaching physical education and wood shop), then to Fairfield, Iowa (coaching Fairfield H.S. football, track & field and teaching physical education then moving across town to Parsons College (coaching football while being Athletic Director) on to Greeley, Colorado (higher education) moving to Albert Lea, Minnesota (coaching Lea College football, athletic director and department professor) with the final stop in Tacoma, Washington (coaching PLU football and department professor). The Westering family grew with five children being born from 1952 to 1960. During this time, Frosty and Donna's love and commitment to Jesus Christ was anchored deeply through their involvement in the Fellowship of Christian Athletes.

Frosty's unique coaching style and philosophy, his public speaking prowess, and his broad community impact are what made him so distinctive. Donna's enthusiasm, joy and wit positively impacted her building relationships with players, coaches, wives, families, as well as her memorable treats that she baked and prepared for every team Frosty coached. The experience of knowing Frosty and Donna comes with an emphasis on "enjoying the trip" and the infamous theme, "Make the Big Time Where You Are," which were foundational in their passions and focus for living life with richer meaning and purpose.

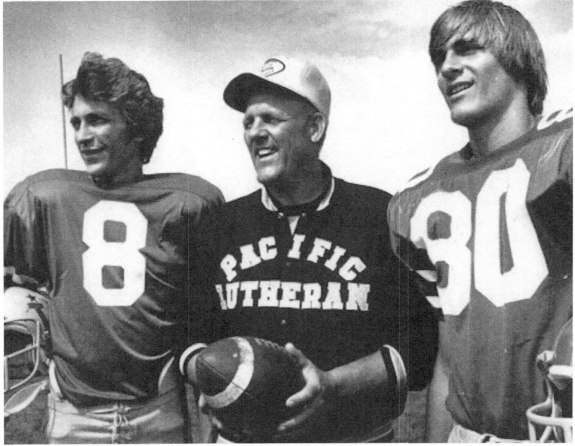

BIO, AWARDS, AND HONORS

FROSTY WESTERING

BIOGRAPHY

Frosty Westering motivated people of all ages with his Big Time message. Frosty taught and coached at Elkader and Fairfield High Schools in Iowa. He was athletic director and football coach at Parsons College in Fairfield, Iowa. Frosty left Parsons to complete a doctoral degree in Educational Psychology at the University of Northern Colorado, Greeley. He then became athletic director and football coach at Lea College in Albert Lea, Minnesota.

Frosty was a professor and head football coach at Pacific Lutheran University, Tacoma, Washington, for 32 years. He was one of the top 10 winningest coaches in the history of college football when he retired with 305 victories and a .761 winning percentage. His teams won four National Championships and he was a three-time National Coach of the Year.

Frosty received Lifetime Achievement Awards from the FCA and Athletes For a Better World. He and his wife Donna were recipients of the John and Nell Wooden Humanitarian Hall of Fame Award in 2004. He was inducted into the prestigious National Football Foundation College Football Hall of Fame in South Bend, Indiana, in 2005.

The scoreboard wins and the awards were not the ends of the story. Those who played for him and were influenced by him can best tell his real story.

TIMELINE

1927	Born December 5, 1927, in Council Bluffs, Iowa; dad was a pharmacist, mom was a teacher
1945	Graduated from Missouri Valley High School
1946	Entered the Marine Corps
1951	Married Donna Belle Jones, July 15, 1951; went on to have five children (Holly, Sue, Brad, Scott, Stacey)
1952-56	Coach at Elkader (IA) High School: 26-8-1
1956-60	Coach at Fairfield (IA) High School: 21-13-2
1960-61	Athletic Director at Parsons College, Fairfield, Iowa
1962	Coach at Parsons College: 10-0 (ranked 6th nationally)
1962-64	Athletic Director/Coach at Parsons College: 15-4-0

1964-66   Graduate School at the University of Northern Colorado; earned Masters an Doctorate Degrees in Health, Physical Education and Educational Psychology

1966-71   Athletic Director/Coach at Lea College, Albert Lea, Minnesota: 29-22-2

1972   Became Football Coach at Pacific Lutheran University, Tacoma, Washington: 261-70-5

1980   Led PLU to their first NAIA National Championship

1985   First foreign trip with the football team to France

1987   Led PLU to their second NAIA National Championship

1989   Second foreign trip with the football team to Australia and New Zealand

1991   Third foreign trip with the football team to China; played Evangel College in Beijing, Guangzhou, and Shanghai: 3-0

1993   Led PLU to third NAIA National Championship

1993   Fourth foreign trip with the football team to Germany; played Hamburg Blue Devils (a team with four PLU alums): 1-0

1999   Led PLU to first NCAA Division III National Championship (4th overall)

2001   Released first book, "Make The Big Time Where You Are"

2003   Won 300th collegiate game, September 20th vs. Chapman College

2003   Retired from coaching

2005   Released second book, "The Strange Secret of the Big Time"

2013   Went to see his Lord on April 12

AWARDS AND HONORS

- Inducted into NAIA College Football Hall of Fame (1995)
- American Football Coaches Association NCAA Division III Coach of the Year (1999)
- Football Gazette NCAA Division III Coach of the Year (1999)
- Chevrolet & Shutt Sports Coach of the Year (1999)
- Lutheran Brotherhood Lutheran College Coach of the Year (1999-2000)
- Hula Bowl Coaching Staff (2000)
- Amos Alonzo Stagg Award
- Fellowship of Christian Athletes Lifetime Achievement Award
- Athletes for a Better World Lifetime Achievement Award
- NAIA National College Football Coach of the Year (1983 and 1993)
- Directed PLU to seven NAIA Division II Championship Games
- NAIA National Championships in (1980, 1987, and 1993)
- NAIA all-time winningest football coach with 256 wins

- PLU's all-time winningest football coach with 261 wins
- Conference Coach of the Year (1985, 1986, 1993 and 1998)
- Northwest Small-College Coach of the Year (1979, 1980, 1983, 1993, and 1998)
- Coached 26 NAIA and NCAA First Team All-Americans
- Member of the Iowa Collegiate Coaching Hall of Fame
- Two-time Tacoma News Tribune Man of the Year in Sports Award
- Seattle Post-Intelligencer Publisher's Award recipient (2000)
- Inducted into the Puget Sound Athletic Hall of Fame (2004)
- Inducted into the PLU Athletics Hall of Fame (2004)
- Inducted into the College Football Hall of Fame in South Bend, Indiana (August 2005)
- Finished college coaching career with 305 wins
- Retired as ninth winningest coach in college football history
- Received the Nell & John Wooden Humanitarian Lifetime Coaching Achievement Award with wife Donna Belle (2004)

COACHING RECORDS

COACHING RECORDS

Overall: 1952-2003

1952-56	Elkader (IA) High School	26-8-1
1956-60	Fairfield (IA) High School	21-13-2
1962-63	Parsons College, Fairfield, IA	15-4-0
1966-71	Lea College, Albert Lea, MN	29-22-2
1972-2003	Pacific Lutheran University, Tacoma, WA	261-70-5
TOTAL		**352-117-10**

Pacific Lutheran University: Year-By-Year

1972 [6-3]

Opponent	Location	Result	Score
at Whitworth	Spokane, WA	W	12-7
Cal Lutheran	Tacoma, WA (Franklin Pierce)	W	31-9
Pacific	Tacoma, WA (Franklin Pierce)	L	7-9
Whitman	Tacoma, WA (Franklin Pierce)	W	34-7
at Willamette	Salem, OR	W	20-12
at College of Idaho	Caldwell, ID	W	46-19
at Lewis & Clark	Portland, OR	W	26-0
Linfield	Tacoma (Franklin Pierce)	L	7-21
Puget Sound	Tacoma (Franklin Pierce)	L	19-37

1973 [6-3]

Opponent	Location	Result	Score
PLU Alumni	Tacoma, WA (Franklin Pierce)	W (exhibition)	27-7
Whitworth	Tacoma, WA (Franklin Pierce)	W	21-6
at Pacific	Forest Grove, OR	W	21-14
at Whitman	Walla Walla, WA	W	36-20
Willamette	Tacoma, WA (Franklin Pierce)	W	41-6
College of Idaho	Tacoma, WA (Franklin Pierce)	W	28-6
Lewis & Clark	Tacoma, WA (Franklin Pierce)	W	42-14
at Linfield	McMinnville, OR	L	22-33
Concordia (MN)	Tacoma, WA (Franklin Pierce)	L	6-45
at Puget Sound	Tacoma, WA	L	2-30

1974 [8-1]

Opponent	Location	Result	Score
at Western (WA)	Bellingham, WA	W	48-0
Puget Sound	Tacoma, WA (Franklin Pierce)	W	38-27
Whitman	Tacoma, WA (Franklin Pierce)	W	47-0
Whitworth	Tacoma, WA (Franklin Pierce)	W	28-7
at Lewis & Clark	Portland, OR	W	30-14
Willamette	Tacoma, WA (Franklin Pierce)	W	37-21
At Linfield	McMinnville, OR	L	14-15
Pacific	Tacoma, WA (Franklin Pierce)	W	49-6
at College of Idaho	Caldwell, ID	W	34-22

1975 [7-2]

Opponent	Location	Result	Score
Western (WA)	Tacoma, WA (Franklin Pierce)	W	42-6
at Puget Sound	Tacoma, WA	L	7-20
at Whitworth	Spokane, WA	W	22-20
Lewis & Clark	Tacoma, WA (Franklin Pierce)	W	28-16
at Willamette	Salem, OR	W	48-3
Linfield	Tacoma, WA (Franklin Pierce)	L	19-20
at Pacific	Forest Grove, OR	W	42-6
College of Idaho	Tacoma, WA (Franklin Pierce)	W	42-6
at Whitman	Walla Walla, WA	W	55-7

1976 [6-4]

Opponent	Location	Result	Score
Puget Sound	Tacoma, WA (Franklin Pierce)	L	21-40
at Central (WA)	Ellensburg, WA	W	48-6
at Lewis & Clark	Portland, OR	L	6-20
Willamette	Tacoma, WA (Franklin Pierce)	L	13-21
at Linfield	McMinnville, OR	W	28-10
Pacific	Tacoma, WA (Franklin Pierce)	W	45-8
at College of Idaho	Caldwell, ID	W	45-0
at Whitman	Walla Walla, WA	W	25-20
Whitworth	Tacoma, WA (Franklin Pierce)	W	21-14
Western (WA)*	Tacoma, WA (Franklin Pierce)	L	28-48

*NAIA District 1 Championship

1977 [8-2]

Opponent	Location	Result	Score
Puget Sound	Seattle, WA (Kingdome)	L	21-23
Central (WA)	Tacoma, WA (Franklin Pierce)	W	41-3
at Willamette	Salem, OR	W	38-0
Linfield	Tacoma, WA (Franklin Pierce)	L	18-26
at Pacific	Forest Grove, OR	W	45-0
College of Idaho	Tacoma, WA (Franklin Pierce)	W	21-17
at Whitworth	Spokane, WA	W	43-7
Lewis & Clark	Tacoma, WA (Franklin Pierce)	W	38-15
at Eastern (WA)	Cheney, WA	W	22-6
Western (WA)*	Seattle, WA (Kingdome)	W	24-0

*NAIA District 1 Championship

1978 [6-3]

Opponent	Location	Result	Score
at Western (WA)	Bellingham, WA	W	45-3
Puget Sound	Seattle, WA (Kingdome)	L	14-27
Whitworth	Tacoma, WA (Franklin Pierce)	W	14-13
at Linfield	McMinnville, OR	L	17-18
at Lewis & Clark	Portland, OR	W	31-6
Willamette	Tacoma, WA (Franklin Pierce)	L	8-23
Pacific	Tacoma, WA (Franklin Pierce)	W	23-0
Eastern (OR)	Tacoma, WA (Franklin Pierce)	W	37-7
Eastern (WA)	Tacoma, WA (Franklin Pierce)	W	13-6

1979 [9-2]

Opponent	Location	Result	Score
at Moorhead State	Moorhead, MN	W	25-23
at Puget Sound	Tacoma, WA	L	14-29
Central (WA)	Tacoma, WA (Franklin Pierce)	W	30-7
at Southern (OR)	Ashland, OR	W	42-12
at Pacific	Forest Grove, OR	W	40-7
Linfield	Tacoma, WA (Franklin Pierce)	W	7-6
at Lewis & Clark	Portland, OR	W	16-14
Willamette	Tacoma, WA (Franklin Pierce)	W	30-2
at Whitworth	Spokane, WA	W	22-13
at Cal Lutheran*	Thousand Oaks, CA	W	34-14
at Findlay*	Findlay, OH	L	0-9

*NAIA Division II Championships

1980 [12-1/NAIA Division II National Champions]

Opponent	Location	Result	Score
PLU Alumni	Tacoma, WA (Franklin Pierce)	W	34-21
Western (WA)	Tacoma, WA (Franklin Pierce)	W	30-0
at Humboldt State	Arcata, CA	W	45-14
at Central (WA)	Ellensburg, WA	W	24-3
Southern (OR)	Tacoma, WA (Franklin Pierce)	W	25-0
Whitworth	Tacoma, WA (Franklin Pierce)	W	39-38
Pacific	Tacoma, WA (Franklin Pierce)	W	41-20
at Linfield	McMinnville, OR	L	19-20
Lewis & Clark	Tacoma, WA (Franklin Pierce)	W	27-0
at Willamette	Salem, OR	W	42-7
Linfield*	Tacoma, WA (Lincoln Bowl)	W	35-20
Valley City St.(ND)*	Tacoma, WA (Lincoln Bowl)	W	32-0
Wilmington (OH)**	Tacoma, WA (Lincoln Bowl)	W	38-10

*NAIA Division II Championships
**NAIA Division II Championship Game

1981 [9-1]

Opponent	Location	Result	Score
Western (WA)	Tacoma, WA	W	23-0
at Southern OR	Ashland, OR	W	29-7
Oregon Tech	Tacoma, WA	W	34-22
at Central WA	Ellensburg, WA	W	16-6
Willamette	Tacoma, WA	W	42-22
at Whitworth	Spokane, WA	W	40-6
at Pacific	Forest Grove, OR	W	51-6
Linfield	Tacoma, WA	W	17-0
Lewis & Clark	Tacoma, WA	W	20-3
William Jewell*	Liberty, MO	L	14-19

*NAIA Division II Championships

1982 [7-2]

Opponent	Location	Result	Score
at Western (WA)	Bellingham, WA	W	39-7
Southern (OR)	Tacoma, WA	W	28-6
at Oregon Tech	Klamath Falls, OR	L	27-45
Central (WA)	Tacoma, WA	W	29-20
Lewis & Clark	Tacoma, WA	W	48-0

at Willamette	Salem, OR	W	29-0
Whitworth	Tacoma, WA	W	45-10
Pacific	Tacoma, WA	W	17-6
at Linfield	McMinnville, OR	L	7-27

1983 [9-3/NAIA Division II National Runner-Up]

Opponent	Location	Result	Score
Puget Sound	Tacoma, WA (Tacoma Dome)	W	13-10
at Western (WA)	Bellingham, WA	W	49-7
at Central (WA)	Ellensburg, WA	L	14-15
Simon Fraser	Tacoma, WA	W	34-12
Linfield	Tacoma (Lincoln Bowl)	L	27-30
at Lewis & Clark	Portland, OR	W	33-15
Willamette	Tacoma, WA	W	42-24
at Whitworth	Spokane, WA	W	47-6
at Pacific	Forest Grove, OR	W	34-3
Baker (KS)*	Tacoma, WA	W	35-3
Westminster (PA)*	Puyallup. WA	W	16-13
Northwester (IA)**	Tacoma, WA (Tacoma Dome)	L	21-25

*NAIA Division II Championships
**NAIA Division II Championship Game

1984 [6-3]

Opponent	Location	Result	Score
at Simon Fraser	Burnaby, Canada	W	27-3
Puget Sound	Tacoma, WA (Tacoma Dome)	L	22-32
Western (WA)	Tacoma, WA	W	24-13
Central (WA)	Tacoma, WA	L	14-31
Pacific	Tacoma, WA	W	45-7
at Linfield	McMinnville, OR	L	10-24
Lewis & Clark	Tacoma, WA	W	34-14
at Willamette	Salem, OR	W	21-8
Whitworth	Tacoma, WA (Lincoln Bowl)	W	38-8

1985 [10-1-1/NAIA Division II National Runner-Up]

Opponent	Location	Result	Score
Puget Sound	Tacoma Dome	W	54-13
at Willamette	Salem, OR	T	26-26
Linfield	Lakewood Stadium	W	14-6

at Oregon Tech	Klamath Falls, OR	W	55-14
Eastern (OR)	Lakewood Stadium	W	50-0
at Central (WA)	Ellensburg, WA	W	41-14
Whitworth	Lakewood Stadium	W	35-22
Simon Fraser	Lakewood Stadium	W	43-8
at Western (WA)	Bellingham, WA	W	52-21
Linfield*	Lakewood Stadium	W	30-12
Findlay (OH)*	Lakewood Stadium	W	40-29
Wisconsin-La Crosse**	Tacoma, WA (Tacoma Dome)	L	7-24

*NAIA Division II Championships
**NAIA Division II Championship Game

1986 [8-2]

Opponent	Location	Result	Score
Puget Sound	Tacoma, WA (Tacoma Dome)	W	22-18
Willamette	Lakewood Stadium	W	49-7
at Linfield	McMinnville, OR	L	17-43
Oregon Tech	Lakewood Stadium	W	28-22
Eastern (OR)	Lakewood Stadium	W	49-3
Central (WA)	Lakewood Stadium	W	42-0
at Whitworth	Spokane, WA	W	64-34
at Simon Fraser	Burnaby, Canada	W	21-0
Western (WA)	Lakewood Stadium	W	49-0
Linfield*	Lakewood Stadium	L	21-27

*NAIA Division II Championships

1987 [11-1-1]

Opponent	Location	Result	Score
Puget Sound	Tacoma, WA (Tacoma Dome)	L	7-24
Oregon Tech	Puyallup, WA	W	27-20
at Whitworth	Spokane, WA	W	28-13
at Southern (OR)	Ashland, OR	W	31-21
Linfield	Puyallup, WA	W	44-20
at Central (WA)	Ellensburg, WA	W	42-16
Simon Fraser	Puyallup, WA	W	42-13
Lewis & Clark	Puyallup, WA	W	55-22
at Western (WA)	Bellingham, WA	T	13-13
Midland Lutheran*	Puyallup, WA	W	40-21
at Carroll*	Helena, MT	W	36-26

| Baker (KS)* | Puyallup, WA | W | 17-14 |
| WI-Stevens Point** T | Tacoma, WA (Tacoma Dome) | W | 16-16 |

*NAIA Division II Championships
**NAIA Division II Championship Game [UWSP forfeit/ineligible players]

1988 [7-3]

Opponent	Location	Result	Score
Puget Sound	Tacoma, WA (Tacoma Dome)	W	30-7
at Oregon Tech	Klamath Falls, OR	W	45-14
Whitworth	Puyallup, WA	W	49-16
Southern (OR)	Puyallup, WA	W	24-10
at Linfield	McMinnville, OR	L	33-35
Central (WA)	Puyallup, WA	L	21-28
at Simon Fraser	Burnaby, Canada	W	52-16
at Lewis & Clark	Portland, OR	W	35-14
Western (WA)	Puyallup, WA	W	41-23
at Oregon Tech*	Klamath Falls, OR	L	35-56

*NAIA Division II Championships

1989 [6-1-1]

Opponent	Location	Result	Score
Puget Sound	Tacoma, WA (Tacoma Dome)	W	35-19
at Lewis & Clark	Portland, OR	L	35-36
Oregon Tech	Puyallup, WA	W	41-12
Central (WA)	Puyallup, WA	T	24-24
at Whitworth	Spokane, WA	W	49-20
Linfield	Puyallup, WA	L	14-24
Western (WA)	Puyallup, WA	W	59-31
at Southern (OR)	Ashland, OR	W	52-50
at Simon Fraser	Burnaby, Canada	W	48-31

1990 [9-2]

Opponent	Location	Result	Score
Puget Sound	Tacoma Dome	W	42-10
Lewis & Clark	Puyallup, WA	W	42-14
at Oregon Tech	Klamath Falls, OR	W	28-7
at Central (WA)	Ellensburg, WA	L	20-31
Whitworth	Puyallup, WA	W	31-9
at Linfield	McMinnville, OR	W	38-24

at Western (WA)	Bellingham, WA	W	21-0
Southern (OR)	Puyallup, WA	W	13-12
Simon Fraser	Puyallup, WA	W	35-6
at Concordia (WI)*	Mequon, WI	W	37-3
Central (WA)*	Puyallup, WA	L	6-24

*NAIA Division II Championships

1991 [11-2/NAIA Division II National Runner-Up]

Opponent	Location	Result	Score
Linfield	Tacoma, WA (Tacoma Dome)	W	9-8
Oregon Tech	Puyallup, WA	W	50-22
at Whitworth	Spokane, WA	W	38-7
at Western (WA)	Bellingham, WA	W	22-21
Pacific	Puyallup, WA	W	38-0
Central (WA)	Puyallup, WA	L	28-45
at Southern (OR)	Ashland, OR	W	35-27
at Puget Sound	Tacoma, WA	W	49-13
Simon Fraser	Puyallup, WA	W	35-16
Central (WA)*	Puyallup, WA	W	27-0
Linfield*	Puyallup, WA	W	23-0
at Dickinson State*	Dickinson, ND	W	27-25
at Georgetown**	Georgetown, KY	L	20-28

*NAIA Division II Championships
**NAIA Division II Championship Game

1992 [9-2]

Opponent	Location	Result	Score
Willamette	Puyallup, WA	W	42-9
at Linfield	McMinnville, OR	L	7-14
at Oregon Tech	Klamath Falls, OR	W	35-6
Whitworth	Puyallup, WA	W	49-7
Western (WA)	Puyallup, WA	W	49-16
Central (WA)	Puyallup, WA	W	39-7
Southern (OR)	Puyallup, WA	W	28-6
Puget Sound	Tacoma, WA (Tacoma Dome)	W	56-29
at Simon Fraser	Burnaby, Canada	W	30-13
Montana Tech*	Puyallup, WA	W	37-0
at Linfield*	McMinnville, OR	L	30-44

*NAIA Division II Championships

1993 [12-1/NAIA Division II National Champions]

Opponent	Location	Result	Score
Linfield	Tacoma, WA (Tacoma Dome)	T	20-20
Eastern (OR)	Puyallup, WA	W	43-13
at Southern (OR)	Ashland, OR	W	50-23
at Willamette	Salem, OR	W	48-36
Central (WA)	Puyallup, WA	W	49-48
Simon Fraser	Puyallup, WA	W	42-4
at Whitworth	Spokane, WA	W	45-13
at Western (WA)	Bellingham, WA	W	37-29
Puget Sound	Tacoma, WA (Tacoma Dome)	W	41-7
Cumberland (TN)*	Puyallup, WA	W	61-7
Central (WA)*	Puyallup, WA	W	35-17
Baker (KS)*	Puyallup, WA	W	52-14
Westminster (PA)**	Portland, OR	W	50-20

*NAIA Division II Championships
**NAIA Division II Championship Game

1994 [11-2/NAIA Division II National Runner-Up]

Opponent	Location	Result	Score
at Linfield	McMinnville, OR	W	21-13
at Eastern (OR)	La Grande, OR	W	27-21
Southern (OR)	Puyallup, WA	W	29-12
Willamette	Puyallup, WA	L	7-10
at Central (WA)	Ellensburg, WA	W	22-20
at Simon Fraser	Burnaby, Canada	W	27-13
Whitworth	Puyallup, WA	W	42-14
Western (WA)	Puyallup, WA	W	35-15
at Puget Sound	Tacoma, WA	W	36-3
Midland Lutheran*	Fremont, NE	W	34-14
Western (WA)*	Puyallup, WA	W	25-20
Northwestern (IA)*	Puyallup, WA	W	28-7
Westminster (PA)**	Portland, OR	L	7-27

*NAIA Division II Championships
**NAIA Division II Championship Game

1995 [5-3-1]

Opponent	Location	Result	Score
at Western (WA)	Bellingham, WA	L	26-30
Simon Fraser	Puyallup, WA	W	35-10
Central (WA)	Puyallup, WA	W	35-32
at Western Oregon	Monmouth, OR	L	16-30
Whitworth	Puyallup, WA	W	37-7
at Lewis & Clark	Portland, OR	W	19-15
Linfield	Puyallup, WA	W	10-7
at Willamette	Salem, OR	T	35-35
at Puget Sound	Tacoma, WA	W	42-28
at Findlay*	Findlay, OH	L	14-21

*NAIA Division II Championships

1996 [7-3]

Opponent	Location	Result	Score
Western (WA)	Puyallup, WA	L	17-34
at Simon Fraser	Burnaby, Canada	W	31-3
at Central (WA)	Ellensburg, WA	W	44-41
Western (OR)	Puyallup, WA	W	49-30
at Whitworth	Spokane, WA	W	41-18
Lewis & Clark	Puyallup, WA	W	28-24
at Linfield	McMinnville, OR	W	26-14
Willamette	Puyallup, WA	L	27-28
at Puget Sound	Tacoma, WA	W	29-3
at Western (WA)*	Bellingham, WA	L	20-21

*NAIA Division II Championships

1997 [7-2]

Opponent	Location	Result	Score
at Cal Lutheran	Thousand Oaks, CA	W	45-23
Western (WA)	Puyallup, WA	W	46-44
at Simon Fraser	Burnaby, Canada	W	27-20
Lewis & Clark	Puyallup, WA	W	53-16
at Eastern Or	La Grande, OR	W	30-26
Whitworth	Puyallup, WA	W	45-24
at Linfield	McMinnville, OR	L	12-28
at Willamette	Salem, OR	L	6-43
Puget Sound	Puyallup, WA	W	52-10

1998 [8-2]

Opponent	Location	Result	Score
Cal Lutheran	Puyallup, WA	W	20-14
at Southern (OR)	Ashland, OR	L	21-58
at Lewis & Clark	Portland, OR	W	48-12
Eastern (OR)	Puyallup, WA	W	34-12
Simon Fraser	Burnaby, Canada	W	35-14
at Whitworth	Spokane, WA	W	34-20
Linfield	Puyallup, WA	W	14-9
Willamette	Puyallup, WA	W	21-19
at Puget Sound	Tacoma, WA	W	26-6
at St. John's*	Collegeville, MN	L	20-33

*NCAA Division III Championships

1999 [13-1/NCAA Division III National Champions]

Opponent	Location	Result	Score
at Cal Lutheran	Thousand Oaks, CA	W	28-26
Southern (OR)	Puyallup, WA	W	47-23
at Eastern (OR)	La Grande, OR	W	41-35
at Willamette	Salem, OR	L	20-29
Whitworth	Puyallup, WA	W	33-7
Lewis & Clark	Puyallup, WA	W	63-10
at Linfield	McMinnville, OR	W	56-23
at Simon Fraser	Burnaby, Canada	W	35-13
Puget Sound	Puyallup, WA	W	49-13
at Willamette	Salem, OR	W	28-24
at Wartburg*	Waverly, IA	W	49-14
at St. John's*	Collegeville, MN	W	19-9
at Trinity*	San Antonio, TX	W	49-28
Rowan**	Salem, VA	W	42-13

*NCAA Division III Championships
**NCAA Division III Championship Game

2000 [9-2]

Opponent	Location	Result	Score
Cal Lutheran	Puyallup, WA	W	49-7
Simon Fraser	Puyallup, WA	W	42-28
at Whitworth	Spokane, WA	W	34-28
Linfield	Puyallup, WA	L	28-38

Eastern OR	Puyallup, WA	W	61-36
at Lewis & Clark	Portland, OR	W	62-6
Willamette	Puyallup, WA	W	48-12
at Southern OR	Ashland, OR	W	33-0
Puget Sound	Puyallup, WA	W	40-16
at Bethel*	St. Paul, MN	W	41-13
at St. John's*	Collegeville, MN	L	21-28

*NCAA Division III Championships

2001 [8-3]

Opponent	Location	Result	Score
at Azusa Pacific	Azusa, CA	L	27-31
Whitworth	Puyallup, WA	L	26-27
at Linfield	McMinnville	W	31-20
at Eastern (OR)	La Grande, OR	W	48-18
Lewis & Clark	Puyallup, WA	W	41-14
Southern (OR)	Puyallup, WA	W	48-38
at Willamette	Salem, OR	W	13-0
Puget Sound	Puyallup	W	62-14
at Whitworth*	Spokane, WA	W	27-26
at Central*	Pella, IA	W	27-21
St. John's MN	Fargo, ND (Fargo Dome)	L	6-31

*NCAA Division III Championships

2002 [5-4]

Opponent	Location	Result	Score
Azusa Pacific	Puyallup, WA	L	42-44
at Chapman	Orange, CA	W	35-10
Linfield	Puyallup, WA	L	21-35
Eastern (OR)	Puyallup, WA	W	24-17
at Whitworth	Spokane, WA	W	21-7
at Lewis & Clark	Portland, OR	W	45-18
Willamette	Puyallup, WA	L	23-30
at Menlo	Atherton, CA	L	29-32
at Puget Sound	Tacoma, WA	W	46-0

2003 [6-3]

Opponent	Location	Result	Score
at Azusa Pacific	Azusa, CA	L	12-21
Chapman	Puyallup	W	31-3
at Linfield	McMinnville, OR	L	10-19
at Eastern (OR)	La Grande, OR	W	27-17
Whitworth	Puyallup, WA	W	28-24
Lewis & Clark	Puyallup, WA	W	48-7
at Willamette	Salem, OR	L	27-36
Menlo (CA)	Puyallup, WA	W	35-28
Puget Sound	Puyallup, WA	W	40-14

NATIONAL CHAMPIONSHIPS & PLAYOFF HISTORY

NCAA Division III
- 1999 National Champions
- 1998 Playoffs
- 2000 Playoffs
- 2001 Playoffs

NAIA Division II
- 1980 National Champions
- 1987 National Champions
- 1993 National Champions
- 1983 National Runner Up
- 1985 National Runner Up
- 1991 National Runner Up
- 1994 National Runner Up
- 1979 Playoffs
- 1981 Playoffs
- 1986 Playoffs
- 1988 Playoffs
- 1990 Playoffs
- 1992 Playoffs
- 1995 Playoffs
- 1996 Playoffs

WRITER'S INDEX

Made in the USA
Las Vegas, NV
25 November 2022

60319469R00149